SUSAN:

Love
Light
&
Laughter
To you!

Mary
:)
9
Dr. Dave

Divinely Touched:
Transform Your Life

Mary *'Divine'* & Dr. Dave DiSano

BALBOA.
PRESS
A DIVISION OF HAY HOUSE

Balboa Press books may be ordered through booksellers or by contacting:

Balboa Press
A Division of Hay House
1663 Liberty Drive
Bloomington, IN 47403
www.balboapress.com
1-(877) 407-4847

ISBN: 978-1-4525-3744-3 (sc)
ISBN: 978-1-4525-3745-0 (hc)
ISBN: 978-1-4525-3746-7 (e)

Printed in the United States of America

Balboa Press rev. date: 6/4/2012

Dedication:

To all of humanity.

*That this book may heal
all in need,*

Physically, Mentally,

*and **Spiritually!***

Cover Art By

IllustriousArt & Graphics

Henry Tamborelli:
Design & Graphics Director
Contact: illustriousart@hotmail.com

Table of Divine Contents

VIII ~ Spiritual Healing   264

IX ~ The Divine Race   294

X Epilogue   309

XI Divine Resources   312

XII A Divine Glossary   321

XIII Divine References   332

Foreword

Most people that meet Mary are immediately attracted to her. Guys are drawn to her physical beauty, woman when they talk to her, quickly see her inner beauty as well. I was no different. However, after a short time with her it became evident to us that we were destined to be together. Our connection became far more than similar likes and dislikes as her spiritual awakening and journey evolved. It became obvious that we completely complimented each other. Just like in the Neil Diamond song, "…she is the words, I am the tune." Everything I had studied, learned, and experienced in my life seemed to be for her, to help her in her journey.

The journey we have been on the past few years still "*blows my mind.*" Especially since I have always come from a scientific background, and I have always taken the "scientific" approach to verifying research and claims. The basis of which, is replicating results from more than one source. This has been the case in Mary's spiritual journey. It wasn't one psychic that told her that she is being attacked by supernatural forces, causing her to be sick, but a dozen from all over the country. It wasn't one psychic that told her she was extraordinary, not of this world, or that she is divinely protected, but all that could see, would tell her that. They would tell her the same thing. These psychics and lightworkers did not know each other. They did not receive any prompting from us. Yet, they were telling her the same things. After a while it even became a test for us to determine how "psychic" someone was, if they knew who Mary was, or if they could feel her energy, after meeting her.

In our journey, as Mary describes in detail, we have met so many extraordinarily wonderful people. We have been led to psychics, lightworkers, gurus, masters, and shamans from all over the world, and across the ages. All the previous thirty years of knowledge of such information that I had had, was eclipsed in a couple of years, after I had met Mary and was on her divine journey as well. The teacher certainly became the student.

The journey she describes may seem exciting, amazing and enlightening to the reader, but it was initiated through her pain and discomfort. It was not one she was looking for. When I had met her, she only wanted a stable, average life and to feel better and normal again.

What transpired was a search for what was making her sick. And, like most people we looked to traditional medicine for answers. Starting with her primary care physician and then going to gastroenterologists, specialists in her type of pain and discomfort, and even allergists. But, they could find nothing wrong with her. All her vital signs completely normal, she was a model of health as far as the doctors were concern. They had no explanations for her abdominal bloating, lack of energy, dry skin, swollen lips, and canker sores on her tongue. Doctors could only come up with perhaps it was a "virus" (what they say when they have no idea of what is causing symptoms) or an allergic reaction. But an allergist could find nothing she was allergic to as well. The answers we found are what follows in her journey.

Through all her pain and discomfort, that sometimes had her in bed for days, few that were close to her ever suspected anything was wrong. She never missed a family event. She continued seeing her clients at her clinic and visiting her hospice patients. She continued being involved in her church. Often, she had to have her abdomen wrapped tightly in order to move. She had to have weekly colonics in order to relieve the pressure in her abdomen so she could function.

Quite often, after going to a family or church function she would be in bed exhausted for the entire next day, or days.

I am sure the pain someone goes through in acute diseases like cancer or chronic illnesses is devastating. Especially, when going on for years. But, to see a loved one suffer, and being unable to ease their pain or discomfort is also significant. So many nights I lied next to her praying to God, calling upon all the Archangels, to come and heal her and relieve her pain. This was the "yang" to our "yin." The downside to her spiritual awakening and the amazing journey that ensued.

Being a scientist, being completely objective, what I have seen being with Mary has been miraculous. The people we have been led to, the knowledge we have been exposed to, her personal transformation, all have been truly remarkable. Being a scientist, being completely objective, I can testify that *Mary is truly, extraordinarily, remarkable. She embodies the Divine!*

Dr. Dave DiSano,
February, 2011

Preface

Divinely Touched is the chronicle of my spiritual awakening. It was not one I had asked for. It wasn't even one I had been looking for. It was one that hit me between the eyes as if someone swung a baseball bat at my head. Many of the amazing individuals I have met in my journey studied and read, and meditated for years and years to awaken their consciousness to their higher self. Many of them were looking to develop their psychic or energy healing abilities. I was not. My journey was one of trying to heal myself and to understand what I was going through. Along the way I met so many truly remarkable people, I learned who I am, and why I am here!

I have experienced things I never dreamed of. Seen and felt things I never wanted to. Many of my religious and spiritual beliefs were changed forever. And, I have been told by many psychics I shouldn't even be alive today. For they were able to look into my soul and see what I went through.

My journey like many, was initiated by medical problems that had no explanations. The medical community had no answers for my persistent abdominal problems. For the waves of energy circulating through my body. For my dry and peeling skin on my face and lips. For the canker sores on my tongue. They did have plenty of drugs for the symptoms. And, if I told them of the visions I was having, most would have committed me to a mental hospital, or at least prescribed more medications.

It is my wish that I might help others to find answers to their unexplained medical issues or their perceived mental illness, based on what I have gone through. That the information from all the lightworkers, masters, sages, and mystics I had come across, may open new worlds and ways of thinking to you that you may have not ever imagined.

Many of the incredible healers and psychics I had met appear in the *Divine Resource* section at the end of the book. They are remarkable individuals from across the country available to help anyone in need. I have, however, changed some of the names as it relates to my personal relationships in my story, to protect their privacy.

I have also included many of the books that have helped me survive my awakening. These are the books that have taught me so much and awakened me to worlds I've never dreamed existed.

Music has talked to me all my life. I loved listening to the music of "Godspell" and "Jesus Christ Superstar" when I was growing up. Throughout this book I have included music lyrics that have spoken to my soul. I believe that many of the writers of these songs were divinely inspired. In my journey I have also been led to a number of inspirational new musicians such as Kristine Wilbur, Dona Oxford, Karen Drucker, and Mark Stanton Welch. Their CDs are listed in the reference section as well.

The glossary I hope, will be helpful for those of you who find the terminology of the *New Age* as "new" as it was for me.

My goal in writing this book was about sharing, healing, and ***changing people's minds about mental illness***. Sharing not only the information I have come across, but all the amazing, wonderful, healers, psychics, and masters that have helped me on my incredible journey. It is my hope and belief that all those that read this book will experience the healing they seek, to whatever the God/Universe/ Source has intended for you!

~ Mary
May, 2011

"Sometimes you have to lose your mind before you come to your senses!"

~ The Peaceful Warrior

Acknowledgements

First and above all, to the Almighty Great One, I AM, for his/her never failing, and never ending, unconditional love and grace.

To my mother for her love, patience, and always faithful support, who I truly believe is a saint. I don't believe that I have told you enough how much I love you! You think I am an angel, but you are the saint sent to me, to help guide me and show me by your example what faith and true love is, so that I might help others from the blessing of your love in my life. I am eternally grateful for all you have endured, to send me and ascend me to my truth.

To my dad who is always with me in spirit. For his great faith and love for me. I know now that for all the tough lessons he put me through, that I thought were so unjust at the time, I see that he did it all to help make me the person I am today. I can now stand up and help heal the innocent, defenseless and broken down.

To Dr. Dave, God has blessed me tremendously by giving me you as a husband. Who could ask for more, you are Buddha and Socrates, all in one. Thank you for standing by me in everyway, for believing in me, encouraging me, and for always being my strength when I was so weak. You showed me what a soul mate is. Thank you for making my life so complete and more than I ever dreamed it could be. I love you eternally, my "Moon boy."

To all my exes, that I know now were sent to help me grow and become an independent woman. I thank the Great One, "I AM" for the gift of having shared time with them and that they helped me with my soul's next step. I now know the ones that have given us our most difficult lessons in life did so, because on the other side they love us, and want us to advance the most.

To my faithful friends that stood by me during my dark periods and never gave up on me even when I didn't return their calls for weeks sometimes. Like my faithful friend Joe, unwavering in his help to persistently call or stop by to check on me, it means more than words I can say. I felt so bad because I didn't have the energy or confidence back then to truly explain what was going on. He is an example of a pure heart, that still cared and stood by me. I know I could always count on him and that always gave me such great comfort.

To my godsend, Joanne "Best Bud." Who would have thought twenty years ago one person from Connecticut and one person from Rhode Island would have a "chance" meeting in Massachusetts. With God there are no limits. God knew the purpose of why we would have to meet. Life is never as it seems at first. From that first encounter we were like sisters. I can't express enough thanks and love for all your care, support and long hours of phone conversations (before there were cell phones). We were so connected from the very beginning. God knew I needed a friend, and He sent me my "Best Bud."

To my dear "soul sister" Claudia; little did I know that during my darkest, self-loathing days that I would meet my "soul sister." You raised me above my "futon state." When we first met I was extremely over-weight, just floating through life. You helped me to see things differently through your genuine love and concern, you always listened and gave me sisterly advice, for that I will be forever grateful.

My dear friend Joanne (Providence); you took a stranger that was your restaurant customer and offered her friendship and thereby helped her through her dark times. I will be forever indebted to you, for you taught me that ***strangers are friends just waiting*** *to happen*. Friends are God's way of taking care of us. They are "earthbound angels!"

So many truly amazing individuals have helped me on my divine journey. They acted as my healers/saviors, mentors, teachers, gurus, colleagues, and friends.

Dr. Dolores Seymour, thanks for all your inspirational articles, free magazines, and your free energy phone line, that is filled with positive messages everyday that truly helped me see more clearly. Dr. Michael Sharp began showing me worlds I never dreamed of, and the way home. My "Amazing" Grace Avila was the first to let me know why I was sick when medical doctors had no cures or explanations of what was going on with me. With her love and support my healing and spiritual apprenticeship began. Heidi Gabrilowitz helped me believe in psychic abilities, angels, and myself. Cora Hayward helped me to realize my soul's next step. Maureen St. Germain taught the importance of practice and how it always produces good results. Joey Stann, you showed me how we are truly all one "family tree." White Swan you exemplified how everything is all "one" to me. Rev. Ian Taylor you freed me from the "robbers of the truth." There are no limits! Robert "Ram" Smith you taught me that anything is possible with God's Grace. Dr. Ysabel Reyes you exemplify to me what a modern-day wonder woman is, in all you do. Michelle Sutton you helped me to believe in myself. Vanessa Riyasat you verified to me who I really AM. Kerrie O'Connor you helped explain the energies and guides that are around me. Pat Hastings your GODincidences gave me faith and support on my journey as well, your divine messages continually encouraged me. Shamans Judy Lavine, Richard Jackson, and Gerry Miller, your healings were beyond ordinary, they, like all of you, were extraordinary!

*God shows his love for us through others.
I feel so blessed that God has sent all these
divine souls into my life that have helped
me get through my divine journey.*

"*...I want the world to know
I got to let it show...
There's a new me coming out
...I'm completely positive!*"

~ *I'm Coming Out*
By Diana Ross

1 ~ Divine Beginnings

Divine: (adj.) of or pertaining to God, sacred, from God, heavenly, godlike.

Am I Crazy?

"You're way too young to be this psychotic," my psychologist told me as she made arrangements for me to be treated elsewhere. She was fine seeing me weekly at $150.00 a session, when I was just discussing relationship problems after my divorce. But, once I started to describe to her how I was seeing people's faces changing, or it seemed like someone else was looking back at me in the mirror, she thought I was delusional and was worried I might hurt myself, and she didn't want to be liable!

So, after years of seeing her, she was shipping me off. Abandoning me when I needed her the most. I thought to myself as I left her office, "Good thing I didn't tell her everything that was going on, or, she certainly would have had me committed to a mental hospital on the spot!"

Nor, did I tell her that what had happened to me before and during the two weeks I had spent in a hospital the previous month, for what my family surely thought was a nervous breakdown. And, at the time, I wasn't sure myself, that I wasn't having one.

Now, as I look back I know what had happened. All the pieces fit together. Everything makes sense now. Just as I had battled the forces of darkness, journeyed to the underworld, I was also saved by the grace of God and led on a divine journey that continues today. Sure, the old saying is hindsight is 20/20. But, I believe right now the most important lesson I have learned though all my trauma, near-death experiences, and hospitalizations is that everything in life happens for a reason, and in my case a *Divine reason*.

To begin making sense of my journey, we have to go back two years before that day when my psychologist was shipping me off to someone else. For I've come to believe:

> *That you can tell a lot about the present,*
> *if you know about your past.*

In my case, everything that has happened to me in my life was to prepare me for the battles with the forces of darkness, that led to my spiritual awakening. That led me into worlds I knew nothing of, or, for that matter, never even knew existed. Worlds of seers, psychics, lightworkers, shamans and avatars. But, before I get into the events that led to my awakening, perhaps I should tell you a little more of where I came from and how I started on this incredible journey.

Growing Up Catholic

I was born in 1962, on May 1st , which I have come to find out is the day of the *Queenship of Mary.* I was blessed by being raised by two spiritually minded, wonderful parents. I had a two-year older brother, and a pet dog named Athena. My father was a college English professor, and my mother stayed home with the kids until I was in elementary school, then she worked in finance for a major corporation in Providence, Rhode Island.

I attended Catholic school from the first through the twelfth grade. I worked hard in high school and was an honor roll student. I started working part-time in a local bakery when I was fourteen, and then at a drugstore through high school. After high school, I had an option to go to school for free where my father was a professor, but I choose to go to another local college that had a better reputation in business and finance. In retrospect, my parents must have been very disappointed in my choice, but they didn't mention it at the time and supported my decision, as they did when after a year in college, I left for a full-time job in a large company in Providence.

My decision to leave college was based on a number of factors. I felt overwhelmed working full-time while maintaining a full academic schedule and because of changes in my home life at the time. I started dating my first husband, Burt, when a junior in high school, having met him through a mutual friend when I was sixteen. We were friends for a couple of years, and we dated for two more years before getting married when I was twenty.

Being the more practical, financially minded one in the relationship, I decided to drop out of college before we were married in order to start saving money for our new life together. Burt was beginning a career as a carpenter and, in what turned out to be a pattern throughout our married life, had an inconsistent income. Using my interest and brief college experience in finance I started out in the accounts payable department in a large company in Providence, Rhode Island.

In the beginning, Burt and I were also your typical young married couple. Both starting new careers, living in a third floor apartment, saving for our own home. On Sundays we would go to church and then have dinner at the parent's. On Saturday night we were out to dinner and a movie with another couple. During the work week I had a nine to five schedule and I would rush home after work to make dinner for us. I would clean up after dinner, make my husband's lunch and get my clothes ready for the next day, and by then, it was time for bed.

To say that we were in a routine after a few years seems to be an understatement. I remember once discussing this with Burt and his response was, "This is life, get used to it!" But, somehow I knew I was destined for more, and slowly came to the realization it would be without him at my side.

Always feeling very connected to God, I remember framing a poster on my own, that I really loved, and that I hung in the den of the first house we owned. The poster was entitled *"My Name Is I Am"* and it read:

> *I was regretting the past*
> *And fearing the future.*
> *Suddenly my Lord was speaking:*
> **"My Name is I AM"**
> *He paused. I waited He continued:*
> *"When you live in the past with its mistakes and regrets,*
> *It is hard. I am not there. My name is not I WAS.*
> *When you live in the future, with its problems and fears.*
> *It is hard. I am not I WILL BE.*
> *When you live in this moment it is not hard.*
> *I AM HERE.*
> ***MY NAME IS I AM."***

Burt's astrological sign was a Leo, and he exemplified a Leo male in every way. He was the king of the jungle (and the house), always right about everything. When we were first married, I guess I was more tolerant with his mannerisms. However, as I grew both chronologically and professionally, I became more and more less tolerant, and less patient with his impatience. And, it didn't help that he seemed to become even more controlling as our marriage went on.

One time, when we were going to a birthday party for one of his nieces I had on a dress that I thought I looked good in. However, Burt didn't like it and told me to change or he wouldn't take me. When I refused to change my dress, to my disbelief, he left without me! Another time, we were discussing something in the car, and when I didn't agree with him he told me to get out of the car, and he took off to go home. I started to walk home. After a few miles it was starting to get dark. I was getting cold, and scared walking by myself, so I decided to call a girlfriend to pick me up. We went back to her house, and a few hours later I called him later to pick me up. When he got there he yelled at me for not walking straight home, telling me that it would have only taken me an hour and half, if I had gone a certain route, and I could have made it before it got dark. He wasn't concerned that I had to walk home, but that I wasn't walking home the right way!

Sometimes, no matter what I did, it wasn't good enough for him. One night for dinner I cooked a meatloaf because I knew he liked it. When he got home and I told him that I had cooked a meatloaf, his response was, "I was at mother's I don't want anything now." As I took it out of the oven, I asked him again, "You sure you don't want any now? It's ready." With that, he grabbed the meatloaf, threw it across the kitchen, and screamed at me, "Didn't you hear me? I told you I didn't want any!" All I could think of was, "Boy, I would love someone to cook me dinner or try and please me!" At the time, I never knew what it was like to have someone serve me.

Professionally, I became a supervisor of the accounts payable department, overseeing five people and millions of dollars in revenue, but, at home, I felt like a maid. Burt was becoming more and more controlling. I was told what to wear when we went out, what to say, and, eventually, he told me what I should be thinking and what I should be feeling, because, if it wasn't what he was thinking, or feeling, I was wrong. I wasn't even allowed to have my own feelings. Eventually I had had enough!

I guess it all came to a head one morning when he started to yell at me for being late for work, as he sat there in his pajamas playing video games. He was between jobs again and, in his controlling way, started to prod me for not being **at** work right at nine o'clock. I wasn't overly concerned because I typically stayed later than five o'clock and put a lot more than forty hours in a week. As our "discussion" escalated, I told him, perhaps, I wouldn't go into work at all that day. His reaction was to throw a glass at me, that shattered on the floor, spraying upwards at me, just missing my eyes. My reaction was to get a suitcase, throw some clothes in it and go to my parent's house. I had had enough of his controlling, egotistical ways, and I was not going to be abused physically, after being abused verbally and psychologically for so long.

It had gotten so bad, my emotions were so frazzled, and my self-esteem was so low, that I started to a see a psychologist towards the end of our marriage. I started to become extremely obsessed with how I looked and would spend hours in front of a mirror staring at my self, picking myself apart. My psychologist diagnosed me with Body Dsymorphic Disorder (BDD). Burt's continued controlling and belittling of me was taking its toll on me. As I was being torn apart by him on the outside, I was tearing myself up on the inside, continually putting myself down.

I guess when you are a teenager or, even in your early twenties, you don't notice being controlled, or perhaps, you accept it more. At least I did. My father was an "old world" Italian male. He did little to help around the house. I grew up watching my mother do all the housework, all the cleaning and cooking, while working outside the home full-time. It just seemed expected at the time to me. So, when I was first married to Burt, it wasn't unnatural that we lived just as my parents did, but, after a number of years in corporate America, talking to other career women, I started to realize that perhaps a marriage should be an equal partnership in every way. Each contributing financially to the partnership and in their work effort at home. My eyes began to open as I grew up.

"There's a new Mother Nature taking over" (finally!)

The next year proved to be extremely difficult. I had been with Burt for close to nineteen years, and suddenly, I was on my own. I had never been on my own or alone as an adult. To say I had second thoughts about leaving him was another understatement. To make it more difficult, he kept asking me not to go through with the divorce. He said that if we got back together, he would change. Even in the courtroom during our final divorce proceeding, he asked me not to go through with it. It was one of the hardest decisions I had ever made. I did love him, but I knew he would never change.

Two years earlier I had left after an argument and stayed with my parents. The second day I was there, Burt came over and pleaded with me to come home, saying that he would change, that he would even go to the doctor's to get pills to help him control his temper (and he hated taking pills). So, I did go home after a couple of weeks. And, things were better, for a while. He tried to control his temper. He helped out around the house, he even considered my feelings, however, after three months the old Burt started to show up again. He was quick to anger, and did little to help at home. He wasn't working, yet he was expected me to do all the housework, all the shopping, and all the cooking, after working eight or nine hours a day.

So, I persisted in going through with the divorce, feeling that he wouldn't change, believing that we just were not compatible.

"We have been conditioned in life to think what is outside is more important than what is on the inside." ~ **Ramtha (J.Z. Knight)**
What The Bleep Do We Know!?

Transition Years

For two years after my divorce, all I did was work and go home to my house and my new puppy, a beagle I named Felicia. My girlfriends all seemed to be married, so they didn't want to (or weren't allowed to) go out with me. And, there was no Internet or Internet dating at that time.

My first boyfriend was Simon, who whisked me off my feet so speak, and wanted to whisk me away period. He was a project manager for a national retail chain store, building new stores for them. He would go into a new location and manage all aspects of the store construction until the store opened. A project might take him six months in one location, then he would be off to the next site. He was from Southern California and looked and acted like it, tall, blond, and easy going, with a great sense of humor.

Simon made being with another man appear easy and natural for me, even though it took quite a while for the scared little girl inside of me who hadn't dated in seventeen years, to subside. He taught me how to date again. And, it was exciting to be wined and dined as an adult But, Simon's project was coming to end after a few months and he didn't want us to end. He asked me go back to California with him and make our relationship more permanent. It was another difficult decision. As attracted I was to him, I couldn't think of leaving my home, family and a secure job. He left, and I was alone again. But, perhaps I was left with a little more self-confidence.

I no longer stayed at home on weekends by myself. I had enough confidence to go out to a restaurant or club on my own, rather than staying home and feeling alone or sorry for myself. That's how my next relationship started.

I was introduced to Peter through a mutual friend I had met at a club I went to on weekends. Peter and I hit it off immediately. He was distinguished, mature and witty. He was a successful semi-retired businessman that loved to go out. Again, as with my relationship with Simon, he was quite a contrast to my married life. It seemed as if I had always had to twist Burt's arm to go out on a weekend. And, then we usually doubled with the same couple, year after year. Now, I was with another man, that, like Simon wanted to go out to dinner every night. I enjoyed forgetting how to cook, and even how to clean.

When Peter and I were out at a restaurant or club we had a great time. However, things started to become a bit more strained when we were at his house. I remember how impressed I was when he first took me there. It was a spacious ranch house, with an immaculately landscaped yard, with an in-ground pool in a private backyard. The inside was even more impressive and immaculate. I soon learned his house was his obsession.

Peter convinced me to move in with him after a couple months of dating. Talk about another contrast to my married life. It was as if I was a queen living with Peter. He wouldn't let me lift a finger. He did all the housework and we ate out every meal. He had a huge kitchen in his house that was spotless because he never used it. I soon realized that his cleaning obsession was in fact a disorder. When it came to his house he was extremely OCD. His Obsessive Compulsive Disorder was to the point that nothing could be out of order. If I opened the silverware drawer, I had to do it carefully so nothing would shift around, or I would hear about it!

Once, I was watching TV and Peter came over to me, took me by the hand and led me to the bathroom. He showed me that I had changed a roll of toilet paper the wrong way; it had to be that the over hang of the roll had to line-up with the line of the nearest tile. After a few weeks of this I moved back home. I was not going to live "walking on egg shells" again (not that he would ever have one on the floor!).

But, leaving him wasn't that easy. Peter called me daily, asking me back. Finally, I agreed to have dinner with him again, and he pleaded with me to move back in. He promised me that he would "change." Even though that sounded familiar, the following week I agreed to give it another try. And, of course, at first he was calmer and appeared a little less preoccupied with his house. But, this too didn't last that long. After a few more months he was getting more and more obsessive. So I left again. Unfortunately, this pattern of back and forth with Peter would last for nearly two years.

In the process of this back and forth relationship, changes occurred in my career. My company was bought out, a new management team came in, and after twenty years I decided to leave. I moved back in with Peter, had rents that covered my home mortgage, and took a break from working fifty plus hours a week.

In the next year, I fell into a routine at Peter's house. It seemed as if everyday was the same; get up when I felt like it, go out to lunch, come back and lie around the pool, watch T.V., go out to dinner. Another contrast to my adult working world. It wasn't long before I started to feel totally useless. Peter wouldn't let me do anything around the house. All he was concerned with was my getting dressed up and looking good so he could take me out to dinner every night. But, I never felt good enough. It was almost as if I was part of his house, I had to be perfect around him. My hair had to be the right color. If it wasn't exactly the right shade he liked, he would send me back to the hairdresser. My dress had to be appropriate for where we were going or I had to change. And "heaven forbid" if I had anything but a French manicure on my nails. He often told me that he was very proud and that, "How I looked was a reflection of him." All this contributed to my self-esteem becoming more and more demolished, and it didn't help my BDD either.

In order to look better, to please Peter more, I started to go for body wraps. Little did I know then how everything happens for a reason. This is how I met my "big sister," Claudia. I started to see her almost on a weekly basis. During my wraps we had numerous conversations about everything going on in our lives. I found Claudia always so helpful, supportive and caring, always genuinely concerned for me. I on the other hand would pour my heart out to her, and exuded depression and negativity. Claudia later told me that I was so depressing to be around at that time, that she would be negative and depressed for days after I left her. It was so bad that Claudia's mother even told her that she shouldn't see me anymore. Claudia's response was, "No, I won't give up on her. There is something about Mary!" And I thank God that she never did give up on me.

During one of our conversations she told me she had a revelation, of why I was so depressed all the time. She told me, "Mary you have no purpose in life. You can't just lie around the pool all day long. You need to find something to do with your life." She was right, I was only in my early forties, a little too young to be retired already, living as if this was it.

Another breakup occurred with Peter over my spilling some water on the carpet in his breezeway where we watched T.V. (his formal living room was too good to use). He went ballistic on me again telling me how I didn't respect his house or his property. He went on and on. It was only water, for goodness sake. Finally, I told him, "You wouldn't have to worry about my spilling anything again because I am out of here!"

Perhaps, this was what I needed at the time. A little impetus to get me to move forward, to start doing something with my life, as Claudia had told me. I moved back to my home and planned to start a career where I could help people. I enrolled in a medical technology program at a local technical school called Lincoln Tech. Coincidently, as I began a new career in the medical field, my father started to become sick and was in a nursing home. I was feeling a little overwhelmed and alone, and called Peter. He was there to comfort me and was always supportive. It wasn't long before I moved back in with him, again.

But, of course, after a few more months he was getting to me again. I believe the final straw came when he started to yell at me because he found a crumb on his door handle. I had served him a piece of cake, and the next day he called me and started to yell at me because he found a crumb. I would had been so elated if someone would had served me cake, yet he was yelling at me! I left for good this time.

The next year I was occupied with going to school working on my medical tech degree, and taking care of my father. His health was declining, and he was back and forth between the hospital and a nursing home. When I was going to school a teacher that was close to my age wanted me to meet his brother, Gordan. I finally agreed to meet him during our Christmas break. Little did I know that my relationship with Gordan was destined to begin to draw me into worlds I never knew existed!

II ~ The Physical Battles Begins

"Wake up you have been sleeping, open those weary eyes....Heaven lies within in you, no more compromise, Won't you listen to your heart? It beckons time and time again. Wake-up, you have been sleeping."

~ Wake-up
By Mark Stanton Welch

That meeting with Gordan was delayed, however. Christmas morning, I woke up feeling fine, and my ex-husband, Burt, called to wish me a merry Christmas to see how I was doing. It had been seven years since our divorce, and he would still occasionally call. He was still single, and I believe he was checking periodically to see if I was too.

A short while after that call, a strange sensation started to come over me. It began with my tongue feeling numb. Then I couldn't feel it at all, and I became terrified I would swallow my tongue! I was feeling dizzy, nauseous and was having difficulty standing. This was highly unusual for me, as I was rarely ever sick. My mother came home in the afternoon, saw I couldn't stand up and took me to the hospital. On the way to the hospital I had to continually stick my tongue, and hold it with my fingers, fearing I would swallow it.

The doctors initially thought it was an allergic reaction. But, I didn't know anything I was allergic to, nor, had I eaten anything unusual that morning, or even the day before. Doctors conducted all sorts of tests, and couldn't find anything wrong with me. Blood tests, blood pressure, heart rate, even a CAT scan revealed nothing wrong. Everything was perfectly normal. Later that evening in the hospital, the feeling started to return to my tongue. I was no longer afraid of swallowing it and they allowed me to go home. But, still not feeling myself, I stayed with my parents the next two weeks resting and helping my mother take care of my father.

I finally went out with Gordan the end of January, after having returned to school. Gordan was a few years younger than I. He never had been married and appeared to be a very stable individual. He owned his own house and had a good job working as an electrician for a college. It wasn't long before we were spending a lot of time together. For Valentine's Day I gave him a big stuffed frog that sang "Rescue Me." Little did I know how relevant that would be in the near future.

Gordan loved to go out and have a good time, and for the next year that's what we did. He was unlike Peter because he liked to go out and do different things, go to different restaurants and places. But, after a while, I started to get the feeling that, that was all he wanted to do, go to work, and go out and party after work. I had doubts that he would ever settle down and be a responsible husband. Not that I envisioned a family at that point, but, I did want someone who was concerned with more than which bar to go to that night.

One time, Gordan came over with a gift for me, which was unusual. Unusual because he didn't often give me gifts, and this wasn't a special occasion. He had been in a gift shop, called *The Land of Ahz* (Oz), and had seen a purple stained glass moon with a green stained glass star together. I told him, "Thanks, its pretty," and I hung it in a window in my den. I would later find out the significance of it, how everything has meaning, and happens for a reason.

The following February my father passed away and my relationship with Gordan became more sporadic. Prior to his passing

I had finished school and was taking care of my father full-time for a few months before he died. That spring, life seemed to be really hitting me between the eyes. My father was gone, my mother was selling her house, I wasn't working or in school, and I had no stable relationships.

It became very easy not to get out of bed in the morning or in the afternoon, or sometimes in the evening too. There were times I didn't leave my house for days. Gordan would still call me to go out. But, I would only see him once or twice a month, again, not feeling that the relationship was going anywhere. I kept in touch with him because I foolishly had let him borrow money. He would come by monthly to pay me and would want to go out, and occasionally I conceded.

Another concern I had about Gordan, which I understand now, but didn't at the time, was when he would have nightmares. They would upset him so much that he couldn't talk about them, or even function at times after having had one. This seemed to be a weekly occurrence with him. He would just tell me they were nightmares, usually not wanting to go into detail. Once, however, he did elaborate about being chased by monsters. But, what really ended our relationship, to my incredible disbelief, was when he stole from me!

After close to two years of seeing him, he started to want to be more serious with me and kept telling me he would change (seems as if I had heard that before). That's when ironically he stole thousands of dollars in jewelry from me. In my closet, I had hanging sleeves of diamond bracelets, and necklaces that had been given to me mostly by my father. When I went to look for a bracelet one day, I couldn't find the entire sleeve. I started to think, who was in my house in the past few months? Who would know I had a sleeve of diamond jewelry? The only person, that knew this, and had been in my house, was Gordan!

The next time he came over, I confronted him about my missing jewelry. His response was, "Prove it!" And, I could have sworn his eyes glowed red when he said the word, "It." So, of course that was it with him. I couldn't believe that someone who said he loved me, who was even talking about marriage, and whom I helped, and even let borrow thousands, would steal from me.

To my surprise, the next week Gordan called and wanted to go out. It was as if nothing had happened. He again started to go into how much he loved me and wanted to be with me on the phone. I was in disbelief that he would think that I would ever go out with him again, but I had a bit of a dilemma. He still owed me thousands from the loan I had given him, so, if I totally broke off with him I felt I could certainly kiss that money goodbye as well. So, I made an excuse about not feeling well and abruptly ended the call. But, he too persisted and continued calling me. And, every time he called I made an excuse, certainly not wanting to see him anymore.

I started to become more and more depressed. Some days I wouldn't get out of bed at all. Everyday I would lie in bed, not listening to the radio, not watching TV, just lying there beating myself up. "How could I be so stupid?" "How could I have let all the men in my life treat me as they did?" "How could all this have happened to me?" For ten days all I did was lie in bed, being depressed, feeling useless and worthless.

Battle of Souls

> *"The people that are the hardest to love*
> *are the ones that need love the most."*
> **~ The Peaceful Warrior**

The following week I started to feel sick all over. It wasn't a cold. I had pressure and intense bloating in my stomach. But, I didn't have food poisoning. My face felt as if it was on fire. My lips were burning and peeling. I had canker sores on my tongue (a first). And, I was extremely exhausted.

I went to my primary care doctor. He couldn't determine

initially what was wrong so he sent me for tests, blood tests, MRI, EKG, blood pressure tests again. And, just like the last time I was in the hospital, two years earlier on Christmas day, everything came back perfectly normal.

Everyday I was feeling worse. The doctors couldn't figure out what was wrong. One day, I felt good enough to go out for lunch, or, so I thought. As I was getting out of my car to walk into the restaurant, I started to feel as if the pressure in my stomach was moving through my body in a lumpy mass. It was like an alien presence moving around in my body, moving from my stomach, to my leg, to my back. I had trouble walking. Somehow, I made it to a table. But, when the waitress came over to me it was as if she was fading in and out of focus. I thought perhaps if I ate something I would feel better, and have more energy and these strange feelings would go away.

I did feel a little better after eating, and I did regain some strength. I made it home and called my mother to let her know I couldn't pick her up from work that afternoon, that I wasn't feeling well. When she got home she checked on me and I started to tell her about energy moving in my body like an alien living and moving around inside me. She said, "Dear, we need to go to the mental hospital." I told her, "I'm not going to a mental hospital I'll be OK. Perhaps, I just need some rest." That satisfied my mother enough not to call 911 to have them take me away.

The second week of my physical misery, still feeling exhausted, feeling as if I was ten months pregnant, my face swollen and red, I got a call from Gordan. I kept putting him off when he wanted to drop by with loan payments, knowing that he still wanted to take me out. However, this time he called and said he would be right over with money for me.

When he arrived, he startled me because his eyes looked like they were solid black. No white around his pupils. I said, "Gordan what's wrong with your eyes?" He replied, "There's nothing wrong with them. How are you feeling? Did you get your test results back?"

They had come back, but, I didn't want him to know anything about my personal life at this point in our non-relationship. So, I told him I hadn't gotten any results yet. But, he was persistent. "Mary aren't you wondering what's wrong? Don't you think it's strange you're so sick?"

I was starting to get a real creepy feeling that he knew more than he was telling me. I told him, "Maybe you should go, I'll be fine." Gordan said, "Really, Mary, will you? Why don't we go out. Maybe you will feel better with a change of scenery." Go out with him at that time was the last thing I wanted to happen, but, again I wanted to stay on somewhat good terms with him because he still owed me money, so I conceded.

So, we went to a restaurant down the street from my house. While we were having dinner, Gordan started to talk about John Lennon, and how he hated the guy who had shot him. He said, if he could, he would shoot the guy that had killed the former Beatle. I told him that would make him just like him. He said he didn't care, and the only reason he wouldn't do it was that he didn't want to end up in jail. I told him that was just the opposite of what John Lennon was all about. He always sang about peace and love. By you doing what that person did to Lennon makes you just like his killer. He should be more like the song "Live Like You Are Dying," by Tim McGraw.

"I loved deeper, I spoke sweeter,
...I gave forgiveness
I had been denying."

He didn't pay much attention to what I said and he then started to pick on our waitress. I saw that she was getting uncomfortable and told him, "Gordan why are you continuing to harass her?" He replied, "Because I can. I want to see how far I can get with her." This was a side of him I rarely saw when we were dating. At that point, I said it was time to go and abruptly got up to leave. Outside

Gordan said, "Lets go somewhere else." He wanted to go to another bar closer to his house. I don't know what "possessed me," but I agreed and left with him.

At the other bar, he, all of a sudden, started to tell me things that no one else knew. He started out by saying, "I know things about you!" I said, "Really? Like what?" "Like the time you stopped by my house to use the bathroom." He described what I had done in there. "And you didn't even pet my dog." My mouth must have dropped open because I remembered a few months earlier doing just that. I had been in the area of his house, had needed to go to the bathroom, had let myself in, which I rarely did, had gone to the bathroom, and being in a rush hadn't stopped to pet his dog. Again, that was highly unusual for me because I love dogs and would always play with his.

Gordan continued, "I know why you're called Mary!" I was dumbfounded. How could he know these things? How could he describe my every move when he wasn't there? What was the relevance of my name?

Perhaps, someone that was calm and in control would have pressured him for more details, but, I was so flustered I merely said, "Oh my God Gordan!" He quickly retorted, "Am I a messenger from God, or am I?" As he said "Or am I," he turned his head away from me, then back towards me, and his eyes glowed a bright red!

I jumped up saying, "My God, Gordan you're the devil! Get away from me!" I got up to leave and he said, "What can you do?" I don't know why but all I said was, "**I AM.**" He waved his hand at me saying, "Come on." As if he wanted a battle right there. And as if that wasn't enough to totally freak me out he then said,

"Mary you're an Angel, but, you are going to HELL!"

I had had enough of him, whoever he was at the time. I didn't care. I just had to get away from him. I left the bar and went outside and called my mother to come get me. During the ride home with my mother, I turned the radio on, and all I heard was, "Come on girl it's the **battle of the souls!**"

Now the radio was talking to me! The ride home and the rest of the night I couldn't help thinking what was going on? At the time, I didn't realize this was in fact, the beginning of the **Battle of the Souls** and of my spiritual awakening. But, I was scared out of my wits, and I had no idea at the time what was happening.

I kept thinking over and over again, "Not only do I have aliens living inside me, not only is my ex-boyfriend the devil, but now the radio is talking to me!" Was I going crazy? Was I having a nervous breakdown? Little did I know, it would only get worse.

When I got home I called my friend Claudia, who in the past few years was like a big sister to me. I tried to explain a little of what was going on to her. She came back with, "Mary, you're scaring me." "Scaring you! How do you think I feel?" I retorted.

"I don't know what to tell you Mary. Maybe you should look up the word *karma*." At the time, I didn't know what that meant. And, talking to Claudia months later she told me she didn't even know why she had said that. Since then I've to come to learn that,

*The **Divine** often talks through people.*

I went down to my mother's. After she had sold her house she moved into the first floor apartment in my house, and I asked her how to look up something on her computer. I was not accustomed to using the computer at all. I typed the word "karma" in and was lead to a Website that was talking about Buddha's levels of enlightenment. It said:

Karma: *Sanskrit word meaning act, action or performance. In Indian religions it is the concept of action or deeds that causes a cycle of cause and effect often through lifetimes.*

The Website talked about of ten levels of beings, starting with hellish beings in the first level to angelic beings in the ninth level. The tenth level was the "Buddha/God" level. Once you reach that level, you don't have to come back (be reincarnated) anymore, you are complete (a perfect ten). In reading this, it just hit me that somehow I knew I was at the ninth level in this life, and Gordan was at the first level.

After printing this all out, I decided to get in my car and go for a ride, as it usually calmed my nerves. As I got into my car, the first song on the radio again said, *"Come on girl this is the battle of the souls."* I was really wondering what was going on. As I was driving I started to think, battle or no battle, I just knew I had to help Gordan.

Good vs. Evil

Over the next week, every TV station I turned on had some kind of battle going on between positive and negative, good and evil. Each day I was getting sicker and sicker, canker sores in my mouth, stomach being bloated, and I was feeling weaker and weaker. I spent most of the day in bed not feeling well at all. I felt as if I had to go to the bathroom all the time, but when I tried I couldn't.

At one point, I walked into my mother's bedroom to ask her something when I heard her TV say, "She doesn't want to be with me I'm going to kill her!" I stopped in my tracks and looked at her TV. Whatever show that was on, started to mimic everything that had happened to me recently. Seeing a doctor, breaking up with a boyfriend that stole jewelry, it even talked about the ex-boyfriend's mother losing her wedding ring down a sink, which had happened to Gordan's mother that very week. I turned to my mom and said, "Are you hearing all this? Its my life exactly! What's going on?" She replied, "Honey, you are making too much of this. It's just a coincidence."

Then the TV said, "All you ever wanted was for your daughter to be safe!" When my mother heard that her mouth dropped open, because that was exactly how she felt. I said, "Still just a coincidence, mom?" and left. It really upset me when my mother was speechless. She never gets upset.

I decided to go out for a ride in my car and when I started the car, the first thing I heard on the radio was

"These aren't coincidences, these are acts of God!"

I ran back into my mom's house and told her what I had just heard. "Is that a coincidence too?" She was still speechless.

Over the next few days every time I put the TV on, it talked to me. The TV printed out on the screen:

I'm going to teach you the power of nature.
I'm going to teach you the power of knowledge.

I was wondering what was going on. I thought maybe a show was coming on. But, that was all there was. As I continued to lie in bed, feeling sicker and sicker, having waves of excruciating pains through my abdomen, feeling more and more exhausted, I saw good vs. evil battles being played out on TV.

Then the TV even started to talk to me. I was watching a show feeling that I had to go to the bathroom, but not wanting to get up when a person on the show turned to me and said, "Go ahead, we'll wait for you!" Then, when I came back, he said, "She's back!"

Another time, I was watching the Tonight Show, and Jay Leno was making a joke of someone being able to think about going to the gym and getting the same effects of actually going to the gym. When he said that I got a feeling to pay attention. And, then it made perfect sense to me, "Yes, just think how you want to be."

The next day I was watching TV, and I said to myself, "I don't believe this, all that's happening to me." Just then the TV showed a smiley face winking at me, and all it said was, "*Believe it!*"

In between these battles on TV, I was getting messages of how to help Gordan. The messages started to come so fast one day that I started to call him with them giving him one message at a time, saying:

"I forgive you."

"I don't care about the jewelry."

"Wake-up. Are you awake?"

"Can't we take a sad song and make it better?"

"For when you let it into your heart, it starts to get better."

He wouldn't pick-up the phone, but I knew he was hearing my messages. Then I heard what he was thinking; "This must be from God, no one else can have this much love!"

The next day he did call and I asked him "Did you get my messages?" "Yes, I did I didn't even go to work, because they were upsetting me so much. What was going on with you?" I said "Nothing, I'm fine now." I thought if he wasn't going to say anything, neither was I.

The following day I was feeling worse than ever, but I couldn't stop watching TV, I was getting so many messages. Thoughts were just coming into my mind. I started writing things down in a notebook:

"Love is all it takes to put up with what we have to face."

"What really matters is what happens in us, not to us."

"God is for us, who can be against? He's the best that's ever been, so I can only win."

"God is my partner, I can't fail. God doesn't fail. He's the best that's ever been and he is the best part of me."

"Good, bad, positive, negative, opposites you choose."

"There are senders and receivers sent to build character, you'll thank me later!"

"In the darkness you begin to see."
"Don't ever underestimate the power of prayer!"
"Don't give up. You're an angel, Don't you want ecstasy? "Don't
you want ecstasy!"

At one point, my mother asked, "Honey, what are you doing?"
I told her, "I'm going to write a book." Her response was, "That's
nice honey. Are you sure you're feeling okay? Did you take your
medication?" I ignored her and kept writing:

"Cause and effect; at the end of life, it does know what you do with
your life."
"It just is."
"What you think and what the thing you are most afraid of will
happen to you!"
"Stand by cause. It will affect where you go in the next world."
"Make a stand for yourself in this life."

The next day, I still couldn't believe that Gordan didn't answer
the "***Call***." I was still exhausted lying in my mother's den. The battles
on TV were becoming more intense.

A show I was watching had a man who was promising to take
a woman he loved away to a beautiful new world. But, he kept her
waiting for him while he took care of all of his needs first. I was
getting upset watching the show because I thought, "Love doesn't
make someone wait!" I got upset and went into the kitchen thinking,
"He should be more considerate of her feelings."

When I went back to the den the show was over. I thought, "It's
too late! I did the wrong thing! The one time I stood up for myself
I missed out on an opportunity to go to a 'beautiful new world'!" I
started to cry and become hysterical. My mother came out to try to
calm me down. She took her bible out and opened it to point where
it was talking about "salvation." I told her, "No, no I did the wrong
thing. I didn't wait for God. I did the wrong thing!"

Then I saw the TV flash *"The Crimson Crusade."* Under that half the screen was showing positive messages, with the other half answering it with negative. There was no sound just words. I took out my notebook and tried writing it all down, but it was going too fast.

"She will be saved."	*"No she's mine."*
"Love is all that matters."	*"Its too late."*
"God is all love."	*"There is no God."*
"She is standing up for herself."	*"No she isn't."*

I couldn't write it all down, but the final message calmed me down. I can stand up for myself. True love doesn't make you wait, or, try to control you. It respects your wants and wishes. I can stand up for myself.

Later that night I got more messages but, they were not positive. I was trying to relax in the den again when I saw the TV flash:

"Don't set the alarms. Don't lock the door.
There's no escape! Coming February 3rd!"

This was the exact day my father had died the year before. Here I thought it was over, but now it was telling me in two days I was going to be taken too. "There is no escape!"

I thought, "All I can do now is wait for the dark forces to take me." I had more canker sores on my tongue. My face was red and raw. I had dark circles around my eyes. I was feeling even more exhausted. I had excruciating pain in my abdomen. My lips were on fire, and I had to keep putting ice on them to calm the burning. I saw more battles on TV. Every once in a while, the TV would flash *"Coming February 3rd!"* I was petrified! All I could do was wait!

The night of February 2nd I was so scared I slept in my mom's bed with her. In the morning, on February 3rd my mother went to work. I woke-up and felt paralyzed, as if a pile of bricks was on top of me. I couldn't move, I couldn't even lift a finger at this point. I was in so much pain, and so scared. I was thinking, "This is it. This is the end of life!" Then the phone ring, and the answering machine picked up the call. It was Gordan, "Hi Mary. Just calling to see how you are feeling. Call me." I hadn't heard from in days, and now he was calling me this morning. I knew he knew what was going on.

After a while, I got up enough strength to get to the kitchen for something to drink, when I heard my beagle, Felicia, growling. I couldn't see what she was upset about. She was going from room to room, growling at the air. This was very unusual for her, she would never growl.

I looked outside to see what Felicia might be growling at, but there was nothing there. Then I sat in a chair in the living room, facing the street. A few minutes later, an unmarked white van pulled up and parked directly across the street from my house. I thought, "It's the 'cleaner' coming to get me." Just like in the movie *Pulp Fiction* that Gordan loved and had made me watch with him once when we were going out. I was paralyzed with fear. Then the man got out of the van, walked into my yard, then went back to the van and just sat there.

I tried to call my mother to tell her they were coming for me. There was no dial tone. I picked up another phone, still no dial tone. Gordan had called me a while earlier, now all the phones were not working! Did the man in the van cut my phone lines? I thought again, "There is no escape!"

I started to hear horrible screams. Screeching animals. Petrifying sounds coming into the house. This is what Felicia was sensing coming toward me. The messages were real. **There was no escape!**

I got on my hands and knees, praying, "Please don't hurt my dog. She never did anything wrong. You can take me. You can do anything you want to me."

The sounds became stronger and louder. The noise was so loud and frightening that I put my hands over my ears to try and block the noise out, but it made no difference. I started praying to God, "God I'm so sorry for everything I did in my life. I'll try to do better. Please give me another chance." At that exact moment, when I had finished praying, the van left and the screeching noises started to become weaker. They started to fade away until they stopped. Felicia stopped growling as well. I thought it was over and said, "Thank you God. Thank you. I'll really try harder to be better." I was so relieved!

I still felt so sick and weak. But, I felt elated that I had made it through the day. "I will move my life forward now." I thought, "I will do it right now. I have been given a second chance. I made it through February 3rd!"

The next morning, I felt good enough to go for a ride in my car. Driving and listening to music always calmed me down. However, all was still not well.

A positive song I love came on "Love Train" but, that was followed by "On Broadway." In the lyrics, it said, *"I won't stop till I reach the top."* I shook my head in disgust, thinking the evil in the world was just like that. They always had to be on top, to rule and dominate. They had to have the power and control. Just the opposite of the "Love Train" where everyone is peaceful and loving. I was thinking perhaps it is not all over.

Just then, as all these thoughts were flashing through my head, out of no where, a **fireball** came at me out of the air! As soon as it seemed to hit my windshield, it vanished. I swerved my car, then pulled over, thinking, "What just happened?" I thought this was over yesterday, but the battle is still going on!

Driving home, I saw a big smiley face winking on a billboard. A positive sign. I got home alarmed that this wasn't over. I went into the den and turned my radio on. It was playing a Michael Jackson song I love:

"We must bring salvation back. Just look over your shoulder, and I'll be there!"

At the point it said, "Just look over your shoulder," I felt a hard tap on my shoulder! I turned around quickly. No one was there. I was home alone. "What is going on? How is this all happening?" I thought.

I then saw an image of Gordan's face right in front of me, as if he was there in person. I screamed. Petrified again, I got down on my knees again praying, "God please help. I don't know what is going on. I don't know how they are doing this. Please make it stop!"

A few moments later my mother came home and saw I was in such a state. "Honey, I have to take you to the hospital." I thought she was part of a conspiracy to get me to the hospital. To put me away. That's how they were going to get me, say I was nuts, then kill me!

So, I just ran out of the house. I started to walk around my neighborhood. As I walked around, every dog I came across started to growl and bark at me, wanting to attack me. This was extremely unusual. Dogs always loved me. I never had had this happen before. I started to cry thinking, "The dogs are sensing evil all around me. They think I'm evil."

My mother found me and told me, "Get in the car, I have to take you to the hospital." I ran away from her. I went to a neighbor's house, rang the bell and told her, "I need help, I have to call the police." She asked why? When I told her I couldn't tell her she wouldn't let me in. I ran to another house.

I went to a house that I knew, knew me, and I knew that they always liked and respected me. They were former tenants of mine. I saw that both of their cars were in the driveway. I could hear their kids playing inside. But, no one would answer the door. I kept knocking and ringing the bell, but, no one came. I was thinking, "No one is going to help me."

I took out my cell phone and called my friend Joanne "Bud." I had known Joanne for over twenty years at that point, and she was always there for me. She was a true god-send in my life through all my marital and relationship problems. God knew I needed a friend and had sent my "best Bud." God knew how much I would really need her, for, in a matter of hours she would save my life!

Even though she lived in Connecticut, I just wanted someone to know what was happening. She wasn't home (of course) so, I left a message, "Joanne I just want you to know if I die tonight that I'm not crazy! There is a conspiracy to put me away. They are out to kill me. If I die tonight I what you to know I wasn't nuts. They are going to make it look like I was nuts. I love you."

"Where am I going to go?" I thought, "Let me go to the lady across the street. She knows me." I rang her bell and Mrs. Tilly let me in. I had never been in her house before, and as soon as I walked in, right in front of me there was a big picture of Jesus on her wall in the den looking right back at me. I thought, "Jesus you're right here with me." Of course, the only one that would help was Jesus! That's why the other houses hadn't let me in.

"With Jesus the door is always open, and you are always welcome!"

She said, "What's wrong dear?" She was a sweet, elderly lady, in her eighties that had lived across the street from me for close to twenty years. "Mrs. Tilly there's a conspiracy out to get me. If anything happens to me, I just want you to know." But, after seeing Jesus I was relieved, and felt I didn't need to call the police. As I left she said, "Okay, dear, take care. Have a nice day." She must have thought I was really nuts.

As I walked back to my house, I saw a dry cleaning hanger in my mom's car with, "We love our customers" on it. I thought, "Yes, Jesus is with me, serving me." That gave me comfort for a moment.

I ran upstairs in my house and started to get feelings and hear voices telling me that if I went to the hospital I would be tortured. They would keep me alive letting me feel excruciating pain, until I could no longer stand it. I thought that there would be nothing I could do about it if I let them take me to the hospital.

But, I could I do something about it! "Yes," I thought, "I can do something about it. I won't give them the satisfaction of letting them torture me to death." I ran to the kitchen and got a large carving knife. "I won't let them torture me to death!" I started to cut my wrists. I, who was deathly afraid of needles, who didn't even have pierced ears, started to cut myself! But, nothing happened! I cut harder and deeper, but no blood came out! I cut into my thigh. But no blood came out! I sliced my stomach, but no blood came out. I became more frantic wondering, "What is going on? How can I cut my body and not bleed? How can this be?" Then the thought came to me, "The dark forces won't even let me kill myself. They wanted to keep torturing me in this life!"

Then the chandelier in my dining glowed brighter and I heard;

"God is the Highest Power!
The meek shall inherit the earth."

Then the chandelier grew a bit dimmer, and I heard, "No, she waits on me!" I started to gag, and go into convulsions after hearing that. Then the chandelier became a bit brighter again, and I heard:

"God is the Highest Power!
The meek shall inherit the earth."

The lights became dimmer again, and again I heard, "No, she waits on me!" I was gagging even more. It was a battle over my soul! At the exact time I was hearing this, I looked down and my body was now covered with blood! I was wondering, "Who was going to win, when would this all end?"

Then my mother came upstairs saying, "Honey, Joanne Bud is on the phone." She took one look at me covered in blood and screamed, "Oh, my God! What have you done?" She dropped the phone on the dining room table and went downstairs to call 911. I picked up the phone and Joanne said, "Mary what's going on?" I told her, "I just want you to know that I'm not crazy. If they kill me it wasn't my fault! It's a conspiracy to get me! I want you to tell everybody what happened. I want who is responsible to *pay* for this!"

Then the chandelier lights went dim. I realized that I had said the wrong thing! It wasn't up to me to judge and decide what is just! It is up to God. Then I hung up the phone. My mother was back upstairs with towels at that point and started to wrap them around my wrists. I ran into the bathroom and shut the door. I heard voices telling me there was no escape and I would also be ganged raped in the hospital! I had made another mistake, second guessing God when I was talking to Joanne. I thought he had left me.

My mother waited outside knowing that the rescue would be there momentarily. When they arrived my mother quickly told the police and firemen what was going on. Then two of them went into the bathroom to get me. I knew there was nothing I could do. When I came out of the bathroom I was shocked to see over twenty men in my dining room. I thought, "All just for me?" Just as I had been told.

They quickly ushered me down into the ambulance. I was surprised that, when being transported to the hospital, only one EMT was riding in the back with me! My mother was not allowed to go with us. Rather than tend to my cuts, this EMT started to fill out a questionnaire asking me my name, address and health insurance information. He had a stern matter-of-fact tone that reminded me of my first husband.

At the hospital several people were tending to me. And, I could tell who was good and who was evil. Some, the evil ones, had red eyes! The others, the good souls, had normal eyes. The other world, the spirit world, was being played out right in front of me in the physical world. When I heard an evil spirit talking to me, a hospital worker with red eyes would show up. When a positive spirit was talking, a person with normal eyes would be around me.

A person with red eyes came over to me and said to another, also with red eyes, "*It's a fallen angel! We haven't had one of these in a long time!*" I thought, "What are they talking about? I'm not an angel."

Then, I was being told by evil spirits that when they were going to give me stitches for my cuts I would feel extreme pain. But, the doctor that came to work on my cuts had normal eyes, and I didn't feel a thing!

I kept hearing the battle being played out in the spirit world. Good spirits (God or my Archangels, perhaps) arguing with evil spirits. I saw a doctor who was in charge of the E.R. staring at me with red eyes and I heard an evil spirit say, "She can see me." Then I heard:

"Light can always see in the dark."

A nurse with red eyes came up to me and I could tell that she was very uncaring and under complete control by the evil doctor with the red eyes who was in charge. She began asking me questions, very matter-of-factly like the ambulance EMT. I was then being showed and told how they are all under control by evil forces. They have to obey these evil forces or this life will be miserable for them.

The Hospital Underworld

After that, they wheeled me down the hall and it kept going downhill, which I thought was quite unusual. Then I saw a sign in the hallway that said *"UNDERWORLD."* I had no idea what that meant. At the time, I just thought it was an unusual name for a hospital wing.

They put me in a room by myself. I was still in unbearable pain. My abdomen felt as if it was going to blow up. My teeth were also in agony. After a few minutes in my room alone, I looked up and in the corner of the room and I noticed a shining ball of light. I thought, "God you are here, you didn't leave me!" Then the thought came to me that he was just here to say goodbye! I had made too many mistakes. He had come to me to say goodbye! How was I going to live without God? He didn't care about me anymore! Then I said to the ball of light crying, "I'm going to miss you." Then it disappeared.

I thought this is what Gordan had told me was going to happen! That, *"I'm an angel but I'm going to hell!"* God is abandoning me! How could Gordan have known?

I was just lying in bed, crying, in excruciating pain. Dark forces were telling me that I would have to live my life in pain and in the cold. This is hell! Then, just at that moment, in the physical world, a nurse came in and put a fan on a chair facing me and turned it on high. I was freezing. It was February, and she turns a fan on me! Then I heard evil spirits tell me that they were going to rip my teeth out without any Novocain. My teeth where on fire at that point.

I was being told that at 11:00 pm I would be "*Taken.*" There was no escape. Then I started to hear those screaming animals coming toward me again. I was thinking, "I would have to be there for eternity. This is hell!" I was in excruciating pain, freezing, by myself, where no one cares. How can I live in a world where no one cares? I said out loud, "I CARE!"

At that point, a male nurse came into my room to sit with me. I told him I had to go to the bathroom, but I knew I wouldn't be able to go. That was part of my torture. To feel as if I had to go to the bathroom but, that you are unable to. They told me, "You will always feel this terrible pain." I was being shown that this is how I would have to live throughout eternity. But, it wasn't eleven o'clock yet, maybe I could go to the bathroom.

When I got up to go to the bathroom, I looked out of my room, down the hall and didn't see anyone. No lights on. No other patients in other rooms. No one at the reception desk. I asked the nurse, "Am I the only one on this floor?" But, he didn't answer me. In the bathroom I began thinking, "I have to get out of here! This is where they are going to torture and kill me!" I ripped the I.V. out of my arm. I quickly pushed the bathroom door open and ran down the dark hall. I got to an elevator and pushed the up button saying,

"Please God save me. Please open." The elevator door opened, I got in pushed the up button, and the doors closed just as the male nurse was trying to get in.

When the doors opened there was light! There was civilization! It was as a hospital should be nurses, doctors, and people working as they should be. Almost as soon as I entered the hall I was on, two male attendants grabbed me by the arms and brought me to another room. As they ushered me down the hall I kept saying "Please don't take me back down there! I don't want to go to hell! I'll be good! Please! Please! Please!"

They brought me to another room on that floor. It had light! That's all that mattered to me. They put me into a bed and a nurse, with regular eyes put another I.V in me, and I believe upped my medication. I woke up a couple of days later. I didn't care the room had light! I was no longer freezing. I was no longer in hell!

When I did wake up, I saw that there was a breakfast tray by my bed. I opened the milk carton on the tray, took a sip, and put it back down. As I looked at it, it struck me that the opened milk carton formed a *smiley* face. I thought that God was still with me. He didn't abandon me!

I got out of bed a little while later to look around the ward I was on. As I was walking down the hall, another patient came up to me and gave me a note saying, "I want you to read this. It's from Mohammad!" I had no idea who Mohammad was, but not wanting to irritate him, I took it and read it. It was a beautiful passage by the prophet. After I handed it back to him, he said, "You know what I'm going to name this?" "No, what?" He said, "I'm going to call it '*The Rise of the Fallen Angel*'!"

I thought, "Oh, my God! How did he know that?" I thought all of these supernatural happenings were over, that I was no longer in the *Underworld*. But, they weren't over. Little did I know this was still only the beginning!

The next few days I met with several doctors and therapists. I tried to explain to them what had happened to me, what had caused me to try to kill myself and leave this world. I told them that the TV and radio were talking to me. That good and evil were fighting all around me. That I was hearing a battle for my soul in the spirit dimension. That I could tell who were good and who were evil by the color of their eyes. That there are unseen worlds all around us! **There was a whole other world going on at the same time within our world, but most people can't see it, or are unaware of it.** But, for some reason they thought I was nuts!

They upped my medication again. I woke up a few days later, again. When I did wake, I weakly opened my eyes, and I saw a nun peeking in to see if I wanted communion. I was so tired that I closed my eyes and heard her leave. But, I wanted communion! Somehow, I got up enough strength to get out of bed and look down the hall. As I did, I saw that she was just getting ready to get on the elevator. I said, "Please don't leave me! I want communion!" She returned and said to me, *"I thought you were awake!"*

I got it. It was my choice to tell God what I wanted. I had free choice. She, (or, God) was not going to force her will on me. She gave me communion. I told her to see me everyday I was there. "Do not pass me by again, and if I'm sleeping please wake me up!"

One day, I got up, planning to take a walk down the hall, and I couldn't find my bathrobe that my mother had brought in for me from home. I thought that it was strange it was not in my room. Then I heard a commotion in the hall and looked out to see another female patient with my bathrobe on. She was lying on the floor as two male attendants were dragging her by her feet and she was screaming, "Please don't take me to HELL!"

On the way back to my room, I noticed on the bulletin board a sign saying, "Are we having FUN yet?" I started to think to myself, "How is this all happening? Everything I am thinking is happening, being acted out, right in front of me." At the time, I had no idea of the power of one's thoughts.

I went back in my room still thinking, "What is going on? It's still happening, even up here!" At that point, another female patient

I had seen a couple of times when we had group sessions, walked into my room and said, "I want you to have this." It was a stuffed hippo with a heart on it that said, "**Love ya.**" I couldn't believe it! I always signed cards to people "Love ya." I told her, "No, I can't take this." She reaffirmed, "It's for you. It's meant for you!" Here again, I thought it was a clear message, good answering evil. This gave me some relief after what I had just been through.

The next day, I had a new roommate. I told her my name and I asked what her name was. She said, "My name is **Karma**." I almost fainted. I laid down in my bed and pulled the covers over my head. "What is going on?" I asked myself. I thought, "Everything that happened before I got here, that I had seen, is coming back! What dimension am I in?"

The day after that, we had another group session. At that session, I saw the girl who had had my bathrobe on and told her, "You know that bathrobe you had on yesterday? It's mine." She said, "Oh, I'm sorry. They just put it my room." Then she got up, went to her room and got it for me. No problem, I thought, what a nice person. I wondered what had happened yesterday to her?

I hated these "group sessions" because all we did was sit around and play board games. At one point, I even asked the head therapist there, "What is the point of all this? We are not learning anything. There is no growth here." He didn't answer me. Why would he? I was the "crazy" one. But, I knew if wanted to get out of here I had to "play their games."

I went back to my room after that session, and I saw a man's winter glove on my tray table by my bed. I asked my roommate, Karma, "Do you know where this glove came from?" She said, "I have no idea." My heart sank. I thought back to when I was first married and my husband wouldn't put the heat on in the winter, and I had to wear gloves to bed. I got freaked-out again. Where did that come from?

I left the room and went to the solarium where other patients were watching TV. After a while, I went back to my room. As I entered my room, the glove was under a wheel of the tray table, being "squashed!" I thought, "Yes, a positive sign. I am not going to be controlled any longer by overbearing males!"

I went into the bathroom and when I came out the glove was gone! "Karma did you take that glove?" She told me, "No, what glove?" I looked around the room, but, it was gone. Not under my bed, or, around the tray table, or down the hall. It was gone. I let go of thinking about where it went and was just glad it was squashed, and gone. "Perhaps, this is it. It is all over," I thought, I hoped! But, it was far from being over!

The next day, after our "group session" I came back to my room and saw a bouquet of white roses on my tray table. It was exactly like my wedding bouquet when I married Burt! It was as if it was saying to me, "No. You are still mine!" I asked the reception nurse where the flowers had come from. She told me, "Your mother dropped them off when you were in group."

I went back to my room thinking I really want to get rid of them, but, I didn't want to just throw them out. Just then the girl who had, had my bathrobe on came in and said, "What beautiful flowers." I thought to myself, "She is so nice, I'll give the roses to her." So, a little later that day, I walked down to her room and gave them to her. She was so thankful, "No one has ever given me flowers like this. Thank you so much." I felt good that I made her happy and that I didn't have a reminder of a negative sign in my room.

One day, the head psychiatrist was interviewing me, asking me, "How are you doing? Are you still hearing or seeing things?" I was well enough to know the correct responses at this point, "No, of course not." Even though I was on their "meds," it was still happening all around me. But, I wasn't going to tell him that. They would never let me out of there.

After my "interview," I went to the solarium, and saw all the other patients were watching a show on TV. In the show, a baby was about to fall out of a window, when someone saved it. The patients watching the show started to clap because the baby was saved. I asked, "What is going on?" One of the patients turned to me and said, "The baby got saved because you walked into the room." Then the other patients turned to me and started to applaud me. I thought they were all crazy. I just left and went back to my room.

I saw Karma packing I asked her, "What are you doing?" She said "I've been discharged. I'm going home." As she was packing, she held up a pair of pants that had sparkles all over them and asked me, "Do you like these?" I couldn't believe it I had those exact same pants at home. I started thinking that was another bad sign.

Right after the other patients told me that the baby was saved because of me, Karma was telling me that I would go home to a life like hers. I had found out that she was a mother of four young children and had a very controlling "Old World" husband. At one point she just couldn't take it anymore and had a breakdown, and ended up as my roommate. Was Spirit telling me I was going back to a life of being controlled? I just lay in bed the rest of the day, feeling sad and depressed.

The next day, I had positive news. A nurse came in and told me I was being discharged. It was February 14th, Valentine's Day!

> *"You have to go through the darkness to see the light!"*
> **~ Debbie Ford**

Awakening From Mental Health

Finally, I was going home, and on February 14th! I said to myself, "Thank you God for letting me go home on the day of love." That morning in the hospital, I had breakfast, went into the bathroom to wash-up, and was surprised to find a card on my tray table by my bed when I returned. There was no one else in my room, my roommate had left the day before, and no visitors were allowed at this time. Most people on my ward were still sleeping. The card had a bunch of golden retrievers on the front, and read:

"I thought love was only true in fairy tales,
then I saw your face.
*Now **I'm a retriever!**"*

As I opened the card it simply said, "Happy Valentines Day," with no signature on it. I knew in my heart the card was from **God!** Later, I would come to find out what "retriever" really meant, that it had nothing to do with dogs!

God was always with me!

Just like in the *"Footprints"* poster, of which,
I have several in my house.

I was glad to be home finally, but, I still felt like a mess, physically and emotionally. I still had canker sores in my mouth and on my tongue, I was exhausted and couldn't get warm. I felt as if I had pins and needles throughout my body, and bloating and pressure in my abdomen. I felt as if I had energy that I had no control of, surging around my body, and I couldn't sit still. My nerves were still frazzled after all I had been through. I was petrified even to turn on the TV. I only listened to music, and then the radio and songs started to talk to me. Like:

"I've been alive forever, and I wrote the very first song.
…My home lies deep within you
And I've got my own place in your soul
I Am music, music, and I write the songs."
~I Write The Songs
By Barry Manilow

After hearing this song I thought to myself, "What did that song just say?" Then the radio started playing "Listen to the Music"… all the time! Right after that, "I Am Everyday People"…. .my own beliefs are in my songs, started to play, and then, "Love Train." As I was thinking, that the songs were talking to me, they, in fact, kept saying "Yes we are talking to you!" Then the next song came on, and I was astonished! "You Sang to Me," came on and it really spoke to me as well:

"…all the while you were in front of me, I never realized.
I didn't see it, but I feel it.
All the words you said to me about,
life, the truth and being free.
You showed me what life needs to be."

~*You Sang to Me*
By Marc Anthony

I started to realize what I was listening to was ***more than just music.*** After having this revelation, I later came to find out there was a song "Music Can be Such a Revelation" by Madonna. The next few weeks, I just immersed myself in music, trying to take my mind off all I had just been through. I took out songs that had spoken to me, to my soul, all my life. Songs like "Brother Love's Traveling Salvation Show," "He Ain't Heavy, He's My Brother," "Heart Light," "Headed for the Future," "You Are The Best Part of ME," from *The Essential Neil Diamond* CD. "Superstar," "Top of the World," "The Rainbow Connection," "Bless the Beasts and the Children," by The Carpenters. "Watch Closely Now," "Everything," "Evergreen," "The Woman in the Moon," "I believe in Love," from *A Star is Born* CD by Barbra Streisand and Kris Kristofferson, and from the *Essential Barbara Streisand,* "People," "Happy Days Are Here Again," "The Main Event," "No More Tears," and "Putting it Together." Songs from the movie *Sister Act II.* And, from the *Sinatra Reprise Collection* by Frank Sinatra, "The Best is Yet to Come," "My Way," and "Fly Me To The Moon."

I would loudly play these songs getting lost in their lyrics, sometimes all night long. My poor mom, who lived with me, must have thought I was crazy (still). I must have driven her nearly nuts, herself.

It was the Catholic season of Lent and the only time I left my house was to go to church, as uncomfortable as I was. I took a wooden hand-carved rosary from the Mount of Olives with me that my mom's boss had brought back from Jerusalem for me (even though he was Jewish). He didn't know I was in the hospital at the time he was buying the rosary. When he returned, my mother told him I had been in the hospital and he told her, "These were meant for Mary."

The next week, I went to see my therapist whom I had seen for years. I had been going to her over the years for issues surrounding my low self-esteem and, bouts with depression and during my divorce, of course, the emotional roller coaster I was on at the time. She had also diagnosed me with BDD (Body Dsymorphic Disorder), a preoccupation with how one looks, that leads to things like depression, anxiety and low self-esteem. This session I went to was a group session at her clinic. It was a small group session with other patients there that had depression or relationship problems. She knew I had been in the hospital and asked me how I was doing. I simply told her fine and didn't want to get into anything with her as other people in the group were coming in. Before the group started, another patient asked her, "Did you get a chance to watch that movie I gave you, *The Possession of Emily Rose*?" I just froze. I literally felt a cold chill covering my body. I had never seen the movie, but, something about the title obviously struck a sensitive cord with me. I told my therapist I wasn't feeling well all of a sudden and left. Before I left she asked for a release from me to get detailed records from my hospital stay for our next one-on-one session.

At my next individual session, I was hoping to get the usual sympathy and compassion I had gotten from her over the years, but, I was quite surprised with her reaction. She had my hospital records and was very upset with me. She said I had put "her" at a high risk. She could lose her license because she hadn't seen this coming on with me. She had just seen me the week before, and I had appeared to be at the best she had seen me in a long time. She was shocked that this "nervous breakdown" had happened to me, and then told me that I was:

"Way too young to be this psychotic!"

I thought to myself that I didn't know psychosis (still wasn't sure what I went through) had an age limit or range. And, in the future I should be more concerned to forewarn her of any psychotic breakdowns I might be having, so as to protect her liability. So, because I could have cost her, her "license" she said she couldn't see me anymore, and made arrangements to send me to a clinic called the Providence Center.

I left her office feeling numb. The one person I had been through with so much, for so long, was abandoning me. Through all my marital and relationship problems, depression, low self-esteem, BDD, she was now going to send me to someone new. I would have to start all over again with a new therapist. I felt so alone and depressed that when I got home I just collapsed in my bed in a torrid of tears. Then I heard a voice in my head:

"When you need them the most you're a liability,
*but you're **never** a liability to **GOD**!"*

"God is always in season!"

"When you're down and troubled and
you need a helping hand
Close your eyes and think of me and soon I will be there
*To brighten up even your **darkest nights**....*
*All you have to do is call, **LORD**, You've got a friend."*
~*You've Got A Friend*
By James Taylor

III ~ Divine Meetings: Soul Mates

"…But if you don't put faith in what you believe in Its getting you nowhere…Two hearts, believing in just one mind….Together forever till the end of time!"

~Two Hearts
By Phil Collins

I never believed much in soul mates. Or, perhaps that I would find mine. It seemed that I had been through so many relationships that weren't right. Guys that only seemed interested in themselves. Sure some had great senses of humor, some were great lovers, and all my boyfriends wined and dined me. But, I never totally connected with any of them. I never felt an inner sense of purpose with any of them. And, all the wining and dining was taking a toll on my body. After all that lying around Peter's pool and going out to dinner every night for a few years, then being with Mister Party, Gordan, for close to two years, I had gone from a size six to a size fourteen.

That's when I decided to do something about my weight. Ironically, at the time I was sitting at a bar eating a Jim Dandy (cheeseburger covered in Russian dressing) and French fries while leafing through a local paper called the *Woman's Page.* There, I saw an article about weight loss through hypnotherapy, written by a Dr. Dave. I decided to give him a call feeling that he could help me.

I found that when I went to see Dr. Dave that he had a practice in a holistic clinic called Waves of Wellness. It was a group of holistic practitioners working together. They had massage therapists, an acupuncturist, a Reiki master, a herbalist, and Dr. Dave, a hypnotherapist.

At my appointment, Dr. Dave greeted me in the lobby of his clinic. He appeared in his late forties, had brownish-gray curly hair, and a confident smile. He took me into his office and explained how hypnotherapy worked, that he would relax me and attempt to change that inner subconscious voice and, thereby, change my habits toward food (no more Jim Dandy's). He would also make me a tape of the session that I could use for continual reinforcement. I, however, went into my story with him of my relationships, my marriage, my divorce, and my father's illness and death. I guess he got the impression that I had a lot more issues than just poor eating habits.

Instead of doing a weight loss session, Dr. Dave tried to work on my depression and self-esteem issues. In his typical session, his patient would lie back in a reclining chair and close his or her eyes as he went through progressive relaxation and meditation exercises in order to get into the person's subconscious and make suggestions. Although, that worked for most, I was so agitated after telling him about my background and my relationships that I couldn't lie back and close my eyes. But I did sit in the reclining chair (staying upright), and I listened patiently while tapping my foot throughout the whole session.

Dr. Dave was unfettered and went though all his relaxation techniques and tried to boost my self confidence as well. He did make me a tape, and suggested that I listen to it before I went to bed; it would relax me to sleep. He arranged a follow-up session for the next week and suggested we go into the weight loss program then.

I liked his professional manner and he left me feeling that he was committed to helping me take control of my life and help me move it forward. At the next session, he did make me a weight loss tape, and even did another follow-up session with me two weeks later. I enjoyed listening to his calm, relaxing voice and positive affirmations he added into the sessions. At our last session, I made a comment that I wish I could just go away somewhere and lose weight. Dr. Dave told me that there were spas that specialize in weight loss, and he would check into it for me. The next week, he called me with the names and numbers of a couple of weight loss spas in New England.

I arranged to go to a spa in New Hampshire the end of September and called to tell Dr. Dave about it. He said that would be great for me to get away for a while and he asked that I give him a call when I got back to let him know how I liked it. The spa I went to was great. Everyday I ate a healthy vegetarian diet, went for hikes through the mountains, had a massage, and swam in the pool. After two weeks, I felt a lot better and lost a couple dress sizes.

I did call Dr. Dave when I got back and he told me to keep the momentum going and stay away from those Jim Dandys. After that, Dr. Dave would call periodically and ask how I was doing, and if I was listening to my tapes. I told him I was, although, I wasn't doing it the way he had suggested. He wanted me to lie in bed and in a meditative state listen to his tapes. However, I would drive around in my convertible and listen to him. After that, I lost contact with Dr. Dave for quite some time.

A Divine Meeting!

*"Don't give up on your **faith**, love comes to those who believe it, and that's the way it is."* **~ Celine Dion**

After I had the battles with Gordan and my hospital stay, I stayed home for the first month sleeping most of the day, listening to music at night as I was afraid to put the TV on, and I rarely left the house. I was lying in my bed feeling depressed and thinking, "When will I find love? When will I be loved?" Then, I heard a new song on the radio by an artist I had never heard before, Josh Groban. His song really spoke to me, and how I was feeling.

> *"Don't give up, it's just the weight of the world.*
> *…When you're lost inside, I'll be there to find you.*
> *…If darkness blinds you I will shine to guide you.*
> *…You are loved."*
>
> **~*You Are Loved***
> **By Josh Groban**

Everyday, I would pray to God, stating and believing that this difficult situation would be turned into a blessing, and then I would recite Psalm 23, just as I was told in my battle:

"Don't ever underestimate the power of prayer!"

When the weather started to get warmer, I started to go for walks. At first, it was around my neighborhood, and eventually, it was for hours at a time. One day when I was driving and, I was thinking of getting into better shape by joining a gym, I saw that the car in front of me had a small sign on it with a number of a personal trainer. I quickly made a note of it and called the number when I got home. I found that the personal trainer was Bill, who was a young man in his early twenties in terrific shape and who was just starting his personal training business. He met his clients at World Gym in Providence, and he arranged to meet me there.

World gym was a weightlifter's gym. It was in an old converted warehouse. It had enormous rooms with hundreds of weight machines and stacks of weights and dumbbells everywhere. Bill developed a weight training program for me and showed me how to do all the exercises. The workout lasted for close to an hour, and I was definitely feeling it the next day. Bill put me on a twice a week schedule, and after a couple of weeks I felt as if I was toning up.

One day, I walked into the gym, and who did I see straining away on a weight machine, but Dr. Dave. He saw me and gave me a hug and said he couldn't believe it was me. I had lost quite a bit of weight since the previous fall and had dropped four dress sizes. He said, "I guess my program worked pretty well for you." I smiled and said, "Like you told me I kept the momentum going." Of course, I thought to myself, "Spend a few weeks in a hospital without eating much, walk five miles a day for a couple of months and work out with a personal trainer twice week for a month doesn't quite hurt either."

My trainer, Bill, came in, and before I said goodbye Dr. Dave asked when did I usually work out? I told him I usually trained with Bill on Tuesday and Thursdays at one o'clock. He smiled and said how proud he was of me, and perhaps, he would see me again here.

The next time I went to the gym, I was looking around and felt a little disappointed that I didn't see Dr. Dave. Bill came in and we went through my workout. However, when I was through and about to leave, I heard a voice behind me say, "Sure, now that you don't need me anymore don't even say hi." It was Dr. Dave, and I was again taken by his smile and quiet confidence. He commented how well I was doing with my exercising and asked how my diet was going. I told him I was staying away from Jim Dandys, and I asked if he had any other suggestions. He said he knew of a place that had a great salad bar and offered to take me there. So we made a luncheon appointment for the next day.

I met Dr. Dave at Ruby Tuesday's the next day and he was excited to show me its extensive salad bar. Being polite, I acted impressed even though I had been there quite a few times before, and the bartender, Naomi, knew me by name. Over lunch, Dr. Dave told me a lot had happened in his life in the past year. His father had died after a short time in the hospital, he had become guardian of his two Down Syndrome sisters, and he had moved into his father's house to take care of them. He also had left his wife after being married for twenty-seven years.

As our "luncheon appointment" continued, I discovered Dr. Dave seemed a lot more relaxed outside his office and that he even had a sense of humor. He still seemed genuinely interested in me and my wellbeing. The more I found out about him, the more I found out all that we had in common.

We loved the same music, movies, boating, the ocean, travel, adventure, and to laugh. I started to think perhaps here was a guy that would treat me like a person. Every time we got together after that luncheon, at the gym, for lunches, for walks together, my feelings grew stronger and stronger. I knew Dr. Dave felt the same way. He often told me how he couldn't believe how great it was to be with someone that liked everything he did. Of course, I would correct him and tell him that he was wrong, he liked everything I did. I felt so right with him. He was sensitive, caring, intelligent, and always concerned with my happiness. He didn't care what color my nails were (I could actually go out and choose my own color unlike in my previous controlling relationships) or what I wore, or even if I went to the hairdresser or not. He was just concerned with my moving forward.

As I said earlier, I never gave much thought to finding a soul mate. I guess I always thought it was an overused concept by lonely women looking for that perfect man. After spending close to eight years in the adult dating scene, I was hoping to find a man that would just treat me with respect and was stable. I wasn't concerned with what he did or, even, what he looked like at that point. I just was looking for someone decent. The thought of finding my "soul mate" wasn't even on my mind.

The other problem I had with the soul mate concept was, in the spiritual sense. In the spiritual definition, a soul mate is someone that you certainly connect with on all levels in this life but, also, one that you have been with in countless previous lives. You travel together from lifetime to lifetime, in search of one another, and often, eventually, you find each other again.

Growing up as that Catholic girl, I followed the Catholic belief system. That we live our life to do good and share the love of Jesus and God, and by doing so we go to heaven when we die. Reincarnation was not a concept talked about or even tolerated in the Catholic Church. And, personally I believed that God was perfect and he would never have to repeat himself by making us live another life. So, being reincarnated or, having a soul mate from a previous life was not in my belief system at the time at all.

That all changed when I met Dr. Dave. It seemed like *magic* the first time I kissed him, as if our souls connected, and that we had done this before. As we spent more time together, it seemed so unbelievable to me how we were so compatible in every way.

Divine Connections

Even though we felt so connected at the very beginning of our dating, I still had a tremendous fear within me. How could I tell him what happened to me? Going to the *underworld* in the hospital. Trying to kill myself? The supernatural battles with Gordan? Being a psychologist, would he think I was crazy? Would he "ship me off" to see someone else and put me on mind-numbing drugs?

Well, just as our meeting and relationship developed in a *divine* manner, so, all my fears were also put to rest. One day at dinner, Dr. Dave started to tell me of an experience a recent client of his had. He had been working with an elderly lady named Debra, who was channeling her deceased soul mate. She was also a psychic and would often give lectures on connecting with the spirit world. She told Dr. Dave that at one of these lectures a woman was questioning her as to how she knew her experiences were real, that perhaps, she was just imagining that her soul mate was with her. At that instant, a fireball out of nowhere, came right at the woman, startling her, but dissolving into the air before striking her. The woman didn't question her further.

Dr. Dave's story of Debra's fireball, being confirmed by someone I didn't even know, was certainly a sign telling me that it was alright to tell him what happened to me. I started to realize he wasn't your typical psychologist. He was very open to experiences that traditional science or medicine can not explain. After all, he did do hypnotherapy, but, the more I talked to him about my paranormal experiences, the more I came to find out that he had psychic experiences of his own (see Chapter V: Divine Signs and Chapter VI: Divine Consciousness). I began to feel that I could tell Dr. Dave anything and everything.

I don't usually pay attention to my dreams, but early in my relationship with Dr. Dave, I had a vivid dream. In the dream, I was standing on a street corner when a bus stopped in front of me. The bus driver opened door and said, "I'm going to take you to the moon." At that point, I woke up feeling elated but not quite sure as to why. What was the relevance? Then I thought of the song "Fly Me to the Moon," by Frank Sinatra. In the song, he ends with…."*in other words, I love you.*" And it just hit me it was about Dr. Dave and me. He was my "moon boy."

I called Dr. Dave and told him about the dream. He said people don't usually analyze dreams like this. But, I felt it in my heart that it meant something. From that point on, Dr. Dave was my "moon boy." He reciprocated after that by saying, "Well, if I'm your *moon* boy, then you're certainly my '*sunshine*'!"

One evening, as I was reading, Dr. Dave brought me some white tea in a red mug that had hearts and the words "Soul Mate" on it, which was unusual because he usually gave me a mug with a beacon on it. As I was sipping my tea, I decided to put in a CD we had gotten from Rev. Karen Weingard that I hadn't heard before. I was surprised to hear her talking about what a soul mate was. I thought the point she made was excellent. She said a soul mate is not someone that likes the same movies or music or has the same interests as you do. That's a friend. Soul mates aren't two people that sleep together, they are two people that *'Awaken'* together. And, I thought, that's what happened to Dr. Dave and me. We were awakened together! On an incredible journey that continues today.

"Let Go and Let GOD"

The Battle Continues...

One day I was out for a walk, and I stopped at store for a bottle of water. As I entered the store my eyes immediately fell on to a free magazine called *ME*. I got a feeling in my gut that I should take one. Later that day when I started to look through it at home, I noticed an article about *Crossroads*. The article talked of how when two opposites meet, that encounter creates an epiphany in both of their lives, changing their lives forever. It becomes a crossroad in their lives. I thought how my meeting Gordan did just that. It certainly changed my life in ways I only started to begin to understand. It was the beginning of my spiritual awakening, and I started to get signs in all sorts of ways.

A few days later, virtually out of the blue, I got a call from Gordan and he said, "Mary, only goodness surrounds you. *The meek shall inherit the Earth,* I'm going to get you!" I don't know how, but I told him, "Gordan what are you going to get?" Then I said,

"Right will always win over might."

Then I hung-up on him. I couldn't believe the conversation, that he quoted the exact words I had heard in my battle when I was home alone. This was months after my battle. But fortunately, this was the last time I heard from him.

I called Dr. Dave in a panic. He consoled me by telling me not to talk to him again. To forget him and move forward. But, again, I couldn't believe Gordan was bringing up exactly what had happened during my battle the previous February, when I had heard Spirit say, *"The meek shall inherit the Earth!"*

Well, the summer took my mind off what I had been through for the most part. Dr. Dave and I had a wonderful time together. We went to the gym, took long walks together, went to the beach, and took my speedboat all over Narragansett Bay. And, the summer flew by.

September came and Dr. Dave went back to his day job as a school psychologist. Losing my day-time playmate, I was planning to do some volunteer work, perhaps at a nursing home. But first I wanted to get my house in order and myself in a little better shape.

One day, while on a walk with my headphones on, I was surprised to hear spiritual music coming out of them. It was not the station I usually listened to. It was playing a song saying, *"…cover thy earth with thy glory."* After the song ended the D.J. said, "This is the Shine radio station. We need volunteers. Are you going to answer the call?"

I thought to myself, "Yes, I'm going to start volunteering." I don't know how this station got on my radio, but, it was a clear sign to me that I needed to answer the call and start volunteering.

In the meantime, in the mail, I received a flyer about a play in New Bedford, Massachusetts. It caught my attention because it had a sun and moon on it (and I thought of my prior dream about the moon). I called and reserved two tickets for Dr. Dave and me to go. It was on Friday, October 13th. I did not realize the significance of the date until later.

On the way there, I saw a billboard advertising the *"The Forces of Nature"* at the Zeitiron Theater, where we were going. I remembered back to the previous February when the TV had told me, "I'm going to teach you the power of nature." My heart sank. I was thinking what were we going to see? I thought we were going to see something to do with the sun and moon, as the flyer I was sent had pictured.

The play turned out to be very "artsy," and I wasn't quite sure what was going on. So, I asked Dr. Dave, and he told me, "They are enacting the Crusades, the Holy Wars." Again, my heart sank a bit lower. Last February on the TV, the day before I had gone in the hospital it had said, "You are in the *Crimson Crusade.*" This was not what I had thought we were going to see. It bothered me, and I was thinking that I didn't want to see battles again between good and evil, but, we stayed to the end.

On the way home I saw another billboard that was disturbing to me saying, "***Pay back to come!***" I had that horrible feeling that my battles with the dark forces were starting again.

The following Tuesday I gave Dr. Dave a card with a butterfly on it that said:

"Just when the caterpillar thought it was going to die… it became a butterfly!"

I wrote in the card, "Thanks to you and God I'm still here." I dropped the card off at his house and went to get lunch. As I was eating lunch, the TV in the restaurant lounge caught my attention, "New on DVD *The Butterfly Effect.*" I had never heard of the movie, and I couldn't believe it, I had just given Dr. Dave a card with a butterfly on it!

I called Dr. Dave and asked him if he had ever heard of the movie, and he said, "Yes, and it is even on TV tonight!" I told him, "No, its coming out on DVD today it can't be on TV." So, he came over that night and we did watch it on TV. The next day we went to the video store to find what was released on DVD.

At the store, we saw that *The Butterfly Effect II, The Phenomenon Continues,* was what was being referred to the day before. After seeing the title I told him, "Its starting again!" He said, "Its just a name of a movie, stop connecting everything together." I disregarded what he said and my eyes were drawn to a poster of the new *Rocky* movie that said:

"Never give up and never, never, never, stop believing in yourself!"

I knew what was happening, what was beginning again. And, I wasn't going to let Dr. Dave dismiss my feelings.

The next few days my condition worsened. Bloating started in my abdomen, my skin started to become drier, canker sores were forming on my tongue again, and my lips were on fire. Things started talking to me again. I began panicking, thinking I was going to end up in the hospital again!

This time, I was more aware of what was happening to me, but, I was still not fully understanding why it was happening to me or what was causing it. However, I was fully aware of where I would end up if I didn't do something different. This time, Dr. Dave was with me, and I knew I could confide in him and he would help me although, he too, also had no idea of how to stop what was happening to me at the time.

One day, while lying in bed (for that was all I could do at this point), trying to rest even though I was in excruciating pain, I was thinking, "What is going on? Why are these things still happening to me? Why am I in such pain?" Then, I heard in my head a voice say, "I chose Mary the first time to deliver Jesus into the world. And, I choose Mary again. But, this time Mary will deliver Jesus into the world as Mary, with Jesus carrying Mary instead of Mary carrying Jesus!" I was in such a state thinking, "What did I just hear? Am I losing my mind?" Then I turned my head and my eyes fell on a card on the bureau that said, "In loving memory." At that point, I just got up and left the room, and thought to myself, "I've got to get out of here." There was no chance I was going to get any rest anyhow.

I decided to get my nails done, be out with people, and try to forget what was going on. As I was walking into the nail place, I was astonished because a guy in the store was coming towards me with a tee-shirt on that said, "In loving memory." I freaked-out and just left the nail salon and went back home. It was happening to me everywhere! There seemed to be no escape, again!

The next few days, I started spending more time looking things up on the computer. And, the computer started giving me messages: "Do you trust me to continue?" I was apprehensive. Was this another good vs. evil battle? But I continued. It said, "Are you in communion?" But, I thought communion is the Eucharist in the Church, so I knew it was okay, a positive sign, I continued. Then the computer said, "The Army of ME!"

I had no idea what it was talking about, but, it had relevance to the *free* magazine I had picked up months before called *"ME"* with an article in it about the crossroads in life, where two opposites meet, have an epiphany, and then go off on new roads. I felt the magazine was really talking to me back then, it was explaining to me what I had gone through with Gordan. It also talked about how it transforms you. The computer then said, "HOPE." That meant Health Opportunities for People Everywhere.

The next day, even though still feeling sick, I was determined to get out and feel better, I went to the gym with my girlfriend Joanne. As we were riding our bikes in the gym in front of a TV, I looked up and saw that the TV said, "Transformation road" with an arrow pointing to the right. Then it came on again with an arrow pointing to the left. I knew the TV was talking to me and "transformation" meant something.

I started seeing the battles happening again all around me, I was getting sicker, and people's face's started changing in front of me. I was seeing a quick glimpse of someone else's face to the point where I was scared to look my mother in the face, being afraid of what I would see. When I would see Dr. Dave, I would scream when I saw his face quickly change (it became very unnerving for him too). I would see fleeting images (like ghosts) all around me, appearing and disappearing.

When I looked in the mirror someone else was looking back at me. It wasn't my eyes looking at me. It felt as if someone else was in me, looking back at me. I was feeling sicker by the day. Sometimes the abdominal pain was so great I couldn't get out of bed. I couldn't stand up straight, I had to crawl to the bathroom. I had waves of pain circulating around my body from my back to my side, down my leg, then back up to my abdomen.

I was thinking/praying everything was going to be fine, maybe this was a positive transformation. But I was feeling more and more pain. Once, when on the computer, I was thinking of the song I had heard a few weeks before: *"Cover Thy Earth with Thy Glory."* I was looking for the words to the song and what came up was *"Cover Thy Earth with Thy Blues."* The computer started answering positive with negative. I hardly knew how to use a computer, and it was really getting me frantic that it was answering me in negative terms, with things I didn't even knew existed. I started thinking that:

"The Meek shall inherit the Earth"

That was from the B-Attitudes. I typed "B-Attitudes" into the computer, and what came up was the *"The Devils B-Attitudes."* I had never heard of such a thing! I freaked out and called Dr. Dave to look at what was happening. He tried to shut off the computer. But it wouldn't shut down, and Dr. Dave knew how to operate a computer. So, he had to unplug everything to shut it off. He started to see that I wasn't doing all this myself, that I wasn't "connecting" too much. This was all really happening to me.

Now, even Dr. Dave could start seeing how sick I was getting. The next few days, he stayed out of work to be with me. And he saw me getting progressively sicker.

At night, Dr. Dave had to return to his house to take care of his sisters, so not wanting to be alone, I went downstairs to be with my mother. I was just sitting next to her in pain, watching TV. I didn't want to watch TV, but she was accustomed to going to sleep with it on, and I was just thankful not to be alone. I didn't tell her what I was going through at the time; she had been through so much the time before with me. As I was sitting beside her while she was sleeping, I was in such pain I was thinking, "Will I be alive in the morning?" The TV kept talking back and forth. I was petrified and in such pain not knowing what to do.

Then somewhere around two o'clock in the morning a one-foot wide purple and pink **butterfly** flew at me from out of the ceiling, came towards me, then went back up into the ceiling and disappeared! "Where had that come from?" I thought.

I looked at the TV and it went back in time to a point five minutes earlier where, in an episode of *The Fresh Prince of Bell Air*, Will Smith's teacher said, "I'm taking formula A and formula B and I'm mixing them together and now I have a ***new creation***!"

I was thinking, "Why is this being shown to me again? What Am I? I'm seeing images around the room again. Am I going to have to live like this? Seeing both worlds at the same time? Am I the new creation? Of Good and Evil? How am I ever going to live like this? Feeling this way, in such pain and seeing ghostly images all around me?"

I couldn't take it anymore. I got up to leave the room and as I did, I looked up at the TV and it printed out on the screen:

"Thank goodness for forgiveness."

I felt a sigh of relief. Maybe I wasn't going to have to live like this. Then I heard a voice:

"I believe in second chances."

I was thinking maybe I was getting a second chance I'll be all right. I called Dr. Dave (somewhere around five in the morning). I told him that I was feeling better, that I had seen a sign from God, that I was going to be all right. He was relieved and said he would be over soon.

Then I went into the den, and I saw two books on a TV stand. I don't know where they had come from, I wasn't accustomed to reading much at the time. One was *Jesus Christ Heals* and the other was *The Road Less Traveled.* I opened the book *The Road Less Traveled.* The page I randomly opened up to had the words to the song *"Amazing Grace."* This really struck me because, in my den I have the words to this song in a frame on the wall. I never really paid attention to the words until I saw them in this book.

> *"I once was lost, but now I'm found,*
> *I was blind, but now I see…..*
> *Grace has lead me safe thus far,*
> *and Grace will lead me home!"*

The book also discussed other things I had never heard of like the *Rhizome Collective.* So, I went on the computer to look up what that was. I found it meant the "true root," or that "God is the root of everything." My eyes were starting to open more and more as I investigated things. But I was seeing with my heart.

The next day, I continued reading more of the book, *The Road Less Traveled.* It talked of terms I was not familiar with, such as transformation, synchronicity, and alchemy. Alchemy I learned was the process of taking something ordinary and making it extraordinary.

But each day I became sicker and sicker. I told Dr. Dave, *"It's happening again!"* At that time, he only knew a little about what had happened the first time when I ended up in the hospital, how things were talking back and forth to me, the TV, radio, and street signs. But this time, even the computer was talking to me. I had to get away from everything for a moment. I went into the den and sat down trying to make sense of what was going on, when a message came through to me, and I wrote in my journal:

> *"So as a Beacon shines for the sea,*
> *so must we, for others to see!"*

As I was trying to understand what was happening, and feeling that no one was listening to me, I asked GOD, "I need a sign now." I thought, "Right now I'm trying to get my life going again, I want to volunteer, to get out and help people. Why am I getting sick again? What is this battle all around me again between good and evil?" I felt compelled to turn the TV on.

As the TV came on, it said, "Beacon Communications, One Beacon Way." I had just written five minutes earlier the passage in my journal about the Beacon. I knew this was real, not in my imagination. I wasn't "*connecting too much.*" The sign on the TV gave me a source of comfort, my sign from God!

I continued reading *The Road Less Traveled* that night and felt excited that I was being saved by God, that I would be all right again, even though I was so sick at the time.

In the morning, I called Dr. Dave telling him I would be all right, not to worry about me; God was saving me. After putting the phone down, I was compelled to open the book again. But, this time the words were being read to me backwards: "Good conquers evil" became "Evil conquers good!" What was positive became negative. I had that sinking feeling again, that I was losing the battle. All I could do was wait now for the darkness to take over me! I kept feeling sicker and weaker. My abdomen was feeling as if it was going to burst again, my eyes, lips, and face were on fire, and that immobilizing exhaustion was coming over me.

Dr. Dave came over later that morning, thinking I was better, that the worse was over, but when he saw me, his fears were renewed. I was becoming more frantic and I was in a state where he couldn't console me. He couldn't rationalize or say or do anything to reverse my fatalistic view at the time. Everything he said to me, I heard the opposite. He would say, "You are going to be all right." I would hear, "You are going to hell." I wasn't even sure that it was Dr. Dave with me. I thought he was in disguise, part of some conspiracy to bring me back to the underworld. As the day progressed, the pain got worse; bloating in my stomach, I couldn't stand up, skin on my face was peeling, black circles formed around my eyes, and my lips were turning black. I felt all I could do was wait to die.

Dr. Dave said, "Nothing is going to happen to you." With tears in his eyes, he said, "I won't let anything happen to you!"

I told him, "You are not the powers that be! You can't control what's going to happen!" As the day went on, I was in such excruciating pain all I could do was wait to die. There was nothing I could do to stop it. I just had to sit and wait to let the "*forces of nature*" take me over.

In the evening, when my mother came home from work, Dr. Dave told me he needed to take me to the hospital, and I told him, "No, I'm not going in the hospital again (fearing I would be taken to the Underworld with no return this time). Whatever is going to happen, will happen right here!"

I kept thinking, "Who am I? What happened to me the night before? The new creation, the butterfly?" Then out of nowhere, and out of my mouth came the words:

"I AM BALANCE!"

Then a calmness came over me. My fears left me. I was still in pain and in tremendous discomfort, but I was able to fall asleep, not fearing that I wouldn't wake-up. Dr. Dave didn't take me to the hospital, seeing that I was finally getting some rest, and he felt I was safe with my mom being home, so he left to take care of his sisters.

As I was resting and trying to fall asleep, I was listening to the radio when a song came on I hadn't heard before. It gave me incredible comfort:

"…Come on and come to ME now
…Let me see you through, 'Cause I've seen the dark side too.
Won't let nobody hurt you…
Take ME in, into your darkest hour and I'll never desert you,

...I'll stand by you."

~I'll Stand By You
By The Pretenders

I Find Grace

"You do not attract what you want; you attract who you are."
~ Dr. Wayne Dyer

The next day, I awoke, thinking more about what I had read in *The Road Less Traveled.* It talked of alchemy and transformation and that in a transformation, being filled with the *Holy Spirit,* is all good. Even though I was still in pain, I was going through a positive transformation. My fears were subsiding.

A few days later, lying in bed, still in pain, I was thinking, "Why is God, who is all love, making me go through so much pain?" I felt I should look up the word "spirit." I went to the dictionary and it said:

Spirit:

1. An animated or vital principle held to give life to physical organisms.
2. A supernatural being or essence as a Holy Spirit; soul; or and often *malevolent* being that is bodiless but can become visible;
3. Specifically a ghost; **a malevolent being that enters and possesses a human being.**

Not knowing what malevolent meant, I looked that up and it said:

Malevolent:

1. Having, showing, or arising from intense often vicious ill will, spite, or hatred.

2. Productive of harm or *evil!*

At this time, I started to think back to the card I got the day I was leaving the hospital with "I'm a Retriever" on it. So, I typed "retriever" into the computer and it said:

Retriever: Remedy from *evil* consequences.

I called Dr. Dave in a panic! I told him that "spirit" also meant "malevolent," and I was being possessed by evil! That is what was causing all this pain. I knew good (God is all love!) wouldn't be causing my pain, it had to be something evil! I told Dr. Dave to get the film *The Possession of Emily Rose.* I remembered that had been brought up to me months before at one of my group sessions with my psychologist, when one of her patients had asked her if she had seen it. She dismissed his inquiry by saying, "It is just a movie." At the time I knew it meant something, but I had just been through so much that I didn't want to think about it right then. Now I was paying attention to what was going on.

Things started making more sense to me. God wouldn't put me in pain; God is all good. Evil was causing my pain!

I went to the video store to get the movie. Just as I was entering the video store I saw a big poster for *"The Omen II."* I freaked-out and left the store. I got in my car, leaving, and the radio in the car was playing Stevie Wonder's song at the point saying:

"The Devil is on his way!"

I was hysterical. I shut the radio off, and I called Dr. Dave, telling him what was happening. He, in his reassuring manner, told me to calm down. Then a thought came to him, "Remember that New Age store you went to last summer? Maybe they have someone there that could help you."

The store was just that, a New Age book and gift store that I loved. It was filled with healing crystals, gems, jewelry, statuettes, books, and herbs and incense. They also had practitioners there that did different types of energy and spirit healings, which I had little knowledge about at the time.

I called the store and told them I wanted to see someone that dealt with energy healing. The woman who answered the phone said, "We have two practitioners here, Linda and Grace." I couldn't believe it, they had a "Grace!" Of course, I said, "I'd like to see Grace as soon as possible." I was soon to find out that she was in fact my **Amazing Grace!**

The next day, Dr. Dave took me to see her. On the way there, I was thinking of what I was going to tell her. I didn't want her to think I was crazy. So, I was planning to tell her I was just not feeling myself. That I wasn't able to sleep. Of the bloating and discomfort I was feeling.

While driving there, when we were stopped at a red light, I noticed a truck next to us with, *"Relax, You're in Good Hands"* on its side. At the same time, the radio started to play *"Angel,"* by Sarah McLachian.

"…You're in the arms of an angel.
May you find some comfort here."

I felt the Universe was speaking to me again, telling me I was certainly on the right track.

As soon as I walked through the door, Grace, who was behind a counter, looked at me and said, "Are you all right? "

She took me into a back therapy room and had me lie down on a massage table. I didn't have to tell her anything. She said as soon as she saw me she could see in my eyes I had an entity in me! That's what she told me at the time. She later told me that she didn't see one, but, thousands in and around me. She knew if she told me what she really saw that I would really have been freaked out. And she was right. I thought I had one malevolent being in me; if she had told me I had thousands, I most likely would have passed out on the spot.

As she worked on me, I was seeing energy again. I would scream as her face changed. As I screamed, it startled her, and she screamed. I was wondering what Dr. Dave and the other person working at the store were thinking. Dr. Dave later told me he was getting concerned over all the screaming in the backroom. After about an hour of Grace working on me, the pressure in my stomach began going down, and my face was less red. She told me she was able to release a lot of energy within me and I made another appointment with her for a few days later.

During the session with Grace, I saw a box on the floor with a label that said "Under The Sun," with a picture of a butterfly on it, a very positive sign to me. As I was paying on my way out at the register, I looked down and saw a sticker, "You're Following A Miracle." Another positive sign. This filled me with much hope and comfort.

While Dr. Dave was waiting for me, he was looking around the store and bought a book that he thought looked interesting, *Healing With the Angels* (1999) by Doreen Virtue. On the way home, I was looking through it. I had never heard, or seen anything like this before. It started to resonate within me. It talked of paying attention to signs around you, of synchronicities (I had just read about that in *The Road Less Traveled),* of messages from angels and God.

A few days later, before my next appointment, Grace called me to see how I was, and she asked if her mentor could also be there at our next appointment. I said of course, if it would help. Much later Grace confessed to me that she had called her mentor because she had never seen a case like mine! For as long as she had been doing this kind of work (that I came to find out was spirit/entity releasement), she had never seen anyone with so many attachments!

The next week, Grace and her mentor came to my house and began working on me. They had me lie down on a massage table, and they both moved around me saying releasement prayers. After the session, again, I was feeling better.

They continued working on me twice a week, which I believe was the only thing that kept me out of the hospital. The third time I saw Grace, she started to tell me, "You know why they are attacking you? They want to kill you!" I got really upset. I told her, "Please, don't tell me anymore; just do the healings." She said, "Did you ever hear of living in the moment?" But that didn't give me any comfort. I just wanted it out of me. I wanted my life back. I didn't realize why this was happening or where this would all lead me, that all this was part of my awakening!

The next week was Halloween, and I was concerned because they weren't able to see me, and Dr. Dave was going to be tied up with his sisters that night. As Halloween eve approached, I was seeing more and more energy around me. People's faces were changing, and I was afraid to look in a mirror for what I would see. I felt pressure in my abdomen again. I thought maybe a massage would help. I made an appointment for a massage at a place near my house called **Heavenly Massage**, (that also had Eternity Photography in the same building). I had never noticed it before.

While there, I saw several signs that had special meaning to me. In the massage room, there was only a small statue of an angel, a picture on the wall of Jesus holding a lamb, and a coat rack that spelled out "lifeboat" on it.

On the way home, I went by a plaza with several businesses listed on a large marquee by the road. One really stuck out at me, *Believe Butterfly* (I had no idea what that business was about). Again, I had never noticed it before, and I had been up and down that road hundreds of times. Being curious about the Believe Butterfly store, I pulled into the plaza to find it. There was no store with that name there. I thought it quite strange that it was listed on the billboard, but nowhere to be found. More signs verifying that my butterfly that flew out of thin air was magic and was real!

Not wanting to sit at home alone on Halloween, I decided to

stop at a nearby Walgreens. As I entered the store, I was shocked by five huge stuffed tigers (each the size of a large dog) on a shelf as you walked in. It petrified me because at the time it symbolized negative forces attacking me. I couldn't believe they had stuffed tigers there; it wasn't a toy store. And on Halloween? Then over the store's intercom I heard a new song by Olivia Newton John. She was singing something really positive about love, and I learned later that the proceeds were going to breast cancer. I left the store feeling that again evil was being answered by good.

I called Dr. Dave to tell him about all that I had seen and the marquee with the *Believe Butterfly* on it and told him to drive by it. He was on his way over to my house with his sisters, so he did. When he came over, he verified that "Believe Butterfly" was listed but there was no store in the plaza with that name!

A Gifted Intuitive

A few days later, I was on my way to a Whole Foods store when I had a feeling I should go to a New Age bookstore, called *White Light* Books instead. I had never been there before but had been by it often. When I entered, I couldn't believe all the books, crystals, jewelry, and statuettes of saints, Jesus, and Buddha there. I called Dr. Dave and I excitedly started telling him about the store. As I was on the phone, a very pretty young lady came into the store and started to shop. Then she came up to me and said:

> *"The angels are telling me it is very important that I talk to you. They are telling me to tell you that you have the light of God inside of you. You are going far, and what you think you will manifest. You are at a very high vibration, and I feel what's going on in your stomach!"*

I nearly dropped the phone and then told Dr. Dave I'd call him back. As it turned out, I was feeling pressure in my stomach again. She introduced herself to me, and I found that Heidi was her name and that she was certainly connecting to spiritual energies around me at that time. She told me she was empathic and could feel energies.

Heidi also told me that she was an optometrist by profession, but that her first love was spiritual healing. I felt drawn to her and knew we would be in touch in the future. She gave me her number, and we parted. I found out that she was in the store buying a gift for a friend of hers. I later learned from Heidi that the friend was someone I had worked with, Cheryl (White Swan), whom I hadn't seen in years.

"Everything is so interconnected."

Before I left the store, I was drawn to two books by Kryon, *Letters from Home* (1999) and *Don't Think Like a Human*. Books! I never read at all. Dr. Dave jokes that before my spiritual awakening all I ever read was the back of hairspray bottles. I had no idea what these two books were about, but while I was looking at all the books in the store, I got that "gut feeling" I get when my body is telling me to "pay attention to something." When I opened the book, *Don't Think Like a Human*, to see what it was about, I randomly opened it to a page and read:

> *"Dear one, if you think you have picked up this book by accident, then you really do not understand how things work. For I am Kryon, and I know you, and you know me. If these words, or those of past writings, seemed to feel like 'home' to you, then it is because your higher self has intuitively recognized the writing of a friend. I love you dearly, as do all entities who are here in service like Kryon.*
>
> *~ Kryon*

I was in awe! It was as if he was truly talking to me, and I thought, I certainly could use the help of an "entity of service," a positive entity for a change.

I left the bookstore with my head still spinning and decided to go across the street to get some lunch at one of my favorite Italian restaurants. I was in the mood for tortellini with red sauce, but the waiter said they were having a special of tortellini with cheese sauce, and I let him talk me into it. He wrote down on his pad that I ordered the tortellini with cheese sauce. But as soon as he left, I was wishing I had ordered what I wanted, the one with the red sauce. To my surprise, when the waiter brought out my tortellini it had red sauce! It came out just the way I wanted it. I couldn't help thinking back to what Heidi had just told me, "What I think, I will manifest."

In one of my subsequent conversations with Heidi, she recommended a psychic named Jackie Eaton. So, I booked an appointment with her the following week. If Heidi, who was so gifted herself, recommended her I couldn't wait to hear what she had to say. Could Jackie shed more light on what was happening to me? Why it was happening to me? Where I was going in life? I wasn't disappointed when I met her.

Jackie was the type of psychic that sat across from you and started telling all about your life. She didn't need to hold my hand or read tarot cards. She just took a deep breath and connected with the energies around me.

Jackie began by asking me, "Are you close to Jesus?" I asked, "Why?" She said, "Because he is standing right behind you! I also see thousands of angels around you and a snake!" The snake was to the left, and Jesus was on the right. She told me that Jesus was also telling her to tell me, "This isn't happening to you because you did anything wrong. You have always done your best. The Catholic Church still has a lot of good points, but it has lost a lot along the way."

One of the things I was feeling guilty about was my premonitions about Buddha (having been that Catholic girl). Of course, Jackie didn't know any of this. Again, I was thinking the snake represented evil, and obviously, Jesus and the angels were good. Later, I found out that the snake, or the serpent, represents a book I was led to, *Serpent of Light beyond 2012* (2007) by Drunvalo Melchizedek.

Jesus then told Jackie to have me pick out a rock from a bowl of assorted rocks she had in her office. My hand was drawn to a heart-shaped rock that I picked out.

If that wasn't enough, Jackie started going into past lives. Now, at the time, I didn't tell her anything about myself, or even that I was seeing anyone. But she saw that I was with my soul mate! She told me, "I see you two married several times in past lives. You were best friends in the military. You were even brother and sister in a previous life." Then she said, "Oh, my God, I see you two are together forever!" I left her feeling even better about my relationship with Dr. Dave.

The next week I started reading the books I had gotten at White Light Book Store. They were the Kryon books written by Lee Carroll who channels a spirit, Kryon. In his book, *Don't Think Like a Human,* it started to explain to me a little of what I had been going through:

> *"You have chosen to be the **warriors of the light.** You are the ones who make the difference and create the change. All the rest of us are in support of you, but you must do the work. Your entire Earth structure, all recorded Earth history, and everything you behold as a human, revolves around this. This is critical work for the Universe."*
>
> *~ **Kryon***

Also in this book, he spoke of how ***"The Meek shall inherit the Earth."*** Did that ever speak to me!

When reading his book, *The Letters from Home,* I was further amazed because he talked of the year I was born, 1962. It started out by saying, "There has been a measurement of this planet's energy and vibrational rate every 25 years, from the first point of time when spiritual humanity came to earth....If you do the numerology on 25, you get the sacred energy of seven, that explains the 25 year period."

Then, I was shocked because he started talking about the year I was born, that, "1962 was a 'nine year,' and the nine has the energy of 'completion.' The 1962 measurement indicated what the completion of humanity, could potentially be."

Kryon stated that three significant years all have numerology meanings. The 1962 year equals nine, completion, 1987, equals seven which is sacredness, and the last measurement is 2012, which equals, five, the energy of change. When you add the three years together (1962 = 9, 1987 = 7, and 2012 = 5; 9 + 7 + 5 = 21; 2 + 1 = 3) you get three. Three is the number of action. These three years together make up the action trilogy.

Kryon then stated that, "People born on these years came back to be here at the very age you are now, all poised for the end. Most of you have lived for eons, lifetime after lifetime, after lifetime. And you have gone through so much! Yet, you couldn't wait to get back because this is it—the culmination of all your work." After reading this I was astounded! I was learning so much of how everything was so related. It started to explain why I'm really here, and why things are happening to me. It started to make sense. I started to learn what was going on with me and the planet.

Also, in his book, he said, "There are those on this Planet who are here in almost their full potential. They have to be here for the spiritual *balance* of the planet." When I finished both books I felt blessed and grateful to God, to Spirit (Kryon), and to all of my family from my real home.

After reading the Kryon books, I felt compelled to go to Barnes & Noble to see what else I could find. I started to follow my intuition. As soon as I walked in there was a huge poster promoting the DVD *The DaVinci Code.* I had the gut feeling I should watch the movie. I went to the magazine section and saw a little magazine called *Angels on Earth.*

As I was looking through it, it referred to a previous issue that said, *"A Butterfly is Born."* I went to a sales clerk and asked if I could get this previous issue and she told me she couldn't order it. So I put the magazine back on the shelf, and as I did, I was drawn to another a magazine that said, *"Enlightenment."* I didn't even know what that meant at the time, but I felt I should get it. I purchased it and brought it home.

When looking through the *"Enlightenment"* magazine, it talked about a CD series called the *Crimson Series* with a song, "This Universe" by Singh Kaur. It took me back to six months previously when the TV had told me I was in the Crimson Crusade, and I had had no idea what that meant at the time, as well. That is why I was led to this magazine, to see and get the Crimson Series. When purchasing the CD, I found, in addition to "This Universe," it had songs entitled "Sparks in the Night" and "The Lord's Prayer." The songs talked about being inspired by *"Beings of Love, these are truths in songs we sing."* I started to realize that the songs we are drawn to are ones that talk to our soul. The songs I loved all my life, the ones I was drawn to, did so for a reason.

When I got home I called and asked Dr. Dave if he knew what *The DaVinci Code* was about and if I should watch it. He said he had seen it before, and it was okay for me to see it because it was about another version of the bloodline of Jesus.

The next day, Dr. Dave brought the movie over. The DaVinci Code made reference to October 13, which we couldn't believe it, that was the date we had gone to *see The Forces of Nature* play.

I was trying to make sense, once again, about what I had been through, lying in my bed, trying to meditate on things, asking the question, "What is this all about? Where am I going with all this?" When a song started to play in my head, *".... Everyone is so helpful, everyone is so kind. We are on the road to Shambhala."* I called Dr. Dave asking him if he knew the song. He told me, "Yes that's 'Road to Shambhala' by Three Dog Night." He later got me the song.

One day, when on the computer to look up something I had read, I was led to a Website by Dr. Michael Sharp. I was in awe reading his Website as it began: *"If you have reached this point, you are standing on holy ground. Take off your shoes."* I was astounded because I didn't even know how I had gotten to his Website. It continued:

"Welcome Home, This is your Christmas Day!"

I couldn't believe it! His writings started to explain to me things I had experienced. He even offered a free book, *The Song of Creation.* A free book I thought. So of course, I printed it out. I was so excited to read this, and then as I'm reading it, it said, *"In great excitement, Spirit sent out a call to the bodies beneath The Veil. NOW IS THE TIME to awake cried Spirit. NOW IS THE TIME to be free. NOW IS THE TIME TO REMEMBER. The ascension will proceed."* The book continued, *"…the warriors awoke, and the warriors remembered. AWAKEN your soul. This is the way.…HEAL YOUR FEAR,…TAKE THIS SWORD…. CLEANSE THIS EARTH. Send forth your light this is the way."* As the book continued, it said, *"Nothing exists outside of ME (striking a cord with the magazine Me I had read earlier, and the Army of Me, I had seen on the computer) I AM that I AM." "…. I AM the fire. I AM the air. I AM the water. I AM all things and at this point in The Unfolding, I AM bursting at the seams with excitement."* At the end of this sentence he had a smiley face.

As I continued reading, it said, *"Thought is creation. Creation is thought. This is the nature of creation. The first two 'Laws of Creation,' energy is without limit, and energy follows intent. Energy is the way it is (i.e. without limit and always following the intent of consciousness) because of what it is.…Energy responds to intent instantly and literally.… Life is but a dream. The dream is as real as the consciousness that dreams it. The only **real** thing in this universe is the consciousness of God."*

I was blown away by how directly his words were speaking to me, how he was describing what had happened to me. He was channeling the **Divine,** and I felt that God sent him to me, in order to help me, make sense of what I had been through. To let me know I wasn't crazy. I ordered the rest of his books that he had on his website: *The Great Awakening, The Book of Life: Ascension and the*

Divine World Order, The Dossier of Ascension, The Book of Light, The Book of Triumph of Spirit, and *The Book of Secrets.*

All his books spoke to me. His book, *The Book of Triumph of Spirit*, really hit home. In the introduction, he says, *"…This book is written for you, not written just for students, artist, lightworkers or practitioners of the Tarot. You see dear one, you are not here by accident, happenstance, or some random turn of fortune. You are here by design. You are here on purpose. You are here because you asked (either consciously or unconsciously) for help on your path of spiritual awakening or, because you are responding to a twingy little feeling down in you gut. Either way, you have come for empowerment. You have come for ascension. Be welcome be in joy. Trust."*

As he continued, it not only helped me at the time, but, as well as in the years to come, as supernatural events kept occurring to me *"…your response to The Call is followed by a variable period of struggle, where the awakening body (you) tear away, piece by piece, the (self imposed) Veil in order that you may reveal to your self the awesome divinity of you."* He continued, *"…the first wave will struggle the hardest and take the longest. It will be difficult for them because they will still be working within the old system. The second wave will also struggle against The Veil. However, their struggle will be shorter. They will awaken to a crumbling old world and the subtle birthing of* **Shambhala.** *The third wave will struggle hardly at all. They will wake-up to emerging divine world order. They will not need to be convinced of the dying old. They will not need to be convinced of The Promise of Shambhala. They will see it with their own eyes." "…remember The Promise."*

Dr. Sharp explained what The Promise (The Sun) was: *"I promise if you work on the ascension, if you sacrifice for Spirit, if you agree to descend beneath The Veil, if you help to lift the universe, if you seek to arrive at a new unfolding, then no matter how far you descend into darkness, no matter how far you travel from your home, no matter how horrible the pain, no matter how unsightly the scars, I will provide a fast path home that will cut through detritus of centuries and return* you to your original spiritual glory and innocence faster that you can say Shambhala. That is my promise. This is my covenant. I will send the Sun. I will send The Light. I will send The Grail. I will train The Lightworkers. I will train the Warriors. I will train the Avatars. They will bring you the paths and you will find your way home. You will be healed. You will return to innocence. You will find joy. You will return to bliss. This is God's promise."

In his book, he talked about the relationship between the moon and the star, and I remembered the stained glass moon and star Gordan had given me, and the time when the thought, "I am balance" came over me and my fear subsided. His words touched my soul: *"The Moon: The energy of completion awaits you just through the gates/portals. The Star: A* **balanced human being** *aligning with the planetary and cosmic energies in preparation to move forward in the great unfolding….the moon and the star have the power of the Sun."*

Also, in one of his books it said, *"I told you I would send you Kryon, I told you I would send you an Avatar, I told you I would send you Sol."* I was in such awe when reading this because I had just finished reading the two Kryon books, I had gotten a few weeks prior to being led to Dr. Sharp's Website. Dr. Sharp is an Avatar, and later on the *Electro-Magnetic Sun Star* spoke to me. I also learned about the Great, Great Grand Central Sun, from Barbara Marciniak's *The Family of Light* (1999), and *Bringers of the Dawn* (1992). In *Bringers of the Dawn*, she talked about as you hold these higher frequencies, that you, "will bring information onto the planet that will astound and shock most of the world." This is what happened to her, Dr. Sharp, and Lee Carroll, and was starting to happen to me, as I would soon find out.

Another time, after reading in Dr. Sharp's books, I found that he was stating that we are in the "ascending times." I started to think back to when this all started, after the butterfly appeared to me and then the TV said in *The Fresh Prince of Bel-Air*, "I have a new creation," and I realized that this new creation was the "ascending creation." All this was going through my mind when I was driving up to a favorite store of mine in Woonsocket, Rhode Island. As I pulled into the store's parking lot, I looked across the street and saw a sign with, "The Call" on it; that was the name of a local newspaper in Woonsocket.

I thought back to when the Shine radio station played, "Are you going to answer the call?" I was thinking that all this was related to what Dr. Sharp's books were about, of what was happening on the planet. If that wasn't an awe-striking revelation, I then looked up and saw that the name of the street I was on was "Ascending Street." I almost fell over. If that wasn't enough, as I pulled out of the parking lot to leave, I saw that the car in front of me was an "Ascender," which I had never seen before or, even knew existed.

In one of Dr. Sharp's book, it gave me great comfort when he said:

> **"If you're reading this you will be alright,**
> **you're going to make it!"**

Indeed, after reading his books, I had such a great feeling of thankfulness that Dr. Sharp was there for me through my awakening. God sent him to me to help me make sense of what was going on, and help me get through it. I was amazed that he described so much of what had happened to me. The "descending into darkness," "the struggle and pain of awakening," "the scars," "ascension," "the ascending creation," "the star, the moon, the Sun," "Shambhala," "The Promise (God's)." He started to enlighten me to worlds I knew nothing of at the time. Shortly after that, while watching TV, I saw a commercial that said, "I *promise* to be there when you wake!" It reaffirmed what I had just read in his books.

These types of revelations started to make me feel that I was in fact moving forward. I was feeling better with my weekly healings from Grace. I was being led to books that were explaining that others had gone through similar experiences. I started to notice things that I had never noticed before. Things around me that had meaning all along, and now I started to see their meaning even more. It was as if layers of gauze were covering my eyes and now they were being taken off one layer at a time.

An example was where I had been to my "big sister" Claudia's house several times and had never noticed a picture frame she had on her shelf that had a butterfly on it and it read:

"There are no endings, only new beginnings."

One day at Dr. Dave's house, while he was watching football, he got up to get something in the kitchen. On the TV, a commercial came on and I saw a black man's face smile and wink at me. I got a feeling that I should pay attention, and I continued to watch. The next thing that came on the TV was "Universal" printed in large letters across the screen. I was just learning that God is also referred to as "The Universal One." Right after that, "The Good Shepherd." flashed across the screen, which was the name of a new movie coming out. Putting this all together, I realized that it was God winking at me. The first time the TV started to talk to me, when I saw the smiley face winking at me saying, "Believe it!" and now seeing "The Universal One," "The Good Shepherd," and the winking smiley face, I understand that all were God talking to me. I was feeling elated at the revelation.

As I went home that night, and walked into my mother's dining room, what did I see sitting on her table, but some flowers in a yellow mug that had a smiley face, with one eye winking. I asked my mother, "Where did this mug come from?" not ever having seen it before. She said, "A girlfriend came over with it this afternoon, while you were out." I told her, "You have no idea what this means to me!" Talk about *Universal Oneness* that I was just learning about. I was astounded and ecstatic over the synchronicities of everything that had just happened. This all confirmed to me that everything I was connecting, seeing, and putting together, was real. They were divine messages coming through to me.

Everything is One!

I felt I should learn more about what energy/spirit healing was about. Grace had told me several times that I was also a healer. But, I had trouble believing that at the time because I was always so sick. I decided to take a course with Heidi in IET (Integrated Energy Therapy). Dr. Dave came with me and we loved it. It was about meditating, learning about healing pressure points on the body, and connecting with your angel guides. We loved Heidi's calm, positive and therapeutic teaching style. After class Heidi mentioned that she was also looking into taking a shamanism class and we decided to go with her to the first class.

I was looking forward to learning more about shamanism. From what I knew at the time, it seemed to be about connecting with nature. The class was once a month on Friday evenings, and Dr. Dave also accompanied me. In the first class we went to, we learned that this type of shamanism was from Peru. It was connecting with the earth, and it was a lot of mediating to drumming and connecting with animal guides. We enjoyed learning about it and decided to return the next month.

In the meantime, I went over Dr. Dave's house one night for a little while. We were excited about the shamanism class we were going to take, and we talked a lot about it. As I walked down his front steps, leaving to go to my car I heard in my head a song playing, "The light of Christ has come into the world; the light of Christ has come." I thought to myself, "Where did that come from?" I hadn't heard that song in years and years.

When I opened the door to get into my car, I noticed that the top of my stick shift was lying on the driver's seat. I had no idea how that had happened. It hadn't been loose when I had driven over to his house, or when I had parked the car. But there it was in the middle of the seat, upside down, sticking straight up at me. If I hadn't noticed it, I would have sat on it, perhaps, not making a pretty picture where it could have landed. I was in shock thinking,

"How did this happen?" Dr. Dave's house was in a secluded area, the car was locked, there was no one around. "How could this have happened?" I got an eerie feeling come over me that it was done by "dark forces" trying to "spook" me, as if that was possible. I was happy singing the song on the way to the car, then when I saw the shift top, it was like the dark forces were saying, "Oh, yeah? Well, f_ _ _ you!"

I ran back up to Dr. Dave's house, telling him what had happened. Dr. Dave tried to calm me down, trying to tell me that, "There must be a logical explanation of how this could happen. Perhaps, your coat got caught on it when you got out of the car." But, I told him, "No, its not possible the shift handle wasn't even loose!" I knew this was a sign. Things were starting to happen to me again. I thought all this was behind me, but, here it was again *Positive* being answered by *negative*!

In The Hospital Again!

The day before our next shamanism class, I started to get those strange energy feelings again. I was feeling bloated, I started seeing faces changing on people around me, and in the mirror. Every time I looked at Dr. Dave, I screamed as his face changed, which was very unnerving for him as well. I asked him to stay home with me that day, which he did.

Dr. Dave put the TV on to try to calm me down; however, it didn't. He said, "Look. It's *The Wizard of OZ!*" But, the part of the story that was on at the time, had Dorothy trapped in the wicked witch's castle when she was pleading with her, "Please don't hurt my dog; she's never hurt anyone!" It was what I had cried to demons coming to me just before I went into the hospital the first time. I told Dr. Dave, "Turn that off. I can't watch it!"

As I was getting ready to go to the shamanism class the next night, I was feeling aching pain in my two calves, as if I had just worked out. I hadn't done much that week, except feel progressively sicker the whole week. I got the thought that I could look anyway I wanted to just by thinking about it. I could change how I looked at anytime. I remembered almost a year earlier watching Jay Leno when he said, "There's a new thing out now. You don't have to go to the gym anymore. You can have a thirty minute workout by just thinking about it!"

As I was taking a shower, I looked at the faucets, and it struck me that they looked like a smiley face. I was feeling better that here is a positive sign. I thought, God is here with me, smiling at me. However, on the way to class with Dr. Dave I started to see positives fighting with negatives again. I would hear on the radio, "You can do this." Then a car would go by with "I can't" on its plate. I felt things were going downhill again.

As I walked through the door, the shaman teacher came up to me and said, "You like to have fun, and not work, don't you?" I thought that was a strange greeting. Then her dog lunged at me, to where she had to hold him back. Again very strange as animals are usually very attracted to me. We went downstairs to where the class was, and we began by sitting in a circle. Our shaman leader started to talk about healing rocks and how to place them on certain pressure points on the body to promote healing. What I heard was that this was a technique of how to cut someone open and place these rocks on them to keep them alive and in pain. I was sitting there in disbelief. My insides were starting to turn over with pain.

Then a woman came down the stairs wearing a tee shirt that said, "Far Away." I took this as I was going far the other way, towards hell! At that point I told Dr. Dave we had to leave. He told the group that I wasn't feeling well (an understatement) and we left. As we left Dr. Dave drove out the driveway and for some reason turned left, when he should have gone to the right. This was unusual for him as he rarely got lost. And this was five minutes from his house. Why was he going the wrong way? As sick as I was, I told him he was going the wrong way, so, he backed into another driveway and started going in the opposite direction. Then as if he was lost again, he turned around again and started going in the wrong direction again. And, I corrected him again.

Then it hit me. Every time I would try to move forward in my life, something would happen, or, I would do something to negate it, and I wouldn't get anywhere. Is this what Dr. Dave was showing me? Was he acting it out, unknown even to him? Every time I tried to go forward, I took a wrong turn or went backwards. Then it hit me, as if to say, "Okay, you got the lesson," and he started to go the right way.

When we got back to Dr. Dave's house, the pain was even worse. As I lay next to him and he feel asleep, I felt as if I was being ripped apart. The pain was paralyzing me. As I lay there, looking around his bedroom, things began frightening me. What must have been a hat on his dresser looked like Darth Vader's head (I hadn't even seen Star Wars at the time). Then I looked up toward the ceiling and I saw three alien beings looking down at me! One looked like a standing reptile with an alligator's face. The other two looked like different reptilian creatures I had never seen before. They were just staring at me, as if they were waiting for the pain to overtake me so they could take me away. The pain kept increasing; I was getting shooting pains in my breasts, my stomach felt as if a basketball was in it, I had bowel pressure, my arms and hands felt paralyzed with pins and needles all over them, my face and mouth were on fire, and I was too weak to even scream or cry. I was like this all night.

I tried to wake Dr. Dave, but he sleepily told me to go back to sleep. I started to think, "Is he in on this? Is Dr. Dave part of all this too?" My mind was going a million miles an hour, "What was going on?" As the morning light entered the bedroom, the reptilian creatures disappeared. Dr. Dave woke up and I told him, "I'm exhausted I have to go home." I was so angry with him. I had had an excruciating night, not sleeping, paralyzed with pain, waiting for alien beings to take me away, and he was sleeping!

As I went to my car to leave, I turned the key, and nothing happened. My battery was dead. I was so upset. I thought, "Was this a trap to send me back into his house? To keep me from going home where I will be safe?" But I had no choice, so I went back to his house and told Dr. Dave that my car wouldn't start. He came out and gave my car a jump start and got it going. When he closed my hood I heard him say, "You were going anyway, I just gave you a 'jump start'!" My heart sank. Was he saying that he was just here to help me go along to hell quicker with his help?

Somehow, I made it home and collapsed in pain in my bed. I was just waiting to die again. Waiting for the dark forces to overtake me and take me to hell. They were telling me that they were going to put those rocks (the healing rocks) on my open wounds leaving me in pain for eternity.

Later, Dr. Dave came over and tried to comfort me by lying next me. I told him that I was just waiting for fifty Marines to come to my house, storm in to rape and torture me. Dr. Dave said, "Don't worry. If Marines are coming I can protect you because I used to be a Marine." That freaked me out even more. I didn't know he was an ex-marine. I thought again, "Who is he? He must definitely be part of this plan, this grand conspiracy to take me to the underworld again."

I told him that the Marines were going to crucify me, leaving me hanging in pain after they were done raping me. I would be hanging on a cross for eternity, in excruciating pain. At that point Dr. Dave got up to go to the bathroom and told me, "Well I'll be around for the next fifty years to see it." Again, I was thinking he was part of this grand conspiracy to torture and kill me. He said fifty years because prior to all this we would often say we were going to be together for the next fifty years. But I didn't hear this as a positive when he said it then. As we lay in bed and Dr. Dave continued to try to comfort me, I heard a song on the radio start to speak to me, one that I had never heard before.

> *"…When there is no place safe and*
> *no safe place to put my head*

> *...I need a sign to let me know you're here.*
> *'Cause **my TV set just keeps it all from being clear.***
> ***...I'm calling all angels, I'm calling all you angels."***
> ~*CALLING ALL ANGELS*
> **By Train**

I turned to Dr. Dave and said, "Did you just hear that song?" He said, "Yes, it was amazing!" That gave me a moment of comfort.

But I continued to get sicker and become more frantic. The pressure in my abdomen was unbearable. I started to go into convulsions. Dr. Dave was holding me up, trying to head me towards the bathroom. I began heaving, but nothing was coming up. All I could think of saying was: *"God is the highest power!"* And I began saying that over and over again:

"God is the highest power!"

Dr. Dave was still holding me up, and he began to repeat it with me hoping it would drive whatever was making me sick out of me:

"God is the highest power!"

After close to a half hour of this, pacing back and forth between my dining room and the bathroom, I stopped feeling as if I was going to heave.

A little while later Dr. Dave left to go and take care of his sisters. I went downstairs to be with my mother so I wouldn't have be alone in my apartment. I lay down, thinking of what is going on again, feeling tired, sick, and depressed, when I heard another song by Josh Groban that came on the radio, that comforted me:

> *"When I am down, and, oh, my soul, so weary.*
> *When troubles come, and my heart burdened be.*

…But then you come, and I am filled with wonder.
…You raise me up to more than I can be."

~You Raise Me Up
By Josh Groban

Sunday Dr. Dave couldn't come over because he had no one to watch his sisters, so I spent most of the day staying in my mother's apartment, in quite an altered state of mind. At one point, I was just walking around her dining room table repeating over and over again, "I could have had a V-8." I must have circled the table a hundred times. I was saying "V-8" because the V was from the V they talked about in the movie *The DaVinci Code* about the bloodline of Jesus, and the eight is a winning number, like when you sink the eight-ball in a game of pool. Later I found out that eight also represents infinity. I was being told that Princess Diana was in Jesus's bloodline and that is why she was killed, so she wouldn't reach her full potential in this life, for if she did, she would have been non-stoppable. I was being told that I too, was in the bloodline and I wasn't going to make it either. If I had had a V-8, it would have changed everything for me.

At one point, going around my mother's dining room table, I looked up and saw a small statue of Santa Claus carrying presents in his sack over his shoulder in her curio cabinet. I was being told that in the future everyday would be like Christmas. People would be able to manifest their desires through their thoughts instantly. There would be heaven on earth. But I would not be here to enjoy it.

I kept telling my mother to leave me alone as I walked around the table, that I knew what was going on, as I kept hearing voices telling me things that were going to happen. After a while I went into her bedroom to lie down. I looked over and saw that some of the handles on her dresser were up and some were down, just as if some were saying "yes," and the others were saying "no." The next time I came into the room, others were up, and different ones were down, all according to my thoughts. They were answering me as to yes or no based on how many were up and how many were down.

I started to become very depressed thinking that I had killed Jesus. If I had done things differently, I could have brought more of Jesus's love, truth, and peace forth onto the planet. I loved him so much, and here I was responsible for his not being here. Now I was being told that God was angry with me. I had killed his Son. They were going to get back at me by taking it out on my dog, Felicia, my baby. Demons were going to use her like a football, kicking her back and forth. There was nothing I could do to stop all this. I kept hearing and seeing this, and my heart was breaking, thinking that I had let God down, and he was so sad and angry with me.

By the next day, I hadn't eaten or slept in three days, and I was in such a state of trauma that Dr. Dave and my mother took me to the hospital, and they quickly admitted me. I'm sure they gave me some heavy duty medications, and after a couple of days I woke up and saw I was in a room with another young woman. I hated the thought of being in the hospital, but the longer I was there the more I saw *why* I was there.

I had my mother bring me some of my books I had started, such as *The Divine World Order* and *The Dossier of Ascension,* by Dr. Michael Sharp. They were giving me some comfort again. I knew I wasn't crazy (I just had to convince my doctors). One day when I was reading in the solarium, a girl in the ward asked me what I was reading. I told her it was *The Divine World Order.* She asked if she could read it, so I let her borrow it.

I found another reason I was there was to open my eyes to what others have gone through. In our daily group sessions, I learned what horrendous lives some of them have lived. At one of our sessions, my roommate said she likes to get admitted to the hospital because she likes taking a bath; she didn't have a bathtub in her home. At the hospital, she gets treated well and gets to have three meals a day. She wished she could stay longer than ten days; it was a relaxing vacation for her. Here I was feeling like a prisoner, and she thought it was a restful vacation and didn't want to go home. I always thought home was supposed to be a safe and happy place, where the heart is. I learned that wasn't the case for a lot of people, especially most of the other patients on my ward.

I found out many of the people on the ward had been there before. This was a safe haven for them. Our society looks at them as being psychotic or losers. If I had been born into their families, or in their place, I would be them. I thought, *"There for the grace of God go I."*

I was thinking, "Is this the life I am headed for? Being looked as psychotic. Maybe because I didn't do the right thing in life?" As I expressed some of these sentiments to another patient he gave me great comfort because he told me:

"God always gives you another chance."

Here was someone that had nothing. He lived in shelters. I don't even think he even owned a coat, yet he was trying to help me. Help me, who had so much. They didn't know that. They thought I had the same background as they did. If they had the life I had, they would have thought they were in heaven. Here were people that had nothing, had terrible lives, but, they were being positive, helpful to one another and still had faith in God. *Another reason I was there!*

I had become aware of paying attention to signs, and so many started to hit me there in the hospital. I was in Roger Williams Hospital, and I discovered who Roger Williams was. He founded Rhode Island in an effort to promote religious freedom. I discovered Rhode Island's state flag is an anchor with the word "Hope" on it. That meant a lot to me because once when on the computer, I was led to the word **HOPE** which stood for: Help Opportunities for People Everywhere.

The "Anchor" is another name and symbol for Jesus. Another book I had read by Dr. Sharp was *The Divine World Order,* which spoke about the ascending time of 2012 and beyond and "Anchoring" the Light back onto the planet. It was all coming together for me, why I was there, to learn even more. *Another reason I was there!*

Another day in the solarium, I noticed a book called *It.* I never picked it up, but I was drawn to "It." I knew it had meaning. Later "It" was revealed to me.

One day in my room, out of the blue (if you believe that), my roommate said, "Have you ever read the book *The Road Less Traveled?*" My mouth must have hit the floor. Out of all the books she could have mentioned, she asked me about that one, the first book I read in my adult life when all of my awakening began. As we talked more, she told me that she heard voices at night, but she didn't want to tell anyone about them because they would think she was nuts. I told her she wasn't crazy, that there are energies out there that only some can hear or see. I gave her the number of Grace, and told her that she could help her when she got out. *Another reason I was there!*

Shortly after that conversation with my roommate, another patient who played the guitar, who would often play it outside our room because we were at the end of the hallway, started playing *"Amazing Grace."*

I don't usually read the newspaper, but one day I looked down and saw a newspaper left in the cafeteria with the headline "J.C. Penney is changing their slogan from 'It's all inside' to 'Hoping Love'." To me this was saying that J.C. Penney, which stood for Jesus Christ and the penny with Lincoln on it were both *hoping* for my life. Abraham Lincoln was an inspiration to me because he had gone through so much, even had several nervous breakdowns, but, he still kept going forward always trusting God, and believing that he could make a difference. In my opinion, he did the best thing ever, freeing people from slavery. I was filled with hope after seeing all these signs.

Five minutes later, another patient came up to me asking, "Mary who loves you?" My first inclination was to say, "God," but, I didn't want to seem egotistical. Then I thought perhaps he wanted to know if I had a boyfriend or husband, so, "I said my boyfriend does." He said, "I thought you were going to say God!" I was amazed at this interchange because I had never even talked to this person before, and it was as if he was reading my mind and verifying my thoughts.

This time I was open to the signs, and my hospital stay taught me so much. This seemingly difficult situation was really a blessing. It opened my eyes to the less fortunate, and it started letting me know I was here for a reason. Everything around me and where I was, was no accident or random coincidence. I left, knowing I wanted to, and was going to **Change people's minds about mental illness!** I was committed! I later learned, as Margret Starbird discovered in her book, *The Goddess in the Gospels* (1998), that less than one-fourth of "mental" patients ever fully recover due to the "therapies" and medications they are put on!

The day I was released, after being there a week, the nurse escorting me out noticed a book I was carrying *The Divine World Order.* I asked her if she knew about it, and she said that her brother in California knows all about it and is part of a group out there called the "Divine World Order." Another coincidence!

"Come stop your crying, it will be alright…
…*They just don't trust what they can't explain*
…*They will see in time we will show them together.*
…Just look over your shoulder, cause I'll be there
ALWAYS."
~*You'll Be in My Heart*
By Phil Collins

A New Beginning

"Don't place a period, where God has placed a comma!"
~ Gracie Allen

I was glad to be home and looking forward to moving forward. I was however, feeling bad about spending Valentine's Day in the hospital. It was strange that a year ago I had come out of the hospital on Valentine's Day, and this year I went in nearly on Valentine's Day. So, I was anticipating setting aside another day and making it special for Dr. Dave and me. He was thinking the same thing and made a reservation at a restaurant in Providence we both loved called the Cav. We had come to find the Cav the previous summer when my friend Claudia told us about the restaurant. We both were amazed when we saw the restaurant's logo, was a ***sun and moon together.***

That night did turn out to one of the most special nights in my life. Dr. Dave had arranged a special table for us. It was in a secluded corner of the restaurant and it had a large bouquet of roses on it. At the end of dinner, the waiter came out with a silver tray with a single rose with a card attached to it. The card had a picture of the sun and moon together on its cover with the words printed *"Here's a riddle for you…."* That was from the song "The Riddle," which we both loved. On the inside it said, "How do the sun and moon come together?…. Answer: for ***eternity*!**"

As I read the card, Dr. Dave was on one knee, pulled a small box out of his coat pocket and said, "My sunshine, I love you. Will you marry me?" I replied, "Yes, of course, you know how much I love you!" And, of course, the box had a beautiful diamond ring in it. He had picked out a ring that had three diamonds on it that he told me represented our *past, present* and *future eternity* together.

This February was turning out different from the past two. A year ago I was in the hospital not knowing what was happening to me. The year before that, my father died. But, now, everything was turning around for me. I was starting to make sense of everything that happened, seeing the signs, I was meeting extraordinary people, and I was on a divine journey with my soul mate!

> *"….That's what love is for, to help us through it.*
> *That's what love is for, nothing else can do it*

Give us strength to try once more.
Baby that is what love is for..."
~That's What Love Is For
By Amy Grant

I had been in the hospital three times with unexplained pains throughout my body. Seeing things I could not make sense of. Encountering signs leading me down a road I had no idea as to where it was going. Now it was all going to be different. That February was the last time I was to be in a hospital, but, my battles were far from being over!

A Divine Wedding

The next week, Dr. Dave asked me when should we plan a wedding. I told him, "I know exactly when, June 16th, which is the Feast of ***The Immaculate Heart of Mary.***" So, we started to look into places to have a wedding. We wanted something by the coast because we both loved the ocean, and Rhode Island has a lot of beautiful coastline and places for weddings. Of course, Dr. Dave was somewhat apprehensive because most weddings are planned a year or so in advance, not a few months. I wasn't!

We had a list of places to check out one weekend in Newport and Jamestown. A place we both instantly feel in love with was a historic hotel called the Bon Voyage Inn, in Jamestown. It had a dinning room just the right size for our anticipated wedding reception that overlooked the Newport Bridge (that was my "Bridge over Troubled Waters," I had been through). When we asked the banquet manager to check on the date I wanted, her response was, which year? Thinking that we were looking at next year or, the year after that. She raised an eyebrow when I said this year. Then, when she did check, she was surprised to tell us that June 16 was available, in fact, the only Saturday she had available that summer season!

Next, we wanted the ceremony to be on or near a beach. We

checked into a park at the end of Jamestown that was near the lighthouse on the island's southern most point. We thought it would be an ideal place for the ceremony. The next day, Dr. Dave called the office of Parks and Recreation for Jamestown and found that of the two lots where we could have weddings, the side we wanted, on the date we wanted, was available! Of course!

One day, when shopping for a slip for my wedding gown, I was driving down a street when I saw the street sign that said "Grace" Street. A minute later, I saw a store called Grace's. The next minute a car, came toward me with a license plate with "Grace" on it. I was so taken with seeing Grace three times within two minutes that I pulled over to the side of the road to catch my breath. As I was thinking of all that had just happened, I looked up and saw a billboard that said only, "The Perfect Gift." I realized I'm being told that I've been given the most perfect gift anyone can get from God, but God's "Grace!"

Another day, when shopping for favors for our reception, when I was checking out of the store, I looked up to see a sign that said, "The Perfect Gift" and another sign that said, "Fun." Then I saw a free magazine that said, "In Touch" with "Does God believe in you?" on its cover. As I was looking at this magazine, a toy machine (with no one around it) behind me said, "It's your turn to win." I turned to see where that voice came from thinking, "Did I really just hear that?" So, I asked a man nearby, "Did you just hear that?" He said, verifying what I had just heard, "Yes, I guess it's your turn to win!" I looked at the toy machine and it said the name of it was the *Electro-magnetic Sunstar*. This was what I had read about in Dr. Sharp's book! As I continued reading the article, it said, "Does God believe in you?…. Yes, do you believe in God?"

One day, when getting my hair done, I was looking at a *Women's World* magazine, and I randomly opened it to the horoscope section. So of course, I looked at mine (Taurus), and it said: "The Universe is in harmony with your thoughts. Think big!" I got that feeling I was being spoken to again. But it was all good! Another message

I would get often, right after reading that horoscope was: **"We're playing your song!"** I would see this often when walking, as part of an advertisement on the sides of buses going by.

Another day, while shopping for some things for our wedding I stopped for lunch. The restaurant had a TV on over the bar area, but I wasn't paying attention to it. As I was waiting for my lunch, I was thinking of everything that had happened to me and what I was supposed to be doing with my life. Then a line on the TV caught my attention saying, "Are you going to help?" I thought to myself, "What do you want me to do? It's just the weight of the world!" Then the TV printed out: "Your world!" I thought, "Yeah, my world." Then the TV said, "But wait!" And the words "Chop Wizard" were on the screen. I thought, "Of course, the real wizard is going to chop through the weight of the world to make everything all right!" I left the restaurant feeling that everything was going to be okay for me and the world. When I got in my car the first song I heard was:

"I am with you. Isn't anyone trying to find you? Isn't anyone trying to take you home? I AM with you."

This made me feel elated. I *was* just having a conversation with God!

The week before our wedding, it was unseasonably cold. We actually had to put the heat on in our house in June. We were becoming concerned that, with our wedding was being held outside, it might be very uncomfortably chilly that day. *Save the Best for Last,* by Vanessa Williams came to us, and it really seemed to fit the occasion:

*"Sometimes the snow comes down in June,
sometimes the sun goes round the moon.
Sometimes the very thing you're looking for,*

is the one thing you can't see.
…Just when I thought our chance had passed,
you go and save the best for last."

But, of course, June 16th turned out to be a beautiful sunny day that was close to 80 degrees. Everything turned out to be a perfectly *divine* day. The next day, my maid of honor, my Bud (short for "buddy") Joanne and her dear husband Dom, spent the day with us in Newport because we weren't leaving for our honeymoon until the following day.

On the way to Newport, I saw billboard that said, "Paradise a gift you can never repay," and I got the feeling I get when I know I'm being spoken to from Spirit. It was saying my life is going to be paradise from this point forward! When we were at the harbor I saw the tour boat sign that gave tours around Newport Harbor was named ***Amazing Grace*** tours. I had been to Newport countless times and had never been aware that that was the name of the tour boat.

After I had that realization, I saw a man walking toward me with a tee-shirt that said, "Come" on it. I was about to point that out to Dr. Dave thinking that was provocatively unusual, when I saw the back of his shirt said, "Home." Just then, we walked by St. Mary's Church, and on its billboard was printed, "I'll never leave you." The very next thing I saw was the "Salvation Army" sign, I was thinking it was all telling me I was home, and this was the beginning of paradise, both worlds were talking to me again. But, this time it was all good.

We got into the car and Joanne put a CD in with a Michael Jackson song "You Are Not Alone." The words were saying, *"You are not alone, I'm there with you, I'm here to stay."* Of all the CD's she could have put in, the one she put in was saying exactly what I was feeling after seeing all the signs in Newport. I was seeing both worlds again. And, now it was saying God is here by my side and will never leave me!

The next day we left for our honeymoon. I was thinking we were going to a yoga retreat in the Bahamas, but Dr. Dave surprised me by first taking me to the Atlantis Hotel in "Paradise" Island for a few days before we went to the yoga retreat. It was truly paradise in every sense. When we checked in, Dr. Dave told the receptionist we were on our honeymoon (which probably was quite an usual happening at that resort) and asked, "Any upgrades available?" And, the hotel receptionist said to our surprise, "Why, yes, we do have a suite available." She gave us a free upgrade! The suite was amazing, two huge rooms, two bathrooms, and a balcony overlooking the hotel's tropical gardens and pool area. I believe the suite was bigger than our apartment back home. It was a breathtaking island and resort, and I was with my soul mate!

One special trip Dr. Dave took me on during our honeymoon, was to swim with the dolphins. It was at a dolphin reserve where they cared for and trained dolphins, about a half-hour boat ride off of Paradise Island. When we arrived, there were about thirty people with us that were divided into three groups of ten. Each group was put in separate areas that had trainers with two dolphins for each group. We just so happened to get in the group that had a special dolphin named *Princess*. Where most dolphins lived to be in their twenties, we were told that she was in her forties, and her trainers couldn't explain her unusually long life.

When at the Atlantis, signs were all around me. I ordered a glass of wine, the waiter instead, brought me champagne. I looked up and saw a sign that said, "Get used to the finer tastes." While walking through the casino, I saw a sign that said, "Earth and Fire." I almost started to panic thinking that the earth was going to be destroyed; but then it occurred to me that the fire wasn't going to destroy the earth; it was the "eternal flame of love," that was being created on earth.

Another time, when Dr. Dave was in the shower, I turned the radio on and a line from a song came on, "I can read your mind chosen one." Right after that, Dr. Dave came out, turned the TV on and it said, "This is the big picture talking." I looked over at the TV and saw printed on the screen, "Dream big. One dream can change everything!" Then "Dream Girls" came on. I realized that God was telling me to dream big, one dream can change everything. It reminded me of what my horoscope told me a couple of months earlier. I was starting to pay more attention to the signs.

After four days in true paradise at the Atlantis, we went to the yoga retreat that was quite different. It was almost like camping-out on the beach. We had a little one-room hut with a public bathroom that was about fifty yards from our room, which we had to use a flashlight to get to at night. Every morning we would get up to a gong at five o'clock for morning yoga and meditation. After that, we had breakfast at eight o'clock in their outdoor dining area that had picnic tables by the beach. We were free to go to the beach and relax for the rest of the day and in the evening we had another yoga class and meditation to nine o'clock.

At the yoga retreat, I started to see and feel things that were making me feel uncomfortable. I started getting that bloated feeling in my abdomen again. On the way to the bathroom, I saw a snake slither past me, making me feel even more uneasy. I started seeing positive vs. negative signs again. I was becoming more and more upset. Here I was in paradise, on my honeymoon, and dark forces were trying to keep me from being happy. I was getting sicker and sicker, thinking I was going to have to be in the hospital again. We became so concerned that Dr. Dave was trying to get an earlier flight out, back home, so I wouldn't have to go to the hospital in a foreign country.

One night, I was too sick to attend yoga class so I was lying in bed in our room and I was listening to CDs in an attempt to calm down. I was listening to a CD by Bruce Springsteen, "I'm on Fire." It stopped at the point in the song were it said, "*I can take you higher.*" In my mind I finished playing it out, "***I'm on Fire***!" I was getting mad at what happened to the CD. Now it was broken. Was this another negative sign? Then it hit me it had stopped at the point where it said, "I can take you higher."

Then I started thinking, "I'm on fire. Fire is going to take me higher, like the sign I saw at the Atlantis, *Earth and Fire*. I'm a Taurus, an Earth sign. Fire is going to take me, the Earth sign, higher. The eternal flame of love will take me higher!" I felt I was going to be fine. At that point, I felt it was the burning fire of "purification-information-revelation," and I knew I was going to be okay. I was going to make it. A calmness came over me. I started feeling better. Dark forces were not going to take my happiness away! *I knew I was going to be taken higher by the fire.*

I was able to stay at the retreat the next two days and leave on our schedule flight home. When home, I continued working with Grace and her mentor for the rest of the summer. They continued to do healings on me and teach me how to do clearings.

> *"What lies behind us and what lies*
> *before us are small matters,*
> *compared to what lies within us."*
> **~ Ralph Waldo Emerson**

> *"Every problem is a gift—*
> *without problems we would not grow."*
> **~ Anthony Robbins**

IV ~ My Divine Journey:

Transformation Begins

"Doctors have come from distant cities just to see me,
stand over my bed, disbelieving what they're seeing.
They say I must be one of the wonders of God's own creation.
…And as far as they can see they can offer no explanation.
…Know this child will be gifted with love,
with patience and faith,
she'll make her way.

~Wonder
By Natalie Merchant

Searching for My Guide

> *"When the explorer is ready, the guide will appear."*
> **~ Himalayan saying**

Looking into Energy Healing: Reiki & Reflexology

In the fall, I was becoming somewhat frustrated. I was continuing to be worked on by others, and I felt I wasn't getting anywhere. So, I decided to take a class that I was drawn to that helped you connect to your angels. It was about opening up to your intuitive gifts.

The class was run by an intuitive, Reiki Master named Nicki. She said she usually started the class with the same song, but said she was told that morning in meditation, to use a new song *"Believe in Yourself."* The previous week, Dr. Dave had given me a basket of *"Angel"* lotion and soap, and a book that said "Believe in Yourself," which he had won in a raffle (he didn't even pick the gift it was given to him). I took this all as a very positive sign of my being at this class.

During the class, I was partnered with another woman who had been to other workshops and had been on this path for a while. I was somewhat frustrated because I wasn't picking anything up intuitively during our exercises together. She, however, told me she got a message from the angels to tell me that, "I was trying too hard." Then she told me she could feel my energy, and saw a white dove on my heart, that I was from the angelic realm. "You are very powerful," she told me. She was so moved by these revelations of me that with tears in her eyes, she gave me a big hug. Although, all she had told me was very complimentary, I still left feeling discouraged. Here I was so angelically blessed and powerful, yet, I didn't get any intuitions, or hear any voices from angels during the class, as she did.

When class was over, I was excited over what she said, but, still down after not getting any intuitions. As I got into my car, the first thing I heard out of my car radio was *"Out of the darkness and into the sun,"* a sign that lifted my spirits. Perhaps, I was on my way, just not quite there yet.

Wanting to learn more about energy healing, and being impressed with Nicki from my previous class with her, Dr. Dave and I signed up for her Reiki class. The class was just one other woman, Dr. Dave and I with Nicki. At one of the classes, Nicki told me that she was getting a message for me from Buddha, who told her my gift to people was "joy." She was concerned at the time because she didn't get any messages for the other people in the class.

In an exercise during the class, the other woman who was attending was working on me and she said, "Mary you are so gifted and talented, but your frustration is blocking you. When your gifts come out you're going to be blown away saying, 'Where did that come from?' Its all just going to happen for you!"

Nicki also told me that each person has a *map team,* a group of spirit guides or guardian angels around them. She told me my map team was Jesus, Buddha, the Blessed Mother and Quan Yin! I was elated on one hand. Who could ask for a better group of guardian angels and guides? On the other hand, I was feeling frustrated again because he while Nicki is telling me what an extraordinary group of guardians I have around me and, the other woman who also had done energy work before was telling me how gifted and talented I was, I wasn't feeling anything or getting any messages!

Nicki also told us about the *silver-violet fire* during the class. This was the energy of St. Germain. It was a higher vibrational energy that has come to the planet now for healing and ascension purposes. At the time, like everything I was experiencing that was new, I thought it was interesting. I didn't think much more about it then, but later, it would make more sense to me.

After the class ended, I was practicing Reiki on my family and friends. But, the more I did it, it seemed the less I felt. It didn't seem as if this was the right path for me. I saw a class being offered in reflexology, and I thought, perhaps, more of a technical "hands-on" healing practice would be what I was supposed to be doing. I told Grace about the class, and she said she would also like to look into it and take the class with me.

Reflexology was about healing by using energy meridians in the body and may be one of the oldest healing modalities there is. However, I still felt there was something missing; I wanted to do more.

I decided to call White Swan, with whom I had reconnected through Heidi. White Swan has an Native American heritage, and I found out that she practices shamanism with a Native American essence. When with her, she began doing an energy attunement on me. When finished, she connected to Spirit and told me that the angels were telling her to put in a music CD and to play a song for me. The song she played was "How Great Thou Art." I couldn't believe it. That was one of my favorite songs that I played on the piano all the time. I asked her, "What is the name of the CD you put in?" She told me, "Its called *Amazing Grace*." I was even more astounded over the connection she had just made.

Then White Swan took out a book and randomly opened it to a passage and read it to me, saying that, "Angels declare that you will be triumphant!" This gave me an incredible sense of peace and relief at the time. White Swan had no idea all I had been through, yet her healing, her song, and her passage all spoke directly to my soul at the time. I left feeling that she was another Spirit Guide sent to me to help me on my journey.

Meeting Kryon

I had a thought one day, when looking through one of my Kryon books, perhaps I could study with him. I asked Dr. Dave to check his Website to see if he was doing any workshops in the near future. To my surprise, Dr. Dave found that he was doing a seminar in New

Hampshire in a few weeks, and was able to reserve us two seats. The seminar was on a Sunday in Manchester, New Hampshire which was about a three hour ride for us.

I was so excited to be meeting Lee Carroll, who channels Kryon, in person. His books were the first New Age books I had read, and were responsible for the beginning of my awakening to new worlds I had never dreamed of.

The seminar was in a hotel conference room that was filled with over a hundred people in attendance. Lee was introduced, and he started out by telling us how he was led on the path he is now on. Then he talked of how scientific concepts, such as quantum physics are proving how psychic phenomenon and conscious intent operate. He discussed the evolution of consciousness on this planet and how the vibrational energy is shifting and expanding and the significance of 2012. Before we knew it, two hours had elapsed.

At the break, I had the opportunity to meet Lee and have him sign some of the Kryon books I had brought with me, and I was able to ask him some questions. I asked him if he was familiar with Dr. Michael Sharp, and he told me, "Yes, he is an excellent resource." I had asked him about Dr. Sharp because his books had spoken to me as much as Kryon's when I first began my journey.

After the break, Lee discussed how his channeling worked and asked the audience to just quietly leave when he was done. He then closed his eyes, took a few deep breaths and connected with Kryon. As Kryon came through, Lee's voice changed, and his eyes remained closed as Kryon talked. Kryon explained his reasons for talking through a human and his vision of where the planet Earth could go in the future. Kryon spoke for close to a half hour and when he was done, he told us to go in peace and love, and Lee remained there with his eyes closed as if in a trance. We filed out quietly as requested, and I felt as if I had truly witnessed and heard a being from another dimension had been speaking to us.

Balancing My Energy

One night, unable to sleep, I started to think back to when things started to change my life, and where I was going, and a thought came to me to go back to my Kryon books for answers. As I opened one of his books, I was drawn to a page where he was talking about the **EMF Balancing Technique**. EMF stands for Electro-Magnetic Field, and I thought back to that toy machine with the *Electromagnetic Sunstar* on it telling me, "It's your turn to win." Perhaps, this was what I should be doing.

Looking into EMF Balancing, I found that it was developed by Peggy Phoenix Dubro, who has an amazing story, herself. She was originally from Norwich, Connecticut, which was only about an hour from my house, but unfortunately for me, she had moved to Arizona. I did find someone who had studied with her, could teach the program, and was still living in Norwich.

So, I scheduled a class with Cora Hayward the next week. On my way to see her, I noticed that the sign welcoming you into Connecticut says, ***"Connecticut welcomes you. We are full of surprises!"*** A good sign! While driving there my mind was replaying some of the incredible events that had happened to me in the past couple of years, when I heard a new song come on the radio that I later found out was "Lost" by Michael Buble.

"…Cause you are not alone, And I AM there with you,
and we'll get lost together.
Till the light comes pouring through
cause when you feel like you're done
And the darkness has won, Babe, you're not lost."

I was immediately taken with Cora when meeting her. She was such an example of God's love. When in her presence you can feel the truth, integrity, and holiness emanating from her. She had been doing EMF Balancing almost from the very beginning with Peggy.

Cora was also a psychic healer that could feel energy. I was so excited to be taking classes with her. Perhaps, I, too, could start learning how to feel energy as she did.

Cora led me to her therapy room, and I noticed a picture on her wall of someone I thought looked very mysterious. I asked her, "Who is that?" She replied, "That's St. Germain." I remembered reading about him when I had taken my Reiki class and how he was bringing the *silver-violet fire* back to the planet.

Cora started by balancing my energy field, doing Phase I of the EMF therapy. She said when she started doing that, that the hairs on her arms started to stand up straight. When she was finished, she told me that had never happened before. I asked what it meant. She replied, "You have so much light and electricity in you; its incredible! I have never come across this before. You are at such a high frequency level!" As I worked with her over the next few weeks, I was so impressed with all she could do and feel. At one point, I told her, "Cora you are so gifted." Her response surprised me. "Mary you are the one that is gifted, you will surpass me." I was thinking again I can't do anything she is doing, yet, she too, is telling me how powerful and gifted I am.

I told her more of what had been happening to me. How I would seem to be moving forward on the verge of a new career, a new life, only to get knocked down again. And, some of the physical sensations and pain were starting to return again. She told me, "Mary don't you see what's going on? You are at such a high vibrational level, such a high frequency level, similar to Buddha and Jesus, and the pureness of Christ consciousness that they possessed. You are going to do such great things in the future. I see that the strongest negative forces are attacking you. They are trying to keep you down so you're not out there. I can feel the negative energies around you. This is really not my area of expertise, but, I know someone that might be able to help you more with what is going on and might be able to heal you." Cora then gave me the name of a healer, Glen, who lived in Rhode Island.

Before I left her, she told me, "Thank you, Mary, for going through all that you have gone through, so I, and others didn't have to. ***Be ready for your soul's next step!***" (Her last statement would stay with me and provide me endless comfort through the more difficult times I was to go through). Then she gave me a CD she had made for me, and I hugged her and left.

When I got home I put the CD in and I couldn't believe it. I had never talked to her about music, yet on the CD she had so many of the songs that started talking to me when all of my spiritual awakening started happening. Like, "Amazing Grace," "You've Got a Friend," and "One Love." I know God was talking through her. We truly are all one!

"God works in us, through us, as us, for us!"

Christian Releasement

The next day, I called Glen and arranged an appointment. When I met him he had told me that from the moment I had called him he had been under "attack" also. He was not feeling right, he was feeling depressed and couldn't understand what was going on. Then it hit him the only thing that was different in his life was my call. He called a colleague of his in Virginia to help him with these energies, and not only was she also being attacked, but her daughter was being attacked as well. He told me "they" were trying to prevent him from helping me.

Glen proceeded to tell me everything that had happened to me. He could see my battles with the dark forces. He told me, "You have been to hell and back! After what you have gone through, you shouldn't even be alive today! You are like one of the stories in the bible where God has really delivered you." I couldn't believe all he knew when just meeting me for the first time. I asked, "What is this all about?" He said, "There are battles going on all the time. Most people have no idea what is going on."

I was in awe! I didn't tell him anything that had happened to me. He told me! I knew he was for real. How could he have known all this?

He said they wanted my power. I thought to myself, "What power? All I have been able to do is be sick!" Then he did some kinesiology testing on me to get more answers over why I was so sick. Glen had me hold my arm out and he tested my resistance to questions. He told me that your body's cells know everything. By asking me a yes or no question and applying a slight downward pressure to my arm while I held it out, he could get an answer from my body. A "yes" answer can be resisted where a "no" response is shown by being unable to hold my arm up, and it would go down with just a little downward pressure.

He asked what percentage of my body was being attacked by dark entities? By starting at ten percent and going up by tens, he found that 90 percent of my body was being attacked. He gave me prayers to say every morning and night and wanted me to come to a special prayer meeting on a Tuesday night at his church. When leaving his office I was very upset and frightened about what was going on. At that moment, I song came over my radio, "***Lean On Me, when you're not strong.***" I looked up to see a car go by me with "Invsbl" (invisible) on its license plate. This gave me such comfort. God was saying to me to "Lean on me and I will help you carry on."

At Glen's church, after the service, a group of three others and Glen formed a circle around me and began praying. This normally would clear someone of negative energies. However, I went home feeling little relief. My pain continued the next day, making me even more frightened and depressed. What do I do now?

The first time I had met Glen he also had given me a name of a woman in New Jersey that did another type of testing. I thought I should give her a call. When I called her and told her what was going on she told me that it was a little beyond her level of expertise and told me she knew a shaman in New Jersey that could help me.

"The things and people you lean on, are the things that don't always last. Lean on ME (God). I AM everlasting!"

"…When tears are n your eyes, and you can't find the way.
…Baby when you're feelin' like, you'll
never see the mornin' light.
…Come to ME, baby you'll see.

~Who Loves You
By The Four Seasons

Shamans to the Rescue

So, I called the shaman in New Jersey and I explained to her what was going on. She was optimistic that she could help me and clear these entities, and she even said she could begin teaching me how to open my gifts up. I was excited that this was what I was looking for and that she could not only heal me once and for all but also help me open these "gifts" people kept telling me I had.

I did a session with the shaman over the phone, but that ended quickly. A few days later I found out that her daughter had unexpectedly died. She was only in her twenties. Her daughter was not sick, and it was a sudden death that upset the shaman so much that she couldn't continue to work with me. I was getting sicker by the day, and started fearing that I would end up in the hospital again or worse. She said she couldn't work with me anymore but, she gave me the name of a student of hers, also in New Jersey, that might be able to help me, a shaman named Joey Stann. I immediately called Joey telling him of my situation. I wanted to get a healing in person from him, but because of his travel schedule, it was a month before he could see me.

To alleviate some of my abdomen pain and pressure, I made an appointment for a body wrap the next day. While driving to the appointment, I noticed the car in front of me, on the highway, had

"I Am" on its license plate. I thought, "Wow, what a great sign!" If that wasn't enough, after my wrap, two hours later, on my way home I saw the same car, in front of me again, with the same "I Am" plate. I thought to myself what a message! *"I Am, is always with me, guiding me."*

In the middle of all this, I had booked a seminar for Dr. Dave and me to go to Boston to see a vibrational healer, Sonia Choquette. She is also author of such books as *Diary of a Psychic, Trust Your Vibes* and *Ask Your Guides*. She is published by, Hay House, and is one of Louise Hay's speakers. I found her seminar to be beyond inspiring. Her seminars were not the kind where you sat there and took notes. It was about connecting to your guardian angels, to your higher self, to believing in yourself. She went on for four hours, but it seemed as if it was forty minutes. Sonia also had Mark Stanton Welch on stage with her whose music connected your soul in a Native American way.

During a lunch break, I was blessed to have an opportunity to meet her and have her sign one of her books I had purchased. As I watched her sign books of the people in front of me she would ask who they were for and signed the person's name, shaking his or her hand and giving a big smile.

However, when Sonia came to me, she stopped, shook my hand, looked up at me and said, "You're a healer!" Then she shook Dr. Dave's hand and told him, "You know why you're here? You're here to keep her grounded!" This gave me such comfort. Here was a woman that knew nothing about me, a world-renowned author and vibrational healer, who could tell I was a healer just by a quick handshake! I didn't hear her tell that to anyone else. Despite all that I was going through, and how I was feeling, this gave me such an incredible feeling that it was all for a reason. God was talking through her, to uplift me once again and carry me on.

A few days later, I was driving and listening to the new Mark Stanton Welch CD I had gotten at Sonia's seminar, and one song I love, "I See You" was playing. As I was singing along with him, a car came toward me with, *"ISeeU2"* on its license plate. I thought to myself, "Thank you God. That was an awesome sign!"

"Everyone needs a Faith Lift!"

That weekend Dr. Dave and I left for New Jersey to see Joey. It was about a four to five hour trip to where Joey lived and we weren't sure how long a healing would take with him so, Dr. Dave reserved a hotel room near where he lived. When we got to his house, Joey came out and greeted us both and told Dr. Dave it would be about an hour. So, he went to check into the hotel. Three hours later, I called him to pick me up. Dr. Dave later told me, "Of course, no one ever spends just and hour with you!"

When I went into Joey's house, he introduced me to Analisa, a shaman that worked with him. The first thing he told me was that after I had called him he was sick for the next two days! He had called Analisa to ask her for her help, and she, too, became ill! He told me that morning he was so sick that he was thinking of canceling my appointment, but, thought I was already on my way, so he didn't. He told me he had never encountered such a reaction, and was wondering who I was. I was wondering myself. Now, not only I, but also the people trying to help me kept getting sick as well!

I found that Joey was a shaman out of the American Indian tradition. He told me he has been a shaman and healer for the past sixty thousand years (which includes several past lives). Joey began his healing ceremony on me by having me lie down on a massage table in a special healing room he had in his house.

Both Joey and Analisa began working on me by walking around me waving their hands over me, trying to feel energy blockages in or around me. At one point, Analisa said should could see dark energy moving down my leg. I knew they were for real because as she said that I was in fact, feeling energy moving down my leg. They began working on this energy trying to bring it up, back toward my abdomen, and up and out through my mouth. But, each time they were getting it up past my abdomen and toward my throat, I would go into convulsions. They would give me a few minutes to catch my breath and they would begin again.

Before I knew it, they had been doing this for close to two hours. At one point during their healing, Joey started to describe what he saw in me. He told me it looked like a dark reptile with long claws and tentacles wrapping itself around my insides, and it had bug eyes that were looking at him as he tried to pull it out of me. I told him I didn't want to hear anymore! I just wanted it out of me. I felt as if my insides where being ripped out. Each time they tried to get it up and out of me, it held on even more.

After two hours Analisa had to leave for another appointment, so Joey continued to work on me alone. He told me it was not going to come out whole so he was going to have to break it up inside me. After another hour of working on me, he felt he had succeeded in getting some pieces of the creature out. Joey said he wanted me to come back the next morning so he could finish. I called Dr. Dave to come and pick me up, and an optimistic but tired Joey greeted him, telling him that they had made a lot of headway but, he needed to finish the job tomorrow. He did confess that he had never encountered anything like this before. Most of the time these dark forces are released in a less than an hour session. With me, two shamans had taken nearly three hours, and it was still holding on!

I was feeling a little more relieved, the pressure in my abdomen had diminished somewhat, but, I was feeling very emotionally and physically drained. We went to our room, and I was asleep in no time.

The next day, Joey had me lie on the floor on an Indian blanket. He used a tuning fork that he would ring and then wave it over my body from head to toe. He told me these negative forces didn't like certain vibrations. He also placed special healing crystals on me, on my forehead, over my heart, and on my abdomen. At one point, during his healing, he went into a trace-like dance beating a small drum and chanting an Indian prayer to release the evil spirits within me. He continued this process, breaking up the creature and pulling it out through my belly button. When he stopped his dancing and chanting and turned to me grabbing at the air over my stomach I could feel him pulling something out of me.

After two hours of doing his clearing/releasing ceremony, Joey told me he had gotten it all out. I was relieved, and felt that most of the unbearable pressure that was in my abdomen was gone. I called Dr. Dave to pick me up. When he arrived, Joey told Dr. Dave what he had taken out of me, and assured him and me, that I would continue to feel better over the next week. We headed back to Rhode Island that afternoon.

The Family Tree
By Joey Stann

We are the children of the Earth, family to one another.
We all have different ways of living,
now we need to bring ourselves together.
Let's make this way of life happen.
All you need to do is to feel the way and to feel inside.
We need a little more understanding,
not ways of being so demanding to ourselves.
Forgive ourselves, give you a reason to live.
And I'd love it when we all come together.
We can change our heart, and ways to learn,
ways to give, and ways to be.
I don't see a reason to fight,
when we have the way to make everything right.
Just understand there's only one,
only one family tree.
There's only one, only one family tree.

Our love will make it all come together,
We can change our hard times into ways to learn,
ways to give, and ways to be one family.
There's only one, only one family tree.

Another Butterfly Appears

On the way back to Rhode Island, I got a call from my mother who said that our house alarm was going off! She was home and for no reason it just started going off, and she couldn't turn it off. We told her to go to the basement and unplug and disconnect the batteries to the alarm system in order to stop it, which she did.

When we got home Dr. Dave checked into the problem and found that when he plugged the system back in it continued to go off, and he couldn't figure out what was causing it to sound, so he left the system unplugged. Later that night when I was in the kitchen I noticed a crack in one of the windows over the sink.

The next day, Dr. Dave took a look at the window in order to try to fix it. When lifting the curtain to take a better look at it he yelled to me, "Mary, you have to come and see this!" When Dr. Dave lifted the curtain to show me the cracked window, we both couldn't believe it. The cracks in the window formed a perfect **butterfly**! We couldn't explain this either.

There was no center hole in the window with cracks coming from one point as if an object, like a stone, or BB, or a bird, had hit it from the outside. There was no hole in the screen that was on the outside, and the window was a thermo-pane (two layers). When taking a close look at it, we discovered that only the inside pane was cracked. Whatever had made the window crack had come from inside the house. And, the cracks filled the window in the shape of a perfect butterfly!

An Amazing Psychic

Over the next few weeks, I was getting my strength back, and I felt I was getting my life back. I started going for long walks again in the late spring sunshine, and I was thinking of volunteering more. I also wanted to finish some sessions with Cora. I wanted her to complete the Master-in-Practice Phases using *"Platinum"* energy with me.

I called her and made an appointment for the following week. At the session with Cora I was telling her all I had just been through in the past month. She told me of another psychic she knew, that she believed was extraordinary. She gave me the number of Kerrie O'Connor in Salem, Connecticut (not Salem, Massachusetts!).

The following week, I booked an appointment with Kerrie hoping she could shed more light on all that had been happening to me and why it was happening to me.

Kerrie was an absolutely amazing, gifted psychic. I met her in her office, and she had me sit at a table across from her. She took out a worksheet and just started writing and telling me about myself. She didn't take my hand; she didn't have me pick cards. She just sat across from me and connected with psychic energies around me.

The first thing she told me was that Jesus, Buddha, Quan Yin, and the Blessed Mother were my guides. I couldn't believe it! That was exactly what Nancy had told me a year ago. They were both telling me the same four divine souls were my guardian angels! She told me that my father recently passed away. She said that I saw the numbers 222 a lot (which I did), which meant, "Your newly planted ideas are growing into reality; everything is working out beautifully." She said these were messages from my father. She ended with telling me that she saw me in purple robes. She told me, "Mary you are royalty, I see purple all around you!"

> *"The journey is what brings us happiness;*
> *not the destination!"*
>
> **~ The Peaceful Warrior**

Getting Reconnected

I started feeling I could now move on with my life, that all these negative events and physical attacks were behind me. I was still thinking about what I should I be doing., when I saw a free magazine called the *Learning Connection*, which had all types of courses you could take on things like self-improvement. On the back cover, there was an advertisement about Dr. Eric Pearl and his **Reconnective Healing** practice, how it was a new form of energy healing on the planet for the first time.

The name "reconnective" just struck a cord with me. It seemed really to hit home for some reason. It might have been that subconsciously, that was what I was looking for, what I wanted at the time, to be really reconnected with God again. In the past few years, with all that I had gone through, I felt, at times I had been abandoned by God. I didn't fully understand why I was being attacked so much.

The advertisement said Dr. Pearl was doing a seminar about Reconnective healing in June in Providence, and I signed up for it. At the seminar, Dr. Pearl talked about how he, a successful chiropractor in Los Angeles, California, was drawn into this new type of energy healing when he observed his patients were starting to have miraculous healings. They told him that they felt his hands on them even when he wasn't near them. Dr. Pearl talked about one patient being used as a channel in a number of different sessions, telling him of what was going on and how he was to teach this type of energy healing to the world.

At the seminar he referred to his book *The Reconnection; Heal Others, Heal Yourself* (2003), that fully described everything that happened to him, and what the Reconnection is. I bought his book at the conclusion of the seminar (also see Chapter VII: Energy Healing). The seminar was an introduction to his healing practice. In order to become a practitioner I learned, I would have to go to a week long training that he held. Unfortunately, none were scheduled in the New England area that year.

I also wanted to experience the Reconnection, and fortunately, there were a few practitioners in Rhode Island that were helping out at the seminar. I asked one of Dr. Pearl's assistants who was available and she told me one of them was Marlene Robinson. On hearing her name, all I could think of was the Simon and Garfunkel song that said,

> "…*Here's to you Mrs. Robinson,* **Jesus loves you**
> *more than you will know!*"

Certainly a positive sign for me.

At the registration desk, I found that she had a practice in Wickford, Rhode Island and excitedly booked a session with her that night. When booking the session with her I was so excited about it that I told her, "I want to see you every week for the next two months." Dr. Pearl was standing behind Marlene and looked at her and said, "What should you say when a client asks you something like that?" Marlene said, "Oh, this is not therapy! Healings occur in two to three sessions at the most." And, the more I thought about it, that fit too. I believe, healing should be instantaneous, or nearly, if you are, in fact, connecting with "divine" energies.

When we got home I had Dr. Dave look into Dr. Pearl's Website, *www.TheReconnection.com* to find where his trainings were being held. As Dr. Dave researched his training schedule he exclaimed to me, "Look at this Mary. He is all over the world! It seems as if he is in a different country every other week." He then found a session being held in August, in Tucson, Arizona. He said, "This will be great. I could go with you. I always wanted to go to Arizona, and I'm still on summer break then!" So, Dr. Dave started looking into making arrangements for us to make the trip.

The next week, I had my appointment with Marlene. I found that she also had a massage therapy practice and her office was in a holistic herbal store called the *Herb Wyfe*. Later, when I told Dr. Dave where it was he said, "The Herb Wyfe, I took a herbal medicine class with the owner, Susan, a couple of years ago. That's a great store."

Marlene did a Reconnective Healing on me. She had me lie on her massage table and began by waving her hands over me. As she did this she told me she could feel energy fluctuation's around me. I found Marlene so genuine, sweet and easy to talk to and we hit it off immediately.

I had Marlene do two more healings on me because I still wasn't feeling 100 percent better. Each time I saw Marlene, she marveled at the energy she felt around me, and I got to know her more and more. Prior to go going to Arizona I needed to have The Reconnection done. It differed from Reconnective healing where The Reconnection was two sessions, two days apart, and it used different techniques intended to "connect one with his or her true purpose in life, whatever that was."

After the last Reconnection session with Marlene, Dr. Dave and I took a ride to Newport for lunch. At a restaurant, that was on the beach, I was telling him about my session with Marlene, when I looked up and saw a man with a tattoo that covered his entire back. To my astonishment, he had a huge sun on his upper left side with rays shining down. The middle of his back had Jesus with outstretched arms, and along his lower back he had The Reconnection logo, which was the two hands with outstretched index fingers nearly touching. This was taken from Michelangelo's painting on the Sistine Chapel ceiling entitled "The Creation." This is where Adam's outstretched hand and index finger is nearly touching God's.

I couldn't believe it! I said, "Do you see this? I just finished having The Reconnection done and I see this!" Right after that another man came walking toward me with a tee-shirt that said, "The Lamb of God" on it. I screamed, "Dr. Dave do you see that?"

God it, to Get it!

After lunch, we went back to our car, and as soon as Dr. Dave turned the car on, the radio was playing "Day By Day" from *Godspell*, which I used to listen to all the time growing up; I couldn't recall the last time I had heard it on the radio. I told Dr. Dave, "Do you see this? (soon to be one of my favorite sayings to Dr. Dave) Its all happening. I just got Reconnected now I'm seeing all these signs."

A week later, I was at a yoga class and I saw another incredible sign. I was warming up before class, and just the instructor and I were there. Then a woman came in wearing a tee shirt that "blew my mind" (not that that was possible). Her shirt just had the Michelangelo creation fingers, very large, on the front of it. I nearly screamed at her, taking her by surprise, "Where did you get that?" She was taken back somewhat but then just told me, "On an Internet tee shirt site." I told her I loved it and that it symbolized a type of energy healing called The Reconnection.

Getting Connected in Arizona

August couldn't come too soon for me; I was so looking forward to learning about The Reconnection. The training session with Dr. Pearl was for five days in Tucson, and Dr. Dave planned some side trips to make it a ten day vacation for us. He planned to take the first part of the training, Level I and II, that were for the first two days, and I was taking Levels I through III, to become a practitioner.

The first session, was actually a repeat of what we had gone to in Providence. Dr. Pearl was giving an introduction to his background and how he discovered the Reconnection. But, this time he gave us some information about what to expect in his training sessions that also contained a suggested reading list. I was so impressed with the list of books he had suggested, because I had already been divinely led to many of the same titles and had already read eight of the ten books he suggested. Then he said he practiced the *Science of Mind* (not Scientology) which is the church we had been going to the past year in Warwick, Rhode Island. I started to think that we were definitely on the same wavelength, maybe I was home, this is what I was looking for, and the next thing out of his mouth was "Welcome home!" Verifying my exact feeling at the time.

The next day, Dr. Dave and I attended Level I training with about two-hundred others from around the country. Dr. Pearl and his staff discussed energy healing and how The Reconnection was different. He also had several of his staff give testimonies of their experiences with The Reconnection, of their miraculous personal healings, and of their miraculous healings on others.

Dr. Pearl also discussed the science behind energy healing and had researchers from the University of Arizona there conducting tests. They were taking readings of various energy levels in the room noting any variations when Reconnective Healing was being conducted. At one point during the day, I noticed a man across the room with a tee-shirt that had the word "Eternity" printed on it. I thought to myself, "How great is that."

Later, during a break, the man I had noticed was walking out of the room at the same time Dr. Dave and I were, and I mentioned to him that I liked his tee shirt. He started a conversation with me, and I found he was from California. At one point, he asked if I had ever heard of a book called *Anastasia*? I told him I hadn't, and he then gave me a copy of the book. I asked him if I could pay him for it, but, he just smiled and told me to pass it along. I didn't see him during the rest of the week there.

That night I began reading the book *Anastasia* (2005), by Vladimir Megre. When reading the book, I was amazed at the story of a Russian businessman, Vladimir Megre, and how he met an extraordinary woman named Anastasia. Anastasia not only had psychic abilities, but, she lived in complete harmony with nature in the wilds of Siberia. Wild animals brought her food and protected her. With no formal education she knew everything going on around the world, and began telling Vladimir how to make it a better world. When we got back home I had Dr. Dave look up her books and found that there is a series of nine books about her called the Ringing Cedars Series. Their Website: *www.ringingcedars.com* sells the books as well as a number of healing products from Siberia. I couldn't believe it when I saw her *Book 4: Co-Creation*. It had a large butterfly on its cover, and in the book, she describes a butterfly as:

"It reflects the perfection and beauty of Nature, and is the ultimate symbol of metamorphosis, transformation and resurrection."

That certainly reflected what I had been feeling about what was going on with me. Perhaps this was why the Universe kept sending me butterflies in all types of forms.

The second day of our training seminar we started to break into small groups. Around fifty or so massage tables that were set up in the room. Dr. Pearl and his staff explained some of the fundamentals of Reconnective healing, demonstrated it to us, and then had us break-up into groups of four or five and go to a massage table. One person would lie on the table, while the others in the group would take turns working on him or her.

Reconnective Healing is a hands-off technique. Healing is facilitated by using special healing frequencies around the various energy layers surrounding the body (see Chapter VII: Energy Healing). As my group conducted its healings, several members commented on the energy waves they were feeling. They noticed that their patients were also feeling the energy and various sensations as they lay on the tables.

I however, was becoming increasingly frustrated because I didn't feel anything while lying on the table or when I was conducting a healing. Others said they felt pins and needle sensations in their hands or, that the energy waves felt like bands of molasses in the air or they felt cold or hot waves. I felt nothing. A few in my group did comment that they felt intense heat from me when I worked on them, and they could feel where my hands were over their bodies as I moved around them. But I felt nothing!

At the end of the day, we were going back to our room when, in the elevator a woman asked how I liked the sessions. I told her that, "I love it but, I still haven't been able to feel any energy." She asked that I put out my hand, and she cupped her hands around mine, moving hers up and down. She asked if I felt that. I told her I didn't, but she told me, "I certainly feel your energy!" That of course, didn't make me feel any better.

After dinner, Dr. Dave and I went to the pool, enjoying the warm Arizona evening. The only other people at the pool to my surprise were the woman I had met in the elevator and her husband. This time we introduced ourselves, and I found out that Bernadette and Charlie Cook were from Canada, and that her husband was also in education. Dr. Dave and Charlie hit it off immediately when Dr. Dave found out that Charlie was a big New England sports fan, and they went off talking about the New England Patriots.

I found that Bernadette was just as excited about getting out and helping and healing people as I was, and we talked about our backgrounds and what brought us to Arizona together. As the evening wore on, she said she was going up to her room, and before she left she made a comment, "You know what mother Teresa said? ***Why follow when you can lead!***" That really hit me because a billboard that stuck out to me on our drive down to Tucson, had on it *"Why follow when you can be the leader."* I felt that spirit was talking through her again, to me.

The next two days, the attendees dwindled down to about fifty people staying for Level III training to learn how to do The Reconnection. The Reconnection was different from Reconnective Healing, where, we learned that when we conduct a Reconnection it is a two session process. It also had a few more technical/ritual components, and, it is intended to connect one to his or her life's purpose.

In the afternoon session, we had to change partners; they wanted us to work with different people, feeling others' energy. Of course, I still wasn't feeling anything! At that time, a woman came from across the room, and said she wanted to work with me. She told me that she was a vibrational healer and had been doing this kind of work for over twenty years, and that she wouldn't work with just anybody. I told her how discouraged I was because I couldn't feel anything. She told me, "Honey I could feel your energy from across the room! Don't worry about anything: you've got it."

We proceeded to work on each other. After I worked on her she told me that she had to do everything she could do to hold back her tears. She said my energy level was incredible. She told me, "You don't feel energy because you were born this way. You have had an incredible vibrational energy your whole life! You just never realized it. You're swimming in it! This is why you aren't feeling anything. Don't worry about feeling it, because you are already there. You are not feeling anything near your level. But, I bet people feel you!" This was all so new to me I just told her, "Thanks. That makes me feel better, but I sure would like to feel something."

As I went back to my room, I thanked God for her comments. I was getting so discouraged I was even thinking of not finishing the sessions and going home. I really needed her to come to me and explain to me what was going on. I thought that this was what The Reconnection was all about, lining you up with the right people, at the right time, for what you needed in life. God was definitely talking through her!

Sedona Energies

After my Reconnection sessions were over, Dr. Dave and I headed north to spend a few days in Sedona. We were looking forward to seeing more of Arizona, and had heard a lot about the energy vortexes in the Sedona area. Dr. Dave had booked a corner suite at the Sedona Hilton that was another beautiful resort. We had a balcony off our room that faced Bell Rock, which was a huge red rock formation. We found out from a very knowledgeable doorman at the hotel that back in 1987, during a celestial alignment of the planets called the Harmonic Convergence, where the sun, moon and six out of the nine planets were in alignment, a thousand people came from all over the world and gathered around Bell Rock. They were holding hands waiting for the "mother ship" to come and take them away. But, unfortunately, the ship never came.

We found the Sedona area amazing with all the red rock formations and its rich American Indian influences. On our first day in Sedona Dr. Dave took me to Angel Valley, which was a holistic-healing resort, that was about ten miles outside the city. He had arranged a "dolphin healing" session for me.

While I was getting my healing Dr. Dave walked around the resort seeing the sights. He was taking pictures of the area and the large walking stone labyrinth there, constructed over an energy vortex However, we realized later that none of the twenty or so pictures he took at Angel Valley came out.

The next day, we went on a jeep safari through the area. Our guide was an American Indian that we found was from the Apache tribe. As he showed us around the area he also told us a lot about his Indian heritage and his perspective on "white man's" views. He told us that Indian tribe names were the white man's terms, that those names given to the Indian tribes were very derogatory terms, similar to the "N" word given to African Americans. The name of his tribe was really Hopi, which meant something like "humans." We even saw bumper stickers when out there that said, "Don't Worry Be Hopi!" He also told us he was writing a book on the subject.

On our last day in the Sedona area, we took a day long trip through the Grand Canyon. We drove up to the Grand Canyon airport and boarded a six-passenger plane. Dr. Dave joked as we were sitting side by side and we both had window seats. As we flew over the canyon the views were spectacular. Dr. Dave said that they were, "Grand." Then we took a raft trip through the Grand Canyon down the Colorado River, stopping for a picnic lunch. Our guide on the raft also had a Native American background and he told us all about the discovery of the canyon and ancient Indian tribes that lived in the area going back a thousand years.

At the time, I may have had trouble feeling energy, but, Dr. Dave and I did experience energies in the Sedona area. Not only did the pictures at Angel Valley not come out, but several of the pictures Dr. Dave took when we went on jeep tour of the Sedona country side did not come out. Dr. Dave complained to me that he had a headache for the three days we were in Sedona. He told me he believed that it was due to all the road construction throughout downtown Sedona when we were there. It was creating disturbances in the energy fields there. And, for some strange reason, the windshield of our rental car, in front of me (on the passenger side) developed a small crack, that kept getting larger everyday we were in Sedona. Neither of us could remember anything hitting the windshield to create or, start a crack. It just appeared and continued growing larger in front of me. Dr. Dave told me, "See what happens when energy meets energy!"

A Divine Offer

On the way back home I was thinking about getting my Reconnective business going and considering where to practice and if I should start out in my home, look for an office on my own, or look to join someone as Dr. Dave had in his Waves of Wellness practice. The next week, to my surprise, Grace called me and told me that her partner wasn't working out and asked if I would consider joining her practice, *Healing Hearts.* Here again, just as I was told:

The Universe lines you up with just what you need!

You don't have to do anything it comes to you.

I was thrilled to be in business with Grace. She helped me so much when all this started. And, now I had the opportunity to be in business with her, helping and healing others. Who better to be in business with than my, *"Amazing Grace!"*

Grace also had a third partner, a, M.D., Dr. Ysabel Reyes, who I found out after meeting her is certainly a "wonder woman." She works full-time at a hospital, raises a family here, as well as supports her family in the Dominican Republic, and is working with us as a holistic nutritional consultant at Healing Hearts. She truly believes in, and promotes a healthy body, mind, and spirit.

The next few months, the three of us expanded the Healing Hearts office and promoted our business with open houses and local advertising. The business grew slowly, and as the holidays approached, our business slowed even more and I was becoming frustrated again. I felt like I had so much to give to others with all that I had been through, and all that I had learned. I wanted to help and heal ten people a day, but, the Universe had other plans for me. My own healing and learning weren't over yet!

An Extraordinary Yogi

In early November, one Sunday after our church service, I was discussing the extraordinary abilities of various masters I had read about in *The Life and Teaching of the Masters of the Far East* (1964) series (four volumes) by Baird T. Spalding with our spiritual leader, Rev. Ian Taylor. He told me about another similar book by Paramahansa Yogananda, *Autobiography of a Yogi,* (1946), that was about a holy man from India and his spiritual apprenticeship and journey with masters throughout India. So, of course, I ordered the book when I got home.

After reading the book I found that Paramahansa introduced a meditative yoga practice called *Kriya Yoga* to the U.S. in the 1920's. I wanted to try it, hoping that it could open me up more, connecting me more to these "gifts" that others had told me I have. I had Dr. Dave check into where there was an Kriya Yoga teacher in New England. The nearest center he found was in Connecticut. When I called them I found that their center had moved to California, but, they told me of another teacher in Rhode Island. I anxiously called and learned that the instructor, Rev. Robert "Ram" Smith was also the East Coast sales manager of a book distributor, and he traveled quite a bit. He told me that he would be in the Providence area the following week and we arranged to meet to discuss Kriya Yoga. He asked me how I found out about him and I told him, "The reverend at my church told me about the book *Autobiography of a Yogi.*" Ram asked, "What church do you go to and who is your minister?" I told him, "I go to Concordia Center for Spiritual Living in Warwick, Rhode Island and Rev. Ian is the spiritual leader there." Ram said, "Rev. Ian! I have been trying to get in touch with him!" (Of course!).

Dr. Dave and I met Rev. Ram at an East Side (in Providence) restaurant the following week and were immediately taken by his amazing personality. He had told us that he studied with Swami Kriyananda, a direct disciple of Paramahansa's, and that he is now the spiritual director of the Ananda Self-Realization Center in Kingston, Rhode Island. Ram went on about his background and we found that he has taught meditation and Kriya-Ananda yoga all over the world. He is also a musician and has five musical CDs to his credit. He told us that twenty years ago he was part of a church choir group that had performed in front of the Pope in the Vatican, and then he sang, in Italian, the song they had performed.

We arranged to have a session with Ram and went down to his house in South Kingston, Rhode Island. There, we found that he had a large studio set-up that had an altar in the front with pictures of Paramahansa, Swami Kriyananda, and Jesus. Ram began his session by telling us more about Paramahansa, and how he came to the US and began his teaching ministry here. During Ram's story telling he also took out a large mandolin and sang a few songs to us.

Ram then led us on a mediation for about a half hour that was very relaxing and clearing. After that he had us get up and he led us through a number of muscle tension and relaxation exercises and yoga. Before we knew it three hours had gone by. When leaving, Ram gave us a book by Swami Kriyananda, *The Art and Science of Raja Yoga* (2002). I found Ram to be an extraordinary soul, and Kriya-Ananda yoga to be very relaxing and therapeutic. But, it was not the quick opening-up enlightening experience I was looking for at the time, especially when Ram told us it often takes a lifetime of study to reach the results I told him I was looking for.

Flower of Life

After the holidays I was questioning what I should and could do to make things happen more, when my eyes were drawn to a book I had read a year earlier called *The Ancient Secrets of the Flower of Life* (2007) by Drunvalo Melchizedek. As I looked through it I saw that it ended with, "See you in Book Two." I realized that I had never gotten the second book, so I ordered it. When reading *The Ancient Secrets of the Flower of Life, Book II,* it talked about Mer-ka-ba meditation, and that one should learn this from a practitioner.

Looking through their Website to find a *Flower of Life* practitioner I found the closest one to me was Maureen St. Germain who lived in New York City. Checking into her Website, I found that she conducted classes all over the world. I wanted to take a class with her but, was unsure about going alone. I found that the only class she had available, which was the exact week Dr. Dave was on a school vacation, was in upstate New York in late February. I called and found that she did have room for me in that class. Here, again, I felt as if the Universe was lining everything up for me.

Maureen's class was in Ithaca, New York which was about a six hour trip for us, so we left a day early and planned to be there for five days. Her *Flower of Life* workshop started on a Friday evening and went through Monday. While I was at the workshop, Dr. Dave was looking forward to the time he could spend in our hotel to update and revise his first book which he did in *Holistic Mental Health-Revised* (2009).

While training with Maureen, I came to realize what an extraordinary, connected soul she is. She truly exemplified the divine! Her wealth of knowledge was remarkable. She had told me she had been on this path for over twenty years and had studied directly with Drunvalo Melchizedek. She made me understand life in a whole new way, opening my consciousness even more.

During our time together, she told me by checking in the **Akashic Records** that, "I'm sorry you had to go through what you went through." She had learned about all the pain and suffering I went through. She added, "You're not crazy. You should consider yourself in '*Wizard Apprentice*' school now!"

The next day, in class she took out several decks of spiritual cards and invited all the participants to pick a deck. To my astonishment, there was an answer to something I had been questioning for a while. For several months before attending Maureen's classes, I kept seeing different signs with the name "Avalon" on it. Each time I saw it, I would get that gut feeling, that it meant something, but I didn't know what. I would see "Avalon" Hair studio, then "Avalon" Restaurant, then see "Avalon" cars always in front of me, and now the deck of cards in front of me said "Avalon." I was astounded! I asked Maureen, "What is Avalon?" She replied, "You don't know what Avalon is? You need to get the book or the movie *The Mists of Avalon.*" When I got home we immediately rented the movie and it revealed so much to me.

After spending a number of days with Maureen, I was amazed at how gifted she was. She could channel the Akashic Records, and she was so connected to her higher self, that she could hear her answers just as if a physical person was talking to her. She told me that by practicing the Mer-ka-ba, anyone can get to this point, that *"Practice always produces good results."* Her knowledge, teaching, help, support, and personal stories, and books are life altering. I felt truly blessed to know her.

An Extraordinary Healer

About a month later, I was starting to feel tired and bloated again and I started to think about getting a colonic to ease the pain. I had gone to a place near Hartford, but, I couldn't think of the name of it. I asked Dr. Dave to help me find it. He called me from work with the number of a place called the Colonic Institute in West Hartford, Connecticut. He was looking at their Website and he thought I would really connect with the owner, Aimee. He read that she was a Taurus like me and had studied in India. However, when he tried to book an appointment for me, Aimee told him that she only worked with chronically sick people. But, she had other associates in her clinic and referred me to Michelle.

Of course, I was *divinely* led to Michelle. I found that Michelle not only did colonic therapy there but she was also a Reiki Master, and very psychic. When she first met me she saw that I had "energies" with me. As Michelle began doing a healing on me Spirit started telling her things about me. She told me, "Mary, they told me why you are getting sick all the time, why they are making you sick. They are trying to keep you from your work! What is it that you do?"

I told her that I do energy healing like she did. Then she went on, "Mary, they are telling me you should be writing a book. Your book will help humanity!"

I couldn't believe it! Dr. Dave and I had been talking about starting to write a book about all I had been going through for a couple of months now. I remembered back to my first battle with Gordan and the dark forces when I was writing and writing notes in a journal, telling my mother (who thought I was quite crazy) that I was going to write a book.

Michelle continued working on me and told me, "You are at such a high energy level!" I thought I sure didn't feel like I was so high. I did feel a lot better after she was done with the colonic and her Reiki healing. The pressure in my abdomen was greatly reduced.

The Best of Both Worlds

At one of my sessions with Michelle, after I told her how amazed I was that she was so psychic and gifted, she told me that her "gifts" paled to that of a friend of hers, Vanessa. She told me I really needed to talk to her about what has been happening to me because that was more of what Vanessa did, as well as remove entities. She gave me her number and Website and when I got home we looked Vanessa up.

On her Website, *www.stairwaytohealing.com,* I found that one of the services she offered where she did a healing and a reading, was called "The Best of Both Worlds," which, of course, really meant something to me. The next day I called her and made an appointment for the next week. Her office was in Cheshire, Connecticut, about ninety minutes from me.

Vanessa was in fact the "***Best of Both Worlds"*** herself. She was an amazing healer and one of the most gifted psychics I had ever met. Vanessa did an energy healing on me as well as an entity releasement. Like Grace, she was able to see entities in and around me. She told me she was able to release several. I felt great relief when she was done. What she told me next really "blew my mind," if that was possible. Vanessa told me,

> "Mary I see thousands of angels around you! I see that you're writing a book" I knew she didn't get that from Michelle because I hadn't told Michelle that I was going to see Vanessa. She continued, "Your book will help heal the world! That you will be able to do magic. Travel the world, healing and helping people. You are gifted, blessed, protected, and tremendously loved! I see Jesus all around you. Every where I look around you I see Jesus's face smiling.

> "Mary, your energy is not human. Your DNA is totally different. You are interplanetary." She told me she had never used that word before. But that so resonated with me because I loved the song by Karen Carpenter "Interplanetary Craft." In it the lyrics said, *"Calling all occupants of interplanetary, most extraordinary craft."* Vanessa went on, "Mary, you are being watched by billions of beings in other dimensions and other universes! I see Jesus and his energy all around you. He is so pleased at where you are going. Your energy aura

is a crystalline-white; I have never seen that before! You are amazing!"

"Me?" I said, "You are the amazing one!" At that point, she gave me a big hug and we both broke down in tears.

A few weeks later, I went back to see her for another *Best of Both Worlds*. When I arrived, she told me that I looked a lot better than when she had first met me. As she did a reading and connected to her spirit guide, she told me, "Mary they are telling me that Jesus is your spirit guide. Also Archangel Raphael is your spirit guide. He is the Archangel of healing. They are telling me you are an *'oversoul,'* a very old soul, and you are in the Holy Family's soul group!"

I was thinking of going to see John of God, and I asked Vanessa to check with her guides to see if I should. She told me, "It will be a transcending experience." She also told me she knew another healer that might be able to help me further, Joanna Neff.

More Divine Happenings

The next day, Dr. Dave and I met with Marlene Robinson. Dr. Dave was doing a past life regression on her as she also did that and wanted to see how Dr. Dave did it. While they were doing that, I was reading a book on ascension. Later we all went out to dinner, and they were telling me about Marlene's experiences during her regression. Marlene told me that when Dr. Dave asked her the name of her spirit guide she just blurted out "Adam." She had no idea why she said that name. I told her, "I was reading about an ascended master named Adam during your regression."

A few days later I had a clearing done by Joanna Neff, who was referred to me by Vanessa. Joanna's specialty was entity removal and soul clearance. She performed this while in meditation from a distance and then sends her client a worksheet reporting what she had cleared. When she sent me my sheet she reported that she had removed thousands of entities from me. She cleared them from my current as well as past lives.

Later that week, I got a call by a man named Greg who said he was looking at my Website and said he could feel my energy through the computer. He told me that he knew he had to call me. He told me that he ran a radio station and would like to help promote what I do. Then he said, "You know why your name is Mary, don't you?" I was shocked that he said that, it reminded me of what Gordan had said to me. Then he said, "Do you believe we will create from the void in the future?" That may have seemed like a strange question coming from someone, but Spirit knew that is all I had been thinking about. My response was, "Absolutely!" After that we had several more conversations on this topic. I found that he is truly a divine and connected soul, and he helped promote our *Divinely Touched* seminars.

The following week I went to Hartford, Connecticut to do a Reconnection on my friend Joanne "Bud" and a friend of hers Barbara. On the way there I took the country route, rather than the highway, and I became somewhat lost. However, I found that you are never really lost. There is always a reason for everything that happens, and there are always signs to be seen. If I had gone what I thought was the right way, I would have missed a number of messages speaking to me.

As I was driving, I heard a message come into my mind, "When you do what no one has done before, then they pay attention!" Just at that point I heard a song I hadn't heard in twenty years, "Magic," by Olivia Newton-John. If I had taken the highway, I wouldn't have been delayed and heard the song saying, "You have to believe we are magic!"

"…you should know me I've always been in your mind.
…You have to believe we are magic
nothing can stand in our way.
…The planets align so rare, there's PROMISE in the air,
*and **I Am** guiding you.*

...*I'll bring all your dreams alive, for you.*"
~*Magic*
By Olivia Newton-John

After the sessions, with Joanne and Barbara, we went out to lunch and when we were leaving the restaurant, I noticed that the car parked next to us had "*won*" on its license plate. When I was on my way home, I saw another plate that said, "unokid." That meant to me, "Number 1 kid," which I also took as a real positive sign.

The next week, Joanne and Barbara were shopping in Mystic, Connecticut and found a store named *Angel Haven.* In the store, they could look up who your Archangel was based on your birthday and make you a small poster of it. They thought it would be a great present for me, so they had mine done. They were as amazed as I was with what mine said. They found out my Archangel is Camael, the sister of Archangel Michael. Her mission is to help people get to their divine destiny! On the poster her caption is, *"I Am Divine; I Am Love !"*

The next day, Heidi called me and said she had met a woman at a conference she had just attended that told her she is an energy healer, but, that she rarely felt anything when conducting a healing. She told Heidi that she doesn't feel anything because she is energy herself, that she is vibrating at a high rate. Heidi told me that she immediately thought of me. She remembered that I often told her when I am working on people I usually don't feel anything. Heidi ended her call saying that because I am at such a high vibrational energy I don't feel lower rates of energy when I do healings. I thought back to the woman I met at the Reconnection conference in Arizona, who had told me the same thing. Just as Michelle a few weeks before had told me. Here were more unrelated people and events telling me the same thing! It started to make sense to me.

Through all my abdominal difficulties, struggling with energies flowing through my body, and continuing in trying to find answers for myself, what kept me going were the amazing results I was getting in helping others. Such was the case when I worked with a waitress that came in to get a Reconnective Healing from me. When Joanne came in she could hardly bend her right knee; it was very swollen and she was in severe pain daily from having to stand on it for so long in her job. She told me that her doctor was recommending surgery, but she wasn't looking forward to it and was concerned with taking so much time out of work, recuperating. As I conducted a healing on her, to our surprise, we saw the swelling disappear before our eyes. She was able to bend her knee without any pain. She left me feeing elated!

The next week, I checked with her, and she told me her knee was feeling fine, even after standing on it all day. She told me she cancelled her surgery. Later I learned Joanne even joined a gym and was doing aerobics and riding a stationary bike there for over a half hour at a time. Cases like Joanne's really made me feel that I was making a difference, even though I wasn't at a 100 percent yet myself.

A Divinely Touched Seminar

At this point in my life, I had met so many amazing and gifted people, and I had been led to such extraordinary resources that Dr. Dave and I decided to put on a seminar in May. We wanted to start sharing with others some of what we had learned and experienced so far. Dr. Dave actually started planning the seminar eight months earlier. He had booked a date at the Crowne Plaza Hotel in Warwick, Rhode Island and started to line up speakers for the event. Our first choice for a keynote speaker, and Dr. Dave heard daily how excited I was that he agreed to do it, was Dr. Michael Sharp, of course. The theme of the seminar was *"**Awakening to Your Life's Potential.**"* Dr. Sharp's talk was on, "Awakening Your Spirit," and he discussed the technical aspects of higher consciousness.

We also had Rev. Ian Taylor, the spiritual leader of Concordia Center for Spiritual Living, in Warwick, Rhode Island. We had come to know and love him since he had moved to Rhode Island the previous summer to lead our church. Every one of his weekly lessons was so inspirational that we wanted him to be able to share some of his insights to others. He spoke on, *"Connecting to Spirit"* at our seminar.

At our church, we had also met a gifted author of *Simply A Woman of Faith* (2007), Pat Hastings. We asked her to be part of our first seminar as well. Her presentation, *"Let Miracles Find You"* was a lot about how she was inspired to write her book and a number of stories that were, in fact, miraculous.

Another speaker we knew we had to have at our seminar, after meeting him, was Rev. Robert "Ram" Smith. We knew that with Ram's spiritual background and his story telling and musical abilities he would be an inspirational speaker as well. We were not disappointed. He spoke on, *"Yogoda: Grounding Yourself Spiritually."*

Dr. Dave also spoke on, *"The Science of Intent."* He discussed the science behind how consciousness can exist outside of the body, blending topics such as quantum physics with psychic phenomena (see Chapters VI and VII).

An Amazing Astrologer

At one of my sessions with Michelle, she referred me to an astrologer named Mark. I e-mailed him and made arrangements for him to do my chart and a reading the next week. He asked for my time, date and place of birth, and we set a specific time when he would call me. Mark likes to call and speak to his client and then afterwards, he would also send a tape of the session.

During our session, he began by saying, "Mary I see so much *magic* and amazing energy, and *electricity* in your chart! I see you becoming clear this summer and your business will really start picking up this fall. Next spring the world will really start to know who you are. I see you in a bigger house next spring. I see you have a book in you. I see you speaking in front of thousands. You are here to shine. You are here to make people see things differently, and you will make them think of things they never thought of before. I also see that you are a gifted healer!"

Mark's incredibly accurate reading amazed me because I had not told him anything prior to our session. I didn't tell him about what I did, or wasn't doing at the time or that we were thinking about writing a book. Again, his reading blew me away. He was verifying what others were telling me, and, I had no doubt that he was connected to and guided by Spirit.

Back to Connect-itcut!

Every time I went back to Connecticut it became **connect - it** for me. And, every time I saw the "Welcome To Connecticut" sign it certainly was *"Full of Surprises!"* which became an understatement each time I saw Michelle or Vanessa.

The next week, when I went back to see Michelle at the Colonics Institute, the first thing she told me was, "Mary, you are glowing, you look great!" I told her about my clearing with Joanna and that I was in fact, feeling a little better. After she meditated on me and connected with her spirit guides she told me, "They are telling me that you will be healing the world. They are asking me if, *'the meek shall inherit the Earth'* means anything to you? They are also telling me your energy in the future will be like liquid light. All you have to do is walk by people, and they will be healed!" What could I say about all that? I was just thinking Connecticut *is* certainly full of surprises!

I also went back to see Vanessa that week, and she started saying just what Michelle had told me, "Mary what have you been doing? You're glowing!" I told her, "Thanks, I feel a little better. I had a clearing with Joanna Neff." Vanessa continued, "I see a line of light coming from your head, extending upward to the *Source!*"

I then showed her my clearing sheet that Joanna had sent me. Vanessa had also had a clearing done by Joanna, and she took her sheet out. When we compared the two, we couldn't believe the difference. I had ten to twenty times more entities cleared than Vanessa did. In each category, where Vanessa had one or two cleared, I had hundreds. Where she had ten or twenty cleared, I had thousands. I had every category filled in; Vanessa had only half of the categories filled in. Vanessa couldn't believe how many more attachments and entities I had compared to her.

Vanessa then continued giving me a reading by connecting to her guides. Vanessa told me that my healings should be taking off in the fall. Then she asked me, "Do you have any children?" I told her I didn't and she said, "I see children all around you in the future. I see multitudes of children around in the future in your schools. You have schools all over the world! You have houses everywhere as well. You are drawn more to California than Arizona. You get more energy there. I see you having your own TV show!"

She then gave me a book about Mary Magdalene and a book of numbers. She hadn't ordered the book; it had just showed up at her doorstep one day. She told me that she knew they were meant for me. As I was looking through the book of numbers, I saw how to assign a number to each letter of the alphabet and how to add up the letters of your name. I found out that in numerology MARY equals the number 3. And 3 is an ascended master number. The numerology book she gave me also talked about 3 being liquid light (just as she saw coming out of me the first time we met)! And, the number 3 stands for supreme *balance*!

A few days later, still not feeling well, I decided to call a naturopath. I made an appointment with Jane at *The Tree of Life* in Seekonk, Massachusetts. I found her to be very pleasant, professional, and thorough. She performed a number of tests and could not find anything wrong with me. Everyone of her tests showed I was perfectly normal, again. Yet I still felt as if I was nine months pregnant again. Believing my problems were more that physical, Jane referred me to a shaman named Judy. I realized Heidi had told me about her a year ago and I had never gotten around to calling her. As I left, Jane told me that I was putting everything together and I was on the path I was supposed to be on. As encouraging as that sounded, I still just wished that I felt better. As I left her office, I notice a plaque on the wall that said:

"Faith is believing when common sense tells you not to."

The next week I went back to see Vanessa, and as she worked over me, she told me that she felt I had a block in my abdomen again. She took out a special tuning fork that she said should break up the blockage. She proceeded to ring it and wave it over my stomach and chest. She continued the treatment for close to forty minutes. When she was done, she told me, "That was amazing, Mary! Normally I only have to do that for a few minutes. Whatever you had in you certainly didn't want to leave!" (That sounded familiar.)

Vanessa then touched my knee and said she was being told that I was going to see John of God this year. I told her, "I don't think so. Grace and I sent our picture to him a few weeks before and we did not get 'X's' back on them, which means that he doesn't need to see us in person. Dr. Dave and I were thinking of going to Brazil next summer to see him." However, Vanessa was somewhat insistent, telling me that she saw us seeing John of God this year. I too was insistent telling her, "I know our travel plans this year, and we certainly are not going to Brazil (little did I know that she would turn out to be right, of course!). As I left Vanessa, she also told me she saw me now filled with platinum light!

A Local Shaman

The next day, I had an appointment with Judy Lavine, the shaman. This time I only had to travel about fifteen minutes from my house as she lived in East Providence, Rhode Island. As I turned into her street, I saw a car with a bumper sticker on it that said, "Grace Happens," certainly a positive sign for what I was about to experience.

Judy had me lie on her massage table, and she began by walking around me, feeling my energy field. Then she told me, "Mary I see you are going to do amazing, astounding things. I see you were a great mystic in a previous life, and you were the leader of many tribes. You have no idea who you are do you?" I told her, "Judy, this is all still so new and unbelievable to me. It seems that everyday it gets more extraordinary."

Judy continued, "Mary, that's a good word for it, extraordinary! You are here to move the world forward. You had to go through what you went through to gain more insight and compassion to what others are going through, to learn what it feels like to be in pain, or have people think you are crazy. That's what you have been going through in this lifetime."

What she told me next startled me (if that was possible at this point!). "Mary I see what is in you that is keeping you sick. It's a demon with long tentacles wrapped around your stomach! These demons keep trying to prevent you from doing what you are here to do." I thought back to what Joey saw in me and got out of me the first time I had met him in New Jersey.

Judy then took out a special rattle and bell and began ringing them over me (like what Vanessa and Joey had done). She said that demons hate these sounds . Judy then told me to do a number of things to protect myself. She gave me a bunch of quartz crystals and told me to put them around the house. She also told me to place CD's in my windows in order to reflect spirits away. Then she gave me an "*Atlantis*" ring to keep me protected. She said that she saw I had Atlantis energy around me. She told me when I heal others that their negative entities are often drawn to me and get attached to me. She said she sees negative entities, demons all around me, trying to get in. She gave me special bell and told me to ring it in every room in my house. She also told me I should read Psalm 91 daily. All these measures would keep these demons away.

Judy also called a colleague of hers that lived in Arizona during our session who told her that she saw that my light is amazing and soon I will be world-wide. My one hour session took over two and a half hours. When I was leaving her therapy room, I noticed a life-sized picture on her door. I asked, "Who is that?" She told me, "That's Sai Baba. He is one of the highest beings on the planet right now. He is a spiritual master living in India. He can materialize anything from the void. If you want a necklace, he puts out his hand and one just appears in it. You need to have a picture of him." Judy then gave me a small wallet-size picture of him to carry with me. As I drove away from her house I saw a car with a bumper sticker that said, ***"God will do it."***

In July, I went back to see Michelle for another treatment. After it, she told me that she saw that I am three-fourths filled with light now. She told me that she was being told I should get the song "Calling All Angels" by Train. I told I did have that song and I listened to it all the time. Michelle also told me that she got a message I should call Richard Jackson who performs exorcisms, that he could help clear me even more. On the way home with Dr. Dave we saw the biggest most incredible rainbow I had ever seen.

The following week I went back to see Vanessa. I told her that we found out that John of God was coming to the Omega Institute in New York in the fall and we were planning to see him then. She reminded me that she had told me months ago that I was going to see him in the fall. At the time, neither of us had known that he was coming to the U.S. Vanessa then told me that Spirit was telling her what my second book will be called. I thought, "Second book? We haven't even begun the first one!"

Vanessa then said, "Mary, Spirit is telling me that you can't even imagine what you are going to be doing in the future. You not only will be able to heal people in their current life, but, you also will be healing all their past lives as well. No one has ever done what you are going to be doing! Even your tears will be like holy water!" Again, I left her feeling amazed at all she could see and what she had told me, and I felt like the one who was blessed by being with her.

No Medical Answers

Towards the middle of July, Dr. Dave and I went to our primary care doctor for an annual check-up. I was still having stomach bloating, and I had some pain on my left side of my abdomen. He performed all his usual tests; blood pressure, EKG, blood work.

A week later my blood tests came back all perfectly normal, again. The medical profession could not detect anything wrong with me. All my tests showed I was "perfectly normal." Yet all the psychics and lightworkers I met knew what was causing my discomfort. They just were not able to keep me clear and healthy by themselves. As least not yet!

In *Spontaneous Healing* (1995), Andrew Weil, M.D. author of over a dozen books on health and healing makes the connection that:

> *"During my travels throughout the world I have met many healers who believe that the primary causes of health and illness are not physical but **spiritual.** They direct their attention toward an invisible world assumed to exist beyond the ordinary world of senses. In this realm they search for reasons for illness and ways to cure it. Some of these people believe in karmic causes of illness (actions in the past or in past lives); others, in the ability of deceased ancestors to affect one's life and health; others, in possession by spirits; and still others, in the possibility of psychic attack by malevolent shamans. It is impossible to talk to most scientists about an invisible world, since scientific materialism looks only for physical causes of physical events. I have learned not to try to discuss the possibility of nonphysical causation of physical events with most doctors, but I do discuss it with some patients and think about it a lot."*

Such was my case. To try to explain that my physical ailments were caused by "spirits" to medical doctors would have been a waste of breath, to say the least. At the worst, it might have gotten me committed to a mental hospital (again). Here was Dr. Weil, an extremely well known and respected doctor, a major force in medicine, the originator of integrative medicine, who doesn't bother talking of "such things" to other doctors. I wouldn't expect a "medical professional" to believe that my physical problems were caused by malevolent entities. Or, to believe in realms that they can't see, unless they had experienced what I had. However, with all that said, my final battle over my health was held in both worlds, the spirit as well as the physical.

The Great White Brotherhood

The end of July, I decided to attend a weekend workshop with Rita Marie Bryant, also who was referred to me by Michelle. Rita lived in New Milford, in western Connecticut, about two and half hours from Providence. The weekend workshop was an induction ceremony to *The Great White Brotherhood*, an ancient mystical society of lightworkers.

The workshop consisted of classes on the society with meditation sessions in order to connect to the spiritual energies. I was in awe when looking through one of the training manuals and saw the *My Name is I Am* prayer that I had framed in my den. It struck me right then that this was why I was led here. In one session, when Rita was performing spiritual cleansing on me, she told me that she had never felt so much energy around someone. In a session on our last day, Rita went into meditation to get some answers as to why I was being attacked so much.

When she came out of meditation she told me, "Mary, I was told that you have been going through so much pain because these dark forces do not want you out there healing the world. They do not like the path you are on." I told her, "There must be something to that; you're not the first one that has told me that."

As I left her house to head back home, my car radio was playing "Awake" by Josh Grobin. The song certainly had special meaning for me. And, the first license plate I saw coming toward me said "Rescue."

Being Exorcised

Still not feeling clear, and still having bouts with abdominal pain, I decided to see what an exorcist could do to help me. I called Richard Jackson (also referred by *Magnificent* Michelle). Initially, I spoke to him on the phone to set-up an appointment. I found that he was not reserved about talking about his expertise in exorcism. He told me that he had been doing this work for over thirty years, he cleared people and homes of evil spirits, he had worked with local clergy, been all over the country, and had even worked with church officials in the Vatican performing exorcisms. He had been interviewed on the radio and TV numerous times.

Richard also told me that these "Ghost Hunting" shows on TV should be banned. That they didn't know what they were doing. Not only were they attracting evil spirits to themselves but also, they were attracting them to the planet. They were causing more and more people to be attacked by these evil entities. He said there are only a handful of people in the world that knew how to do what he did.

Just by talking to me over the phone, Richard said that he could feel that I am such a bright light, that I am being attacked because of my purpose here. Here too, I hadn't told him what I did. After three hours on the phone (he had told me he never talks to anyone more than fifteen to twenty minutes), we set up an appointment to meet in Mystic, Connecticut, which was about half way for both of us, the next week.

At that meeting in Mystic, Richard began by telling me more about his work. He told me he had done an exorcism on a family that had had a curse put on their great grandfather. After he cleared the house and his descendants, the woman who had initially contacted him came back to see him the next week, and she looked fifteen years younger!

During my session with Richard he had me sit back on the park bench we were on and he had me close my eyes as he guided me through a short meditation. He told me to visualize swallowing a white pill that would bring a cleansing white light throughout my body. As I was doing that, he said a number of prayers and gave me a number of blessings to protect me. In all, the session lasted a couple of hours. When he was done, he suggested that he do a house clearing as well. He told me that he did not travel more than an hour anymore, but for me (over two hours away from him), he would make an exception. We set-up the appointment for the following week.

Dr. Dave and I were amazed at how thorough and professional he was during our house exorcism. Richard went to every room in the house reciting prayers in English and Latin. As he did this, he would burn incense of myrrh and frankincense he had gotten in the Vatican. When he was done he gave us a dozen rosaries and told us to put them on our doors and around our bedroom. He also gave me an eagle and hawk feather to invoke positive Native American energies.

After that, he joined Dr. Dave and me in our backyard, and he did a healing on me. He had me lie on a lounge chair and he meditated, prayed and waved his hands over me. He told me later that he could feel that negative entities had entered me in my throat chakra and had flown down to my stomach chakra, making me sick. I believe I had told him about my stomach problems in a previous conversation, but, I know I had never mentioned that often at night I would wake up feeling as if I was choking, having a difficult time breathing. Richard told me that he cut and released those energies that had been initiated by previous relationships I had had.

The three of us (mostly Richard) then had a discussion about why these negative entities attack humans. He said that the collective consciousness has created evil beings like Satan by thinking of it and believing in it over the past two thousand years. These evil entities, that were never human, were created by man's fears and thoughts.

That they now attack humans because they are often jealous of people being happy. Richard said that some entities are lost souls, deceased people that did not go to the Light, and are trapped in the earth dimension. Whatever the origin, whether never human or, a lost soul, he is able to release them *"into the Light."*

Richard was confident that I would be feeling better and better, that he had rid me of any negative forces in me and in my home. At one point, in our discussion, he turned to Dr. Dave and said, "I see a job change for you this fall." After he had left, Dr. Dave commented to me that he didn't see that that was possible. He had been in the same position as a school psychologist for the past ten years, and his job was very stable. But, amazingly, he would find that Richard was right when he returned to school in September!

A short time later, I randomly opened *The Complete Ascension Manual; How to Achieve Ascension in this Lifetime* (1994) by Dr. Joshua David Stone and began reading about Sai Baba, the man from India, whose picture Judy Lavine, the shaman, had given me. I was amazed when reading his story of the miracles he was able to do. He is one of the three highest beings on the planet right now. The chapter then continued about Lord Maitreya, who is another one of the three highest beings. The chapter stated that the third that would be revealed, would come from the East Coast of the USA!

The next day I was listening to *Spiritual Madness,* by Caroline Myss and I could not believe she talked about praying to Sai Baba. One of the miracles he does is to materialize healing ash out of the air. After Caroline had prayed to him a bottle of his healing ash appeared at her front door!

A couple of days later a friend of mine, Karen, asked me to look at an e-mail, from the *Wisdom of Light* she was receiving talking about a woman who was channeling a spirit. She didn't know why she was getting the e-mails, she didn't sign up for them, they just started coming to her. She sent me a copy because she wanted to know if it was okay to read it. After reading it, I couldn't believe that the spirit being channeled was Dr. Joshua David Stone! I had read all of his books and really wanted to meet him and was very disappointed that he had transitioned to the spirit world in 2005. I felt that Karen's e-mails were a divine message to me.

More Divine Predictions

In September, Dr. Dave returned to his job as a school psychologist and got a surprise! He had been reassigned to two elementary schools in his school district. He was initially upset, having over twenty years experience working with high school students, but as always, he quickly adjusted and made the best of it. He told me it was quite refreshing working with young children. Then we both remembered Richard Jackson's "out of the blue" prediction a month earlier, that he saw a job change for Dr. Dave in the near future.

The next week, I went to a psychic, recommended to me by Marlene Robinson, Miss Rose, who had an office in Warwick, Rhode Island. She used tarot cards as well as channeling by Spirit during her reading. After she had me shuffle her cards, she laid them out, closed her eyes, and began telling me amazing things. She said, "Mary, I can't believe all you have been through! Your metamorphosis is taking so long. I don't understand why. Most experience what you have for only a month, maybe three at the most. You have been going through this for years. But, I see you coming out of this so balanced.

"I see you have had two marriages. The first to a Leo, and the second to a Gemini! Your husband now, is a doctor, he has curly brown hair, and I see that his mother's spirit is with him often when he is driving.

"You two are both so much on the same wave-length. I see you two going on forever! I don't see this often. It's incredible that the two of you are so in synch in life and in your careers. You are both going in the same direction in your work, expanding and growing together. I see you speaking in front of large audiences, doing seminars, being the voice for women because of what you have gone through. I see philanthropy all around you."

What could I say? I told her she was amazing and she said, "No, you're amazing." Then she gave me a great big hug.

John of God

At the end of September, Grace, Dr. Dave and I went to see John of God at the Omega Institute in Rhinebeck, New York. Because it was about a five hour trip for us we went up the day before and stayed overnight.

I had first heard of John of God from Cora Hayward. In one of my discussions about healing with her, I had told her, "When I do healings I want instant results!" Her reply was, "The only one I have ever heard of doing that, besides Jesus, is John of God. But, you have to go to Brazil to see him." At the time I logged the information away and felt that I would in fact, make the trip some day and see him. Nearly three years later, we found out that once a year he comes to the US and performs healings here. So, I was excited that I would finally meet him and see what he does. Dr. Dave was excited we didn't have to go to Brazil.

The sessions with John of God started at 9:00 am at the Omega Institute. We were surprised to see so many people there. There had to be at least two thousand. They had a large tent set up with a stage in it. The day began with a number of John of God's colleagues telling of his work. Then they had some people give testimonies of how they had miraculous healings by John of God. One person even said he was nearly blind before going to see him in Brazil. But, after staying at the "Casa," as they called it in Brazil for a number of weeks, his sight returned. Today he does not even need to wear glasses!

Shortly after that, John came out and blessed everyone there sitting under the large tent. We were then directed in sections to file into a building where we would pass in front of him. As he touched our hand, he would direct as to what kind of intervention we needed. He would tell you if needed a physical or a spiritual healing, and in the afternoon, you would go back for the appropriate session.

After over an hour of waiting in line, we finally came to the area where he was sitting. I was amazed at what I saw. He was sitting back in a trace-like state with his eyes rolled back looking upward. As you extended your hand toward his, he would take it, without even looking at you, and direct you by saying something in Portuguese (he spoke no English) to his staff as to what you needed. He directed Grace, Dr. Dave and me to all come back for spiritual healings. Later, we learned that about one-third of the people there were told that.

In the afternoon, we were broken down into smaller groups of about a hundred people. At the session we were directed to sit in a smaller hall with chairs lined up in rows that also had an altar in the front, as if in a church, where John was seated. During this session, he said a number of blessings and then asked that we stay and meditate for a while. After our spiritual healing John gave us very specific instructions that included not eating any pork, or hot peppers, not drinking any alcohol, and not having any sex for the next forty days. He told us to drink blessed "holy water" daily that they supplied us with as well. He also directed us to get plenty of rest the next few days.

We were all done by 3:30 that afternoon, so we headed back to Rhode Island. The next day Grace and I had no problem getting plenty of rest. Actually, I did not hear from Grace for four days. Only later she told me that she was in bed for the next three. Dr. Dave, however, did not want to take anymore time off, so he went back to work the very next day. He told me that night when he got home, that late in the morning he was walking upstairs (not another soul in sight!) in the school he was in and he felt as if someone had punched him in the back. It was so hard that he lost his breath and dropped to his knees. He just stayed there for ten minutes until he was able to get up and go back to his office. He told me that it seemed to be a clear sign from spirit to slow down. Which he did for the rest of the day. When he got home, he went directly to bed and did not move until the next morning.

Anastasia

"There is a law of the Universe which says: A single Creator inspired by love is stronger than all the sciences combined, which are deprived of love."
~ **Anastasia**

In October, Dr. Dave and I took Ram Smith and his wife to dinner and, as always, found his conversation to be quite enlightening. He was telling us of a series of books that are flying off the bookstore shelves called *Anastasia* (2005) by Vladimir Megre. I told him I had the whole series of nine books and agreed with him that she is amazing. He told us that he has been taking cedar nut oil and eating cedar nuts that he was getting from their *www.ringingcedar. com* Website.

I thanked Ram for the information and I remembered back to the previous summer when I had read the series and I had wanted to get cedar nut oil but didn't know where to get it. We then had a great conversation about spirituality and how the consciousness of the world will continue to raise in 2012 and beyond.

Connecting To Your Higher Self

Towards the end of October, we had our second Divinely Touched Seminar with Maureen St. Germain as our keynote speaker. Our seminar topic was ***"Building a Connection to Your Higher Self."*** Maureen's talk was about trusting in your own intuition and connecting to your inner wisdom, your higher self. We also had Ram speak on *"Yogoda: Materializing Your Dreams,* and Dr. Kelly Taylor-Bentz who spoke on *"Your Human Guidance System; Are You Connected?"*

After the seminar, we had dinner with Maureen and she talked more about the Akashic records with us. She told us that they are like a record vault, located in another dimension. In this case, she said they are located in the eleventh dimension. They contain personal records of each individual, telling of their past, present, and future. By meditating and accessing them, she can go into your personal records and tell you of your past lives and where you are going in this life.

Maureen told us that often these past life memories or feelings can be relived on an anniversary date, with someone you were with before in a past life, or when visiting a place you lived before in another lifetime. She told us that she had an experience when she was in France. She felt as if she was having a heart attack, but when she calmed down and checked the Akashic Records she found that she was reliving a death she had experienced from a stabbing in a previous life there.

The next day, Maureen met with me individually for a couple of hours before she headed back to New York City. She clarified a lot of things for me. Again, I was asking why so much had happened to me? Why was there so much pain and suffering here? Why did children and women get abused? Why did people have to suffer horrendous illnesses or tragic losses? She told me, "Mary, we all come here at different evolutionary levels in our soul's growth. We all come here to learn different lessons."

Maureen gave me a simple example. "Lets say different colors represent our soul's evolutionary growth. And, lets say that red souls may be here for the first time, blue is a little more evolved, and green souls are the most evolved beings on earth. Green beings return here to help the planet. Mary you are a green soul." Maureen then meditated for a few moments. When she returned she opened her eyes and told me that she checked further by going into the Akashic Records. She told me, "Mary you are not of this earth! You are from a star system beyond Vega (way out there).You were one of the 144,000 light beings sent to Earth to bring love and light to this planet."

Maureen was not the first to tell me (nor the last) that I was not from this planet, which could really "blow your mind." However, I had heard so much by so many different psychics at this point that I found what she said very helpful in answering my questions and explaining more of what was going on with me.

Nature's Wisdom

In November, I decided to look into a new type of therapy called ASYRA. My good friend Claudia had gone there and raved about what it could do. It was being offered at Nature's Wisdom Wellness Center in Westerly, Rhode Island. I found out that ASYRA uses homeopathy and computerized technology to determine what is going on in the body (see chapter VII: Energy Healing).

I discovered that Nature's Wisdom was a delightful holistic clinic. Carol Stanton, the owner of the center was a former RN and a now a holistic healer. She was also a naturopath and a reflexologist. The ASYRA testing she conducted there used a remarkable machine. By holding two probes that were hooked up to a computer it could read vibrations in your body. It would then program these vibrations into a vial of water that would heal the body, based on homeopathic principles.

Carol's testing determined that I had a number of allergies that she said conventional testing could not (and did not) detect. It was reading my energy fields. She programmed the vial of water for me and told me I needed to take several drops twice a day and to see her in a month for a follow-up visit to make sure the therapy was effective.

On a follow-up visit Carol's ASYRA machine also identified a specific tooth that I was having trouble with that when we checked is directly related to stomach problems. The dental chart she gave me indicated what body organs are related to each tooth (*www.drfarid. com/chart.html*). Just like energy meridians, acupuncture points, reflexology points, and chakras, even our teeth are all related to energy pathways, and affect our health.

Carol also saw that my ASYRA readout was very devoid of any cancer symptoms. She said if she saw a series of repeating numbers, it would indicate a potential for cancer. I had none, which she said was excellent, and very unusual. I told her I certainly had enough other problems. Carol then gave me a copy of *The China Study* (2006) by T. Colin Campbell, Ph.D. She told me how one aspect of the study found a link with high protein consumption and cancer (as in a Western diet). I told her how ironic. Many of my friends were always so concern that I eat very little protein because I follow a primarily vegetarian diet, yet they have far more health problems than I do.

ASYRA also said that a number of my vertebrae were out of alignment and recommended I see a chiropractor. Dr. Dave suggested someone he had worked with at Waves of Wellness, Dr. Robert Marzilli Jr. At my appointment with him, I found Dr. Bob to be extremely knowledgeable and professional. He explained to me how the vertebrae can influence all types of body systems that includes organs as well as muscles and bones. He did find a few of my vertebrae that were slightly out of alignment when he examined me. After his adjustments, I asked him if he had ever heard of the ASYRA system. He told me he hadn't. I showed him Carol's print-out and he compared it to his findings, and they matched perfectly. Every vertebrae that the ASYRA computer had said was misaligned, were in fact, the ones Dr. Bob had worked on.

Ishmael

In the middle of November, I went back to see Michelle. Besides the bloating increasing in my abdomen, now, I was having trouble sleeping. I would feel my whole body constantly vibrate. My hands and legs had a continual pins and needles feeling, and I would be jolted awake several times during the night as if I was being given an electric shock. Michelle did a healing and again walked around me meditating and connecting to her spirit guide. She then told me, "What is happening, Mary, is that 'they' are working on you at night. They are downloading vibrational energy and light into your cells. This transmutation of energy is infusing your cells of the memories of who you are. It is being done gradually. If they did it all at once you would explode!"

I told her, "I guess that makes sense. I thought it was something bad going on like negative entities not wanting me to get any rest and trying to wear me down." "No, Mary, its all good. But you can tell them to slow it down. Or, that you want a night off to get some rest." I told her, "I'll try that tonight, I could use a rest!"

Michelle then told me, "They are saying 'Ishmael' to me." I said I had never heard of it and Michelle said she hadn't either, but the message came through loud and clear. Then we looked up Ishmael up on her computer in her office and found out that there is a book named *Ishmael*. Michelle then told me, "There must be a message in that book that Spirit wants you to see!"

When I got home, we ordered the book, *Ishmael An Adventure of the Mind and Spirit* (1995) by Daniel Quinn. I'm not sure if the opening message was coming through to Michelle when spirit told her about Ishmael, but it sure came through to me. The book started off with:

"Teacher seeks pupil. Must have an earnest desire to save the world."

This was exactly my frame of mind. Nearly everyday, I complained to Dr. Dave, that all I wanted is a teacher to show me the way. I didn't care if I had to go to Peru. Brazil or India and study for a year. I just wanted to be shown how to open up my "gifts," these extraordinary abilities that every psychic, shaman, and lightworker I was coming across was telling me I have, or, will have in the near future.

About a week later, I woke up with a song playing in my head, as so often happened to me. I asked Dr. Dave to find the lyrics for me.

"I hear the drums echoing tonight...
...There's nothing that a hundred men or more could ever do.
I bless the rains down in Africa.
Gonna take some time to do the things we never had."
-Africa
By Toto

The line, "Gonna take some time to do the things we never had" seemed to be a message from Spirit to me, that what I really needed now was patience. I needed to remember that, even if every time I heard that word it reminded me of a plaque my friend Claudia has *"God grant me patience, but please hurry!"* What I still needed to do was to concentrate on healing myself, and believe that when I was ready a guide would appear. I still wasn't quite buying what Dr. Dave was telling me that, perhaps, there was no one on earth other than me, to lead me to where I was going!

It Keeps Going On

I made it through the holiday season feeling good enough to do all that was asked of me by family and friends. No one suspected that anything was going on with me. We even went to Disney World to be with Dr. Dave's brother Dan, who lived in California, as he was turning sixty and wanted the family together for his birthday.

However, when we got back home, January hit me like a ton of bricks. I was exhausted and slept for days. I even came down with a cold, which was very unusual. My old symptoms were returning. I was feeling drained again, my skin was becoming more dry and flakey, and my lips were on fire. My stomach was swelling again and I was having trouble sleeping. My eyes were even swollen and red, which really bothered me, because before, even when I was feeling exhausted and in bed, I could still read. Now it bothered me even to do that.

I called Grace to do a healing on me. As she worked on me, she saw me in a previous life. She was seeing me having a baby back in the 1600's. The baby was born breeched and not alive, and I, too, died during the delivery. Grace told me that she kept seeing the number "48" during this vision, and she believed I was forty-eight in the previous life when this happened. I told her, "I'll be turning forty-eight this year!"

Grace responded, "This is why you're feeling so much abdomen pain. It's like a parallel window being opened with a previous life. The trauma of what you experienced is still attached to your soul. When you experience a healing in this life, it should close that window."

After Grace's healing I did feel a lot better. The swelling in my abdomen went down significantly. Before leaving Grace at Healing Hearts, to go home, I went to the bathroom, and I was surprised to find that I had just started my period. I was not due for another two weeks.

The next week I saw Vanessa, and she said that she could see I had attracted several attachments again! She told me that she could see a gargoyle-type creature in me with tentacles wrapped around my stomach (again I thought, just as Joey and Judy had seen). Then she meditated, connected with spirit and said, "Mary you have had a lot of stomach trauma in your past lives. You have died in childbirth. In another life, you committed 'hari-kari' by killing yourself by falling on a sword. And in another life, you were shot six times in the stomach!"

Vanessa then proceeded to clear me and told me that I needed to protect myself better. She told me, "I see you will be clear this summer, and by September you will be very busy, and you will have a fantastic 2011!" As always, I felt better physically and emotionally after leaving Vanessa.

Shamans Continue to Help

However, after a few weeks later I was starting to have that exhaustion feeling come over me again. I was concerned I wasn't 100 percent clear again. I decided to call a shaman that Michelle had referred me to. She highly recommended him telling me that he had studied in Peru. I called and made an appointment with Gerry Miller, who also lived in Connecticut, about an hour from me. Dr. Dave took me as it was an evening appointment.

We could not believe his office when we saw it. It was a large two floor building that was like a museum from the Amazon. The first floor had so much stuff in it you had to follow narrow paths to walk around all the antique furniture, bottles, books stacked up on the floor, artwork and artifacts. As we went up stairs to his therapy room, it was like entering a clearing in an Amazon jungle. It was dimly lit but we could make out stars painted on the ceiling and more artifacts from Peru all over the place.

Gerry had what looked like Peruvian clothes on and what seemed like a hundred necklaces made of beads and bones around his neck and down his chest. He told us that he had started out as a young artist going to the Amazon but was quickly taken in by the indigenous people's culture and began studying with medicine men there. He had been back and forth to the Amazon for the last forty years. He showed us pictures of him in rituals there with elder shamans and one of a huge sacred tree and some bark he had from it.

During our session, he had me sit in a chair. He put on some music that was chanting by Peruvian shamans, and then he took out special rolled tobacco from the Amazon. He lit it, and as he went around me meditating, he would blow smoke at me from the rolled tobacco. He also had a large fan made out of plants from Peru, and he would occasionally hit me on the head or front or back with it. Several times during his ritual, he would suck something out of my eye or neck and then go to a corner of the room and spit it into a vat.

When he was done he told me, "You are a great spirit and very strong! I saw many little demons hiding in you, in your eye and throat." He described the little demons as shriveled up monkeys. I hadn't told him of any discomfort in my eye or throat prior to our session. Yet, he was able to tell exactly where a lot of my pain was. I was still waking up at night, feeling as if I was choking, and often had trouble breathing.

The next week, I went back for a follow-up session with him, and he performed the same ritual. This time, he said that he saw and released an "incredible demon" from me. I asked him how I could prevent this from continuing to happen. He told me that I should be all set because he had released all that was in me, and then he placed a protection prayer around me. I felt better, but quite smoky after leaving him.

Feeling better but not quite myself still, I called Judy Lavine for another session. In this one (that also took two hours), Judy meditated and then told me what she thought was a revelation. "Honey, you are being attacked so much because dark forces don't want you out there healing the planet! You are not of this world! You have been sent here by God to help heal the world, return it to light. If doctors really looked at your insides, they would discover that you are not human!" I thought, she is just telling me what I have heard from so many others.

Judy then told me in order to keep these dark forces away, I should prepare a special glass jar, and bury it on the north side of my house. She then placed a large box of protection around me and said I should not have any further problems with being attacked. When I got home I had Dr. Dave bury the glass jar, as Judy described on the north side of our yard, which just happened to be under our bedroom window.

Acupuncturist Try To Get Answers

In late February, I decided to see what acupuncture might be able to do to relieve some of the symptoms I was still having. I called Dr. Chris Carlow, who was an associate of ours at Healing Hearts. His office is in Coventry, Rhode Island only about thirty minutes south of Providence.

Dr. Chris started his exam by looking at my tongue. He told me that in Traditional Chinese Medicine (TCM) the tongue is a map of the body. But, after examining my tongue he couldn't see anything wrong with me, my tongue was perfectly normal. However, when I lay back on his exam table, he waved his hands over me from my head to my toes, and told me that he felt an incredible ball of energy and heat over my abdomen. He said that he believed that I was out of balance, where I should have been fire and water, I was all fire. He had never seen anything like this before. He told me he wanted to confer with some colleagues and asked that I come back next week. He also referred me to a book that he thought I would identify with *Black Elk Speaks.*

The next week, when I went back to Dr. Chris he confirmed to me what he had thought the week before. "Mary, I checked with some colleagues as well as ancient texts I have, and what is going on with you is extremely rare. There have been no reported cases of something like this for the last two thousand years. It seems as if your root charka is backing into your other charkas. This can be caused by significant trauma and fear (like visiting the underworld, I thought). Your root charka is the source of energy to the body. Your energy is being depleted for some reason. The texts describes symptoms of this condition as pain in the abdomen and difficulty breathing." And I certainly had a lot of that. Dr. Chris suggested that I start eating a lot of root foods, beans, seaweed and cinnamon, and stay away from hot spicy foods.

More Messages

In March, I went back for another session with Kerrie O'Connor, the psychic in Salem, Connecticut. I was so impressed with her when I first saw her nearly three years ago that I wanted to see if she could see what was holding me back. I could not believe how she started out. Her eyes began tearing, and became painful and itchy for the first four or five minutes of our session, she couldn't stop rubbing them. Then she took a deep breath as if clearing that energy, or whatever it was away, and her eyes returned to normal. She said, "Mary, they were trying to keep you from seeing." I told her, "That was going on last January. My eyes were so red and swollen I had to place paper towels soaked in ice and milk on them. You were just feeling what I was going through!"

Kerrie continued, "Mary you were an amazingly gifted seer in a past life. You need to continually visualize that you are cleaning your second sight vision and aura. You can do this as if using Windex to clean a large projection screen in front of you. Clean it by using an infinity figure-8 motion. Also, you need to be more grounded. Go outside and hug trees more. I see *'Avalon'* energy all around you. That is the female goddess energy. You are very close to getting where you should be." Again, I thought she was amazing. Just the fact that she felt my pain in her eyes, I thought was so incredible. And, she talked about "Avalon" energy around me, which is what Maureen St. Germain had told me about a year earlier!

A week after that, I met with Heidi and she did a healing on me. After she was done, she told me, "I was being told that the discomfort you are feeling is really an expansion. You are changing inside." I guess that made me feel a little better, but it didn't exactly put an end to my abdominal pain and bloating.

Later that week, I went back to see Jackie Eaton, the psychic in Cumberland, Rhode Island. I was still seeking answers as to when things would start happening at a faster rate for me. She started by saying, "Mary, your third eye is wider than most, it's huge. I can't believe you can't see as much as I." Then, she paused and got more messages from Spirit and said, "It's because of all the trauma you have had in previous lives. Because you were such a great seer, a great psychic, you were killed, hung and burned in past lives for using your abilities, and this soul trauma is still holding you back in this life."

Jackie then started to get choked up, as if she was reliving one of my past hangings. When she composed herself she continued,

"I see you as a world healer and teacher in the future. Your book (I hadn't told her I was writing one) will really help change the world. I see you and your husband as an amazing pair. You two compliment each other so well. You are an inspiration to others. I see Archangel Michael behind you. I have never seen him so large. He is protecting you as well. He is so impressed with you saying that you didn't have to do all this and go through all the pain and suffering you have been going through, but you chose to do it to help heal the planet." As I left, she hugged me and said again, "You are so extremely connected."

In April I went back to see Vanessa. The first thing she told me was, "They are telling me your book is about 70 percent done." I told her, "That's exactly the percentage number Dr. Dave used last week!" She continued, "I see your book taking off next year. You are filling seminar rooms talking about your book. The 'Sacred Order of the Rose' is coming through. You should look that up, as well as information about Mary Magdalene. You are in her soul/spirit group. I see you doing healings in the future by just being there. Just your presence will heal others!"

After my session with Vanessa, Dr. Dave and I took her to lunch. She explained what 5D consciousness was to Dr. Dave and then told us a story that had happened to her recently. She told us that water from all the rain we were having started to come into her basement. So, without thinking she started to vacuum it up. Then she stopped and thought, "This water is coming in because of me. I am in 3D consciousness." She then meditated and got her mind into 5D consciousness and looked down to see that the water had stopped coming in, even though it was still raining outside!

Vanessa then told us that we often see in this world what we want. She told us a story of how she bought a purple blanket to go with her purple comforter on her bed. She was enjoying it for weeks until her boyfriend was over one day and asked why she had a *yellow* blanket with her purple comforter. At that instant Vanessa said she saw the purple blanket turn yellow in front of her!

At one point during our lunch, Vanessa turned to Dr. Dave and said, "I see a lot of Archangel energy in you. I see why you were sent here to help Mary. You are here to ground her." Just what Sonia had told us, I thought. Vanessa and I then discussed signs we see, and she said something we thought was very profound:

"Everything is Something!"

~ **Vanessa Riyast**

The FINAL Battle!

Where God guides, She provides!

For my birthday, Dr. Dave took me to New York City to see Rev. Karen at the Creative Light Church. It was a wonderful weekend. He booked a room at the Michelangelo Hotel, and we had dinner at the Beacon Restaurant the night before going to see Rev. Karen. Before dinner, we went for a walk down Broadway, and I stopped into a gift shop. It turned out to be a large souvenir shop as well. In the store, I was drawn to a small crystal *Statue of Liberty*. Dr. Dave commented, "Why do you want that? It's kind of expensive for something so small." I told him, "I don't know I am just drawn to it; I have to have it."

The next morning, we drove down to see Rev. Karen and of course, with cars lining the both sides of the streets around her church, we found a spot right in front. Rev. Karen was amazing and so inspirational. After the service we bought a copy of her book *I Am The Party* (2009), and she signed it for us. On the way home, at the first red light we came to, I was elated to see that the car in front of us had, "Where ever You go there's I AM," around its license plate.

The next day, as part of my birthday present Dr. Dave had bought another reading from Mark the astrologer for me. We had arranged a 2:00 p.m. reading from him where he would call me.

However, that morning I awoke thinking of the words to a song in my head, but I wasn't sure of the name of it. I called Dr. Dave at work and asked him if he knew what the name of the song is, that began with:

"My eyes have seen the glory of the coming of the Lord…?"

He said, "That is a really old church song. I believe it has to go back a couple of hundred years. I think that's the name, "My Eyes Have Seen The Glory." And, I think the second verse is:

His truth is marching on!"

Just like everything that comes to me, I knew it had special meaning, and I knew it would eventually reveal itself.

That afternoon, Mark called as scheduled. But, what he said surprised me (if anything could at this point). He said, "Mary, this morning in meditation, my spirit guide told me this is not going to be your typical reading. Its going to be unlike anything I have ever done before!"

A couple of days before, I had e-mailed him some questions including ones asking why a number of the things he had told me a year ago hadn't come true. Mark told me that after reading my questions it puzzled him too. He remembered telling me that he had never seen so much "magic" and "electricity" in someone's chart. And, he couldn't understand why I wasn't further along as well. During his "reading" with me our questions were answered.

Mark's spirit guide told him that I had an extremely high vibrational dark entity in me. It was draining my power. Not only was he draining power in this life, in this dimension, but this dark entity was using this energy he was getting from me to hurt others in another dimension! This draining was blocking my energy, keeping me from my reaching my full potential. He called this entity a "trickster" because it kept hiding and changing its appearance so other psychics and shamans couldn't see it or work on getting it out of me.

This explained why every other psychic healer I had met over the past three years thought he or she had gotten everything out of me and thought that I was clear when I had left them. The other healers also couldn't understand why I wasn't doing more when most of them could see or feel my energy field.

Mark told me that he could hear his guide yelling at the trickster entity to leave. They began fighting back forth and were arguing so hard and so fast that Mark said he could hardly keep up with the conversation. Mark told me he could hear the Trickster saying, ***"She's mine*****!"** and his guide saying, ***"She belongs to the universe!"*** He said they were going back and forth screaming at each other. I was astounded! This was what had gone on years earlier in my first battle, which I had never told him about!

His guide finally got it out of me and banished it. Then his guide put a protection prayer around me so it could never get back in to hurt me. Mark said in all his years of doing readings (thirty plus years) he had never encountered anything like this before. After the trickster entity was gone his spirit guide told him, "Mary is ***liberated*** now!" And, to tell me that, ***"So shall it be."***

I told Mark, "I can't believe it! I say *'So Shall It Be'* all the time. I even have it on a plaque on my wall in the kitchen!" Mark told me that I had just been in a battle and over the next few days I might feel it, but that my energy should be returning in a couple of weeks. Things should start happening over the next month, as he had foretold to me the previous year. He told me again that, "This was amazing Mary. I'm an astrologer, not a spiritual or psychic healer. I've never had a session like this before!" I thanked him again and thought to myself, "How many times over the past few years have people told me 'I have never encountered anything like this before'?"

When I started to tell all this to Dr. Dave he said that the previous week he was watching an episode of *Supernatural* on TV and it was about the two demon fighters in the show and how they finally got rid of an archangel type demon called the "trickster!" Then we both understood why I had been drawn to the crystal Statue of Liberty I had purchased a few days earlier. Whether we know it or not:

Spirit is always talking to us.
We are drawn to things for a reason!

Over the next few days, I did in fact feel like I had been through a battle. The next morning I woke up with cuts on my upper lip and under my eye. I felt drained. My stomach became bloated again. My arms and legs had black and blue marks all over them.

I went to see Michelle at the Colonics Institute for a colonics and a healing. It had always helped with my bloating pain, and I wanted to hear what Michelle had to say about what was going on with me this week, as she too was so gifted. When I got into my car to go to her, I was in so much discomfort, and I felt so depressed that I was crying. As I turned the car radio on, I heard:

"Why do you look so sad? Tears are in your eyes. I'll stand by you. I won't let anyone hurt you. I'll never desert you."

It was from the song, "I'll Stand By You." I felt immediately comforted, knowing God is always with me, watching out for me.

When Michelle saw me, she gave me a hug and just said, "Mary, are you all right?" I told her, "Not exactly." And I filled her in on a little of what Mark had told me. When Michelle started working on me by waving her hands over me (doing her Reiki) she said, "Mary your insides are all torn up! Your aura is a mess and it's as if you shouldn't even be alive!"

That was not what I wanted to hear, but it was certainly how I felt, as if I had been in a head on collusion and I was feeling the after effects of the accident. After the colonics and Michelle's Reiki healing I did feel better.

However, a couple of days later, I had a horrendous night. I hardly slept. I felt every time I was about to fall asleep I would be jolted awake, as if I was getting an electric shock. I had feelings of pins and needles in my arms and legs, and my abdomen was becoming more and more bloated again.

An Epiphany!

The next week, I went back to Michelle at the Colonics Institute for another colonics and healing. However, when Michelle greeted me this time, she had a very different reaction from the previous week. "Mary, you look so clear!" she said speaking of my aura she was seeing, and reminding me that a week ago it hadn't looked like that. She proceeded to give me the colonic treatment which always greatly relieved the pressure in my abdomen.

When she was done, I started to tell her how discouraged I was feeling, "Michelle all I want to do is get out there and help and heal people, yet every time I think I'm moving a little forward, I get knocked down and end up being the one needing healing!" She told me she didn't understand why this was going on, but perhaps, I needed to be more patient. "Easy to say," I thought, "if you aren't in so much pain everyday."

After that she did a healing. Michelle walked around me in deep meditation like she always did, waving her hands and placing them periodically on various points on my body. She continued for a half hour.

When she was done, she just stopped with her mouth half open, starring at me. I said, "Michelle what's wrong? What did you see or hear?" thinking again that she had seen something terrible in me. She exclaimed, "Mary I had an *epiphany!* Spirit told me you have been healing thousands and thousands the past few years! Every shaman and psychic healer that has worked on releasing entities from you has released thousands of lost and trapped souls into the Light. Every time they worked on you, they were healing them and sending them on their way to fulfill their own destinies! You have been healing the Universe, and clearing and lifting this planet from lower negative vibrations. You are helping higher frequencies and light to be able to come through more easily. You are helping to accelerate the planet's evolutionary shift." Then Spirit told Michelle to tell me, "Mary, you're like Joan of Arc!" At that point I interrupted, "Who's Joan of Arc?" Michelle explained to me who Joan of Arc was; then she continued.

"The physical pain you have been going through, the pressure, the pins and needles feelings, the electric pain, are because of information being 'downloaded' to you by your spirit guides. At times, this energy may be coming too fast for your physical body to handle it. Tell your guides to slow it down, that its okay to take a night off so you can get some rest. Mary, every time you were sick you were healing thousands, sending them to the Light."

When she was done, Dr. Dave came in, and Michelle told him all she had told me. He said, "Mary that's what Grace told you in the very beginning of all this, that she and her mentor were releasing thousands of trapped souls in and around you. Peeling them off like layers in an onion. Mark's spirit guide got to the last one last week. The darkest one with the highest vibrational energy he finally got out of you. And, that's why you have been feeling like you were in a physical battle all week!"

I felt better after the colonics and almost elated after what Michelle had told me, except that I was feeling very drained. On the way home, Dr. Dave and I discussed how everything was finally fitting together, finally making sense.

The next day, I finally had a chance to ask my mom about the song that had come to me at the beginning of the week, and she said it was from the Civil War era. The song was "The Battle Hymn of the Republic." How fitting I thought. I had been in such a battle that week one held in the spirit dimension over my soul, so to speak, and

I had felt the physical reality of it. As the song stated, **"His truth is,** (indeed) **marching on!"** This was the final battle!

The next week I had a follow-up reading with Mark. He told me his spirit guide said that all my physical problems had been caused by dark entities. I told him I was still feeling tired and bloated. I was seeing energy outside my body again. When I looked at my hand, I had the feeling that it was not mine. It seemed bigger and hairier than normal.

Mark checked with his guide and found that what I was seeing energy around me, and not in me. He said that his spirit guide was still working on keeping evil entities away from me that I was clear and would be getting more open soon. In a couple of weeks, I should be really clear, and people would start being drawn to me. I would be glowing! Mark ended by again, telling me that he couldn't believe the previous reading with me. He had never had a spiritual healing session before!

The Final Piece to the Puzzle!

Being impatient that I was still not feeling recovered from my last spiritual battle, I decided to call a medical intuitive that Michelle had recommended to me earlier in the month.

After several days of playing phone tag, I finally connected with Anthony, who lived in northern Maine. Although Michelle told me that he was an amazing medical intuitive, that he was able to diagnose exactly what was wrong with you over the phone, Anthony simply told me that he only considered himself a medical consultant. I found that he was truly remarkable.

Anthony started our session by first meditating and connecting to spirit. He then told me (without having asked any questions or taken a "medical history") that I had a very unusual yeast infection. I told him that I had been to a gastroenterologist, he had done every test available and could find no infections or abnormalities with me. I told Anthony that all the doctor could come up with was that I had IBS (Irritable Bowel Syndrome), that perhaps, I was eating too much broccoli! I told him that my husband, Dr. Dave had said that, that was a rule-out diagnosis that they give when they have no idea what is wrong with you. Anthony laughed and said, "That's right, but there is no medical equipment out there yet that can detect what you have. Maybe technology will catch up in ten or twenty years. This infection is feeding off your energy, causing you to be weak, gassy and bloated. You feel as if you're on fire on the inside, yet your hands and feet are always cold."

I told him, "That's exactly right! I wear socks to bed at night because my feet are always cold, but I usually feel as if I'm on fire in my abdomen." Anthony continued, "This infection also is allowing entities in that have been taking advantage of your weakened state and are fueling the infection and your discomfort to make you more weak and exhausted. I see that you have been putting up with this for a while and that you are, in fact, a very strong individual, that you are very special."

Anthony then outlined a plan to rid me of this super yeast infection once and for all. He directed me to go on a dairy and wheat free diet and to get specific herbs, juices and vitamins from certain suppliers over the Internet. He told me to order from _www. internationalherbs.com, www.ambayagold.com_ and _www.pureplanet. com_. He told me that the program he was putting me on, would clear this infection in a few months.

Here again, I was divinely led to someone with extraordinary gifts. I didn't have to tell him what was going on in my body. He knew, and he knew why.

On a follow-up call to Anthony, he told me to get a natural antibiotic called oxysilver. When it came in a week later and I opened the package, I screamed to Dr. Dave, "Look at this. I can't believe it!" When I took the bottle out and looked at it I was amazed, and thought, of course, this makes perfect sense. It was a purple bottle that had the Michelangelo "**Reconnection**" hands on it! Looking at the bottle more closely I saw the number 528 on it. The 5 stands for change, and 28 means "the warrior of the *sun*!" Then in faint print, the bottle had the words "Love," "Thanks," AND ***Divine"*** on it!

When I called Anthony to ask him when to start taking it and tell him how I couldn't believe what the bottle had on it, he told me that, "Well out of all the products I could have recommended to you, Spirit told me this one would 'sing' to you." "Sing!" I told him, "Do you know how special that, in itself is?" I then asked him how long I had to be on this diet and continue taking all the supplements he was recommending, and he told me, "Mary, your body has been fighting this infection and entities trying to tear you down for years. Between the two, it's surprising that you are even alive!"

I asked him, "Why do you think they are attacking me so much?" He told me, "Because they want to keep you from doing what you are going to do, to make a difference in this world." "But, Anthony when all this started I was just leading a normal life." "Mary, Spirit, in this case, dark entities, knew what you were going to do in this life before you were even on this path. They wanted to stop you from getting to the point where you are now. They don't go after regular people, having a 'normal' life. They go after people that are going to make a difference in this world. They want to stop them from making a positive difference in the world, and they want to keep the world in pain and darkness, where they are."

Mt. Shasta

In July, we had planned a trip to Mt. Shasta, California. I had wanted to meet Amorah Quan Yin, author of *The Pleiadian Workbook* (1996), and feel the energy of the mountain. Mt. Shasta is where St. Germain appeared to Godfre Ray King in the 1920's as described in *Unveiled Mysteries* (1939), and is said to have many sacred energy vortex sites. Dr. Dave had been planning the trip for eight months. We were going to visit his aunt and uncle that lived in Seattle, Washington; drive down to the Mt. Shasta area, spending five days there; and then leave from San Francisco, where we would spend a few days with his brother Dan and his wife, Fay.

I had been looking forward to the trip up until May. That's when I had the final battles fought out with Mark's spirit guide, and started working with Anthony and being on a special diet. In May and throughout June, I had very little energy and was in a lot of abdominal discomfort. My stomach and abdomen was feeling as if I had a washing machine constantly churning inside. I was wondering how I was going to make the trip at all. Constantly feeling drained, I needed a nap after doing something as simple as going to church.

These feelings didn't subside until the week before we left. I felt I was clear of entities and Anthony's diet began working wonders. The rumbling in my stomach finally stopped, and my energy was returning. I began looking forward to the trip and seeing Dr. Dave's West Coast family, and couldn't wait to see what Quan Yin had to say about what was going on with me. I was not disappointed.

The morning of leaving for our trip, as I was packing, I thought to myself, "I should take some socks; it may be cold in Seattle." I opened my sock drawer, and right on top I saw a pair of socks that I had bought months earlier that said "Jesus Saves!" I put them in my suitcase. Later when we were driving, a car passed us with a bumper sticker with a big S on it that had "Jesus" in the top part of the curve, and "Saves" in the bottom part of it. A minute later, another car passed us with "Magic" on its license plate. We drove up to Boston, where we were leaving from, and as we parked at Dr. Dave's cousin Janice's condo (she was taking us to the airport), one of our favorite songs, *"I Melt With You,"* by Modern English, was ending with:

> *"Dream of better lives the kind which never hate*
> *Dropped in the state of imaginary Grace*
> *I made a pilgrimage to save the human race!*
> *There's nothing you and I won't do."*

We first flew to Seattle, Washington, to spend the weekend with

Dr. Dave's Aunt Carol and Uncle Ed. It was the first time we had both been there and his aunt and uncle were amazing hosts taking us all around the area. Everyone had always told us how rainy it usually was there. However, the weekend we were there each day had beautifully clear, sunny skies with temperatures in the eighties. It was great spending time with his aunt and uncle, in the "Emerald City," it truly was like being in Oz.

We then headed down to Mt. Shasta. I had arranged a private session at Amorah Quan Yin's house, which was about a half hour away from the town of Mt. Shasta. As I got out of our car to go up to her house, Dr. Dave rolled down the window and called me back to the car, "Mary, listen to what's playing on the radio!" When I walked up to the car I heard that "Instant Karma" by John Lennon on the radio. I just smiled and said, "Of course."

When I went into her house, I found it warmly decorated with religious and Far Eastern statues of Jesus and Buddha all over her living room. After a brief hello, she asked me to sit down across the room from her and close my eyes. She began by connecting to her higher self and calling upon the *Cities of Light,* and then told me, "Your aura is huge! You are 'way out there' most of the time. You also have a lot of *karmic* contracts that need to be released. There have been a lot of domineering males in your life. I see your father and your first husband were very adept at keeping the women around them in submissive roles. We need to release that. I see that you are at a very high angelic realm. When you were a child you were very psychic, but your parents kept discouraging you until you forgot about your gifts. You shut down your psychic energy so you would "fit in" with other children. But, you never did feel that you fit in growing up."

I was amazed of course. Everything she said was 100 percent correct. Then she continued, "Dark entities keep wanting to attach to your energy to use your energy for their purposes. They also want to keep you from your purpose, your truth. Your whole geometric energy field is in shambles! Its been torn apart by them. I see a dark cord going up your anus into your abdomen, into your third charka causing you discomfort and draining your energy."

Amorah then told me she was going to rebuild my geometric energy field. She called upon the *Cities of Light, Archangel Michael, the Pleiadians and Sirius,* and began to wave her hands in the air. After she was done with that, she told me that she was going to put a cocoon of protecting white light around me. The cocoon also has a tube of white light connecting to *divine* energies.

When she started to clear me of the bad karmic energies I still had and as she placed the protecting cocoon around me, the phone began ringing. Later she told me that that was strange because she had turned her phone off. When she was done, she told me that she was connecting to the Akashic Records. "Mary, I see Spirit giving you a gift, a shield and a sword, and you have roses over your heart!" When she was done she told me she wanted to give me a hug, if she could (she had severe allergies), but said she would hug my energy field. I told her I would do the same to her.

Dr. Dave picked me up an hour and half after he had dropped me off at her house, and I told him how truly amazing and gifted I thought she was. She just knew everything I had been through, exactly what kind of pain I had been through, and was in, and what kind of healing and protection I needed. I felt as if I had received just what I had wanted and needed from Amorah.

A Divine Guide

The day before we were to meet a guide that Dr. Dave had arranged to take us around Mt. Shasta, we headed into the town of Mt. Shasta to look around. As we left where we were staying at Steward Mineral Springs in Weed, we noticed a gruffy older man with a large backpack, hitch hiking with a sign that read "Mt. Shasta" on it. We went by him and a about a half mile down the road I turned to Dr. Dave and said, "Why don't we go back and get him? We are going that way. Our ego and fear is what prevents us from helping strangers all the time. We should just trust in God, and rise above our egos." With that Dr. Dave turned the car around and went back to pick him up. When he got in the car, we learned that he, Ted, was going to spend a couple of weeks camping out on Mt. Shasta. He told us that, that morning he had prayed for a perfect ride to pick him up. And when we went by the first time, he noticed that the woman in the passenger seat was "glowing," and he thought to himself, "What is that about?"

We found Ted to be a remarkable soul. He told us that he had lived in the Mt. Shasta area for the past ten years and is a caretaker of someone's house near where we were staying. He said he had been all over the country, physically, and to places like India, when he astrally projects. He then told us that he writes poetry and recited a number of poems to us on the way into town. We asked him where he wanted to go and he said that he needed some supplies in the town first before going up the mountain. So, we brought him to the market, and then we brought him up Mt. Shasta as far as the road would go.

As he was going to leave, I asked him, "How do you survive out here? Aren't you worried?" He simply smiled and told us, "God provides!" I thought, "He is right, he certainly did get the 'perfect ride' today."

The next day, we went back to the town of Mt. Shasta to meet our guide. We had a little extra time, so we went into an amazing store called Soul Connections. It was filled with religious statues, pictures, crystals and novelties. In the store, I found a bumper sticker that said:

"Everything is Connected."

We were to meet our guide at Berryvalle Grocery store that had a small café attached. As we were waiting, I was looking through some of the things I had gotten at Soul Connections, including the bumper sticker, when who walked in but Ted, the hitchhiker. He told us that he needed a few more things and he had gotten another ride down the mountain. I was just in awe that he was there right when we were. Everything is certainly connected. At that point, our guide, Andrew came in, and we introduced him to Ted, and Andrew told us, "Of course I know Ted!"

From the very first instant when we met Andrew Oser, I knew we were (of course) divinely led to him. Andrew is a spry man in his fifties with curly dark hair and a broad smile. As he greeted us I couldn't believe a shirt he had on that had printed on it *"Live, Laugh, Love."* I told him that we have that all over our house. He told us that he had been a guide in the Mt. Shasta area for years, usually living there eight or nine months a year and the other months in Maui. He was also a personal coach and he conducted personal development seminars and workshops all over California and in Maui and Hawaii. He had planned to go to Harvard Law School after he had graduated summa cum laude from Princeton University. But at that point, he read *The Inner Game of Tennis,* and it changed his life, initiating his own spiritual awakening. He decided to teach tennis rather than be a lawyer.

He is also an author of *How Alternation Can Change Your Life; Finding The Rhythms of Health and Happiness* (2010). Not only did we find out that he was so knowledgeable of the area, but he knew every spiritual author and master I had read about, and he had met several in the past thirty years. He had even taught tennis lessons to Master Joshua David Stone's mother!

The first site he brought us to was an area about half way up the mountain called *Ascension Rock.* It was a series of large boulders piled up for thirty or forty feet. As we approached the area, what did we find flying around? A butterfly! I asked Andrew, "Is this normal? Do you often see butterflies around here?" He said, "No, not really."

We headed toward the rocks and that butterfly kept flying around the rock we were about to climb up on, as if it was waiting for us. When got to the top of the rocks and sat down, the butterfly kept circling around us. Andrew had us close our eyes, and he led us in a meditation. He said, "I would like to invoke the great **I Am** presence. To help all that are here to connect to universal energies. To release any blocks and to be able to connect to all universal energies." I thought his meditation was amazing. I had not told him what "I Am" meant to me or even that I had any blocks.

As we left Ascension Rock and continued up the mountain that butterfly followed us for another hundred yards and, then all of a sudden, flew into my chest, into my heart, as if to say, "I'm here; follow your heart!" And then it flew away. Andrew, then, took us up to another area that he said was a vortex site. He had us sit and he conducted another similar meditation. The air was clear and cool there, and there was hardly a sound to be heard except for his soft words and a slight rustling breeze through the tall pine trees on the mountain. I didn't see or hear any visions there, but I certainly felt a calm peace cover me.

The next day, Andrew took us to an area where there was a spectacular waterfall that flowed down to Lake Shasta. As we sat on a large rock by the waterfall he led us in another meditation. Then we waited out by the waterfall to feel its energy. After that Andrew changed his shirt putting on one that had printed *"Om Sweet Om."* I told him, "I can't believe it, I have that sign in my dining room." He said, "Spirit told me what to wear this morning. That it would talk to you."

Andrew then took us to an area where a spring flowed out of Mt. Shasta. He told us that it was the head water of the Sacramento River. It was where the river began. He told us that it was pure spring water from the mountain, and we all filled our water bottles. He said that if we brought the water home and added a couple of drops of this spring water to water we drink, then we would carry the energy of the mountain with us. And when we ran out of the water, it was time to come back to the mountain.

After two days with Andrew, we felt incredibly connected to him. He exuded confidence, knowledge, sincerity, and connection to Universal energies. We knew this would be the beginning of a long relationship. Dr. Dave summed up how I felt when we said goodbye to him: "Andrew, it would have been great to have seen a vision of St. Germain when on the mountain, but Mary and I talked, and we know the real reason why we came to Mt. Shasta, was to meet you."

Further Revelations

I met Terry Wildemann at an open house we had at Healing Hearts. She did a talk on "Empowering Women" for us and I was extremely taken with her. I was very impressed with her business sense, learning that she conducted seminars in helping women develop self-confidence and how to run their own businesses. She also gave workshops for large corporations on being more efficient. But after talking to her I knew I wanted to meet with her privately when I found out that she was intuitive and channeled the *Call of the Rose,* which is Quan Yin, Mary Magdalene, and the Blessed Mother. I met with her the following week in her home office in Middletown, Rhode Island.

She began by telling me that the people I have been meeting will be part of my "tribe." She said that she was being told by her guides that, "I had come such a long way, and all that had happened to me was for my call for guidance, direction, and healing. Without what I had experienced and the terrible times I had gone through (I hadn't told her anything about my story) I would not be in a place to have the amazing joy I would now be experiencing."

Her guides continued by telling Terry, "I should trust that my journey might have felt like a rowboat going against the current, and uphill at times. But now I would be flowing towards the things I wanted. I would be in my truth as a teacher. My message would find the listeners that need healing, hope, and trust. Those in power in leadership are fearful of the energy that's in my world. I would be helping those with mental health problems, and I would be able to discern those who are suffering from those who are divinely guided. I was nearly in my true magnificence. The spotlight would be on me in many ways. I should declare my goals, and my guardian angels would hold a perfect divine space for me."

Terry then asked that I pick a deck of cards. I saw that one of the decks she laid out for me was *Ask and Its Is Given,* which were cards by Esther and Jerry Hicks who channel Abraham. She told me to take the deck in my hands and fan the cards out with their backs toward me so I couldn't see the faces of the cards and to randomly pick out a card. The fist card I picked had; "I am attracting its vibrational essence." Terry told me that it meant, "That which is like onto itself is drawn. Whatever you give your attention to is unfolding in your experience."

The next card I picked had the words: "But whose truth is the truth?" Terry said that it meant, "With enough attention to anything, the essence you have been giving thought to will become a physical manifestation." The last card I turned over had a picture of a queen with her body as mother earth. Terry told me that it stood for my getting my power back and my trek up the emotional scale being now, not only possible, but also relatively easy. I thought the cards were so incredibly meaningful and, of course, reaffirmed what I had heard so many times before.

Terry ended our session by telling me that her guides were telling her, "That I was the *Magic* that the future would depend upon." I left knowing that Terry was also for real. The words that came through her from her guides were what other psychics had told me. She definitely passed my "psychic test."

Another amazing psychic I met with shortly after Terry, who also spoke at a workshop we had at Healing Hearts, was Stephanie Miller. Stephanie is an intuitive and also communicates and heals animals. Because I wanted her to work with my dog, Felicia I had her come to my house. Felicia was getting on in years and had difficulty being left alone, barking continuously when by herself. She would also spend all her time in my mother's apartment on the first floor and rarely ventured upstairs to visit me anymore. Stephanie began working with her by holding Felicia and whispering in her ear. Then she took out a crystal and began rolling it over Felicia's back.

When she was done, she asked that my mom and I join her in leaving the apartment. We were amazed that Felicia stayed behind and didn't bark at all. Stephanie also told us that she felt that Felicia's bowels were very impacted (she could tell when she rolled the crystal on her back). The next day I was surprised to see Felicia upstairs visiting me, and a few days later my mom took her to the vet, and he did, in fact, have to clear her bowels out as they were very impacted.

After Stephanie was finished with Felicia, we went upstairs to my apartment, and she began doing a reading for me. She told me that she saw me moving to a warmer climate in the next year. Things would start to happen more and more for me in the coming spring and really take off in the summer, and by December I would be really in my purpose. Then she said she saw that Dr. Dave and I were so interconnected, so intertwined, unlike anything she had ever seen, that it was as if we had the same DNA." Stephanie also said she saw that someone named Lucy would be an important part of my inner circle. I knew that Stephanie was for real also. She again, reaffirmed what so many others had told me.

"Knowing the path is different from walking the path!"
~ Morpheus in the Matrix

In retrospect, I feel I was divinely led to all of these amazing healers and psychics that have helped me in so many ways. When doctors could not help me, psychic healers and shamans like Grace Avila, Joey Stann, Judy Lavine, Gerry Miller, Joanna Neff, Richard Jackson, Vanessa Riyasat and Amorah Quan Yin were able to clear entities from me that were making me ill. Individuals with psychic abilities like Heidi Gabrilowitz, Kerrie O'Connor, Jackie Eaton, Michelle Sutton, Maureen St. Germain, Vanessa Riyasat, Mark the

Astrologer, Anthony Williams, Terry Wildemann and Stephanie Miller were able to explain to me what was going on, who I am, and to clarify the divine life path I am now on.

It still amazes me, but certainly seems so fitting that my final battle was fought in another dimension. Thanks to Mark's spirit guide I was finally cleared. And, it is just as fitting that my physical problems, a high vibrational infection that was undetectable by the medical profession, and caused by dark entities in order to keep me exhausted and in pain, to keep me from my purpose in this life, was detected and healed by a medical intuitive, Anthony!

What Have You Learned Dorothy?

To coin a line from the scarecrow in the *Wizard Of OZ,* I certainly had an education through my divine journey. Prior to my journey, I didn't even know what an avatar was or even that earth angels existed. Now, I feel as though I have a graduate degree in the New Age world. In the Divine Resource section I listed many of the amazing healers and psychics that had helped me. A few remarkable souls are not listed, they had intended a different direction for their lives.

In my journey, I had also experienced many "not so real" psychics and lightworkers. Obviously, I did not discuss them or recommend them. To separate the real lightworkers (includes alternative healers, psychics, shamans, channels, mediums, gurus and life coaches), from the not so real, keep in mind:

- Are they telling you facts? True psychics know things about you by just being in your presence. They are not being overly general, as in; "Someone in the audience has lost a relative whose name begins with a 'J' or, 'J' sound, through an illness."
- You shouldn't have to give them any information about

yourself. The will tell you specific things that have happened to you, that they had no way of knowing.

- When they "see" spirits around you, they can accurately describe them. If they tell you your deceased mother is by your side, they can tell you what she looks like and usually her name.

- They should be sincerely interested in helping you. Joey Stann once told me, "Your outcome is more important to me than my income."

- They do not charge outrageous fees for their services. Many of the lightworkers that had helped me had no set fee, and simply asked that I pay, "Whatever was in my heart."

- They do not advertise excessively. Amazing lightworkers are extremely busy. Most of their business comes from referrals from others they had helped.

- They may be difficult to get an appointment with. Because they are so good at what they do, you may have to wait weeks or months (as I often had to) to get an appointment with them.

> *"You are not defined by your past…*
> *You are prepared by it."*
>
> **~ Joel Osteen**

Divine Moments

Dr. Michael Sharp & Mary

Pat Hastings & Mary

*Dr. Dave, Pat Hastings, Mary, Dr. Michael
Sharp, Dr. Ysabel Reyes, Grace Avila,
Rev. Ian & Laurie Taylor*

Mary, Rev. Ram Smith, & Dr. Dave

Grace, Dr. Dave, Mary, & Maureen St. Germain

Michelle Sutton & Mary

"Amazing" Grace Avila & Mary

Mary & Vanessa Riyasat

Mary & Joey Stann

Marlene Robinson, Pat Hastings, & Mary

Richard Jackson & Mary

*Mary & Andrew Oser
on Mt. Shasta*

Mary with Ted the Hitchhiker

Mary & Joanne "Best Bud" Fammartino

Mary's Mom, Pat & Rita helping at a Conference

Good friend Claudia Rathbun & Mary

Good friend Joanne Corry & Mary

Dr. Heidi & Mary at Heidi's backyard labyrinth

Rev. Ian giving Words Of Wisdom to Mary

Our Cracked "Butterfly" window

Miss Butterfly

V ~ Divine Signs

"…everything around her is a silver pool of light
The people who surround her feel the benefit of it,
it makes you calm….She got the power to be, the
power to give, the power to SEE."

~Suddenly I See
K.T. Tunstall

Through my spiritual awakening, I began seeing signs everywhere, all the time. Some people with psychic abilities, like Grace and Vanessa, can see energy or spirits. Some psychics like Heidi, Michelle, Maureen, Jackie, Kerrie, Terry, and Stephanie, connect with their intuition and feelings and can tell of past or future events. Although, I see energy on occasion; a changing image in a mirror, or when looking at someone, most of my signs come through obvious things all around me. The TV, radio, songs, license plates on cars, billboards, signs on trucks, what people wear, an animal, all continually talk to me. Life can be a breeze, if you just observe all that is around you. Spirit is always talking to you. People often never see what is right in front of them. They are too wrapped up in themselves to notice. They ***choose*** to look the other way.

When I was in the "battle of souls," signs were talking back and forth to me. Negative was answered by positive, evil by good. While driving I would see a negative sign, like 666 (usually associated with the devil), and look up and instantly see a billboard saying, "Jesus

Saves." I would get into my car turn the radio on and hear a song talking to me, answering a question or feeling I had had earlier. The signs were too often, numerous, and intense for me not to pay attention to them.

Divine Happenings

Carl Jung, (1875-1961), a Swiss psychiatrist and considered founder of analytical psychology, coined the term *synchronicity*. To explain events he witnessed that he believed could not have happened by mere chance, he developed the term and concept of synchronicity. He stated that events that first may appear to be coincidences, when examined further, are "incoincident." They could not be simply a chance event, and perhaps, there were other forces at work. Of course, being a traditional clinical psychologist, he was not specific as to what the "other forces" were.

Not being a "traditional clinical psychologist" I have no problem describing these "other forces" as *Divine* forces. When I look back at the events of my spiritual awakening, I believe they go far beyond incoincident or synchronistic happenings. What I experienced can best be described as *Divine Happenings*.

At first, it was hard to believe what I was experiencing wasn't just a number of coincidences. But when they continued, it became more than evident that they were messages from God, *Divine Happenings*!

One or two or, even three events that happen over a day or two might be easily dismissed as a coincidence. But, when events happen all day long and everyday, it goes far beyond mere chance. I would be thinking of a song and get in my car, and it's playing on the radio. I'm lying in bed, thinking about how various spiritual channelers, like Lee Carroll have changed my life, and on TV, it flashes, "A channel can change your life!"

Dr. Dave and I enjoy watching old episodes of *Seinfeld,* and a couple of times, the *divine happenings* were uncanny. Listening to a tape of my astrological chart by Mark the Astrologer, I heard him make several references to "magic" in my chart (see Divine Journey). That night, after my reading with Mark, we were watching the Seinfeld episode where Jerry dates a Miss America contestant, Miss Rhode Island, who was a blonde, with brown eyes, (like me) whose talent was magic.

Another time, I had just finished my volunteering application process with Beacon Hospice and called Dr. Dave to tell him how it went. His response, jokingly, was, "Well, I hope the first client you get is not like the one Jerry had when he volunteered to be with a senior citizen." Of course, that night when we were watching *Seinfeld,* it was that episode where they were volunteering with senior citizens.

Once, when on the way to doing a follow-up healing session with my Aunt Norma, I saw a license plate with "GODS" on it. When I arrived, I was pleased to see that she was getting around the house without the use of her walker, which she had used for years. As I left her house, the first song my radio was playing as I turned my car on was, "Every little thing she does is *Magic*" by The Police. Then, as the song was playing, I saw a license plate that said "AWESUM" (awesome) and another one that said "ALTRUI" for altruism, and then a van went by with "Crimson Rose" on it. Sometimes, it just never seems to stop with me.

My cousin, John David, was like a younger brother to me growing up (by the way, Dr. Dave's middle name is John, as in 'David John,' and he also has a younger cousin, named John, who was like a little brother to him as well). Shortly after John David's mother passed away, he had an apartment for rent. The tenant he found for it was from Egypt. John had always been drawn to Egyptian culture all his life, and even had a curio cabinet filled with Egyptian statues and artifacts. He then found out that his new tenant's birthday was the same day as his mother's. He felt as if his deceased mother had sent him his perfect tenant. When you just have too many coincidences, it's a ***Divine Happening***!

I love it when my clients tell me of *Divine Happenings*. I had given a Reconnection session to Barbara, who told me she felt great after it (Reconnecting also connects one with his or her life's purpose). However, her son didn't believe in the whole process and told her it was "all a big scam."

Barbara felt as if her faith in me was shaken, and asked God for a sign. The next day with her son in her car, she stopped at a store, and a car pulled in next to her with "Amazing Grace" on its license plate. She turned to her son and said, "See there's my sign." Her son retorted, "That's just a coincidence, mom."

So, Barbara told me she asked for another sign. The rest of the day she saw nothing extraordinary. She was about to go to bed, feeling depressed about the whole process, thinking that maybe her son was right, but before she turned off the TV she saw that the first daily lottery number that came up was *3*. Her attention was really drawn to the screen when the second number was *3*. Barbara knew that 333 was a divine number used in the Reconnection, and she thought to herself, "This could be the sign I was looking for. If the third number comes up a *3*, then Mary was right, if not, perhaps I was hoping for too much and my son was right." The third number was drawn and it was a *3!* The **333** that came up that night confirmed Barbara's belief, she went to bed elated!

Another example of a *Divine Happening* with numbers occurred with Dr. Dave's father. The week his mother died, his father mentioned to Dr. Dave that he had been seeing the number 442 quite often that week for some reason. He told Dr. Dave he saw it on license plates in front of him, in the news, on billboards, and didn't know what it meant. At the time, Dr. Dave could offer no help because at that point we were not yet together, and he had never given such "signs" a second thought. Dr. Dave said he and his father couldn't believe it, when their question was answered at his mother's funeral. They saw her plot number was 442!

The first day I volunteered at Beacon Hospice, I met with two delightful elderly women that had early stages of Alzheimer's. As I was leaving the nursing home the car parked next to me had "PAM-1" on its license plate. Dr. Dave's mom's name was Pam, and she also had had Alzheimer's!

Sometimes it seems as if all I see is *Divine Happenings*. Another day, on the way home from my weekly visit with the two ladies at the nursing home, a car passed me with "EMPOWR" (empower) on it's license plate, at the same time the disco song, "I've Got The Power," came on the radio. The next car that went by had "UNITY" on it's plate, I had just finished reading a chapter called "Unity" the night before. A few cars later, I saw a license plate that says "Fatima 1." The blessed mother is also called *Our Lady of Fatima*, and that also happens to be a hospital near my house (on "High Service" Avenue). Then, I passed a van with the word "signs" painted on it's side. The next song that came on the radio was "I Saw The Signs." I went home to tell Dr. Dave everything that just had happened, and he was watching one of our favorite TV shows, *My Name Is Earl.* We both love the show because its about, as Earl puts it, "righting karma" and "trying to be a better person."

In one of the episodes of *My Name is Earl,* he was telling a visitor from France what was so good about America. He said, "We have football, the Statue of Liberty, and we even have a 'black winking Jesus doll'!" I couldn't believe it when he mentioned the doll, because that was a sign for me when things started to talk to me. I never knew such a thing even existed, but I had made the connection several times during my awakening, and here it was again!

A good friend of mine, Pat Hastings, who is also author of *Simply A Woman of Faith* (2007) tells of amazing synchronicities throughout her life. In her book she calls them **GODincidences**. She talks of getting messages from the divine in seeing signs or hearing that special song of having her prayers answered, and, in some cases, not answered only to have something better happen.

One of the reasons I love Pat is that she always trusts her intuition and acts on it. She is so connected to *Divine* energies. In her book, she describes one instance of getting a message from God to go and talk to a woman that was sitting by the ocean. As she acted on that message, she found that the woman was considering committing suicide at that moment. She was sent to help that woman when she needed it the most.

I can't tell you how many times she called me to tell me that she just got a message from God to tell me something, and it concerned an event that had just happened to me. For instance, once I had just come back from a psychic telling me I had a thousand angels around me, and, at the same time, Pat had left me a message, saying that she was told (by Spirit) to tell me that there were angels all around me.

Another time when I was away at a weekend seminar (unknown to Pat), I was starting to get very discouraged, and thought of leaving. I wasn't "understanding" what they were taking about, and I was feeling I had wasted a lot of time and money (the seminar was in New York) going to the seminar. I was even getting upset with God thinking, "Here I am trying everything I can do to get me to my purpose in life, and its not happening." At a break, I went to my room to call Dr. Dave to tell him I was going to come home early. As I picked up my phone I noticed a message on it, it was from Pat. She said, "Mary, I came by your house to tell you a message that came to me loud, and clear from God, but you weren't home, so I had to call you with it; *'Trust in the Lord with all your heart, and rely not on your understanding!'* I'm not sure if it means anything to you but I had to tell you now." I couldn't believe at the exact time I was feeling this way, she received a message from God answering my thoughts. It gave me a source of great comfort. Because of her message, I stayed the rest of the weekend, and things did start to make sense, and I did feel the weekend was worthwhile in the end.

Signs are all around us constantly giving us messages from the **Divine.** They may come in a variety of ways asked for or not. Sometimes they are answers to questions you have may not even thought to ask. Once, when feeling frustrated because things were not happening as fast as I wanted them, I walked by the den where

Divinely Touched: Transform Your Life

Dr. Dave had the TV on, and I heard, "Don't tell me nothings happening." The next day I opened one of Kryon's books, *Lifting The Veil,* and a page jumped out at me, "Don't tell me nothings happening!" At that point, I felt it was a clear message from the Divine just because I couldn't see what was happening, it didn't mean that nothing was.

> *"I saw the sign and it opened up my eyes,*
> *I saw the sign.*
> *…No one's dragging you up to get into*
> **the light where you belong."**
>
> *~The Sign*
> **By Ace of Base**

Types of Signs

Signs come in all forms in the physical and not so physical realms. They are messages from your guardian angels, who could be deceased loved ones or relatives, your spirit guides, or from even higher spirit dimensions, such as ascended masters or the Universal One/God/Source.

What constitutes a sign? Sometimes, it can be something to which you have given special meaning, like Barbara's *333.* Other times it can be something that is recurring, as in Dr. Dave's father's 442. For psychics, it is a voice in their head, a vision, or a feeling.

I have had the opportunity in my travels to meet many people that are true psychics, and even more with psychic abilities. The difference is that psychics usually use their gift in a business. But many of the people I've been in contact with in my spiritual journey have psychic abilities. They get flashes of insight, hear a voice, or get an occasional feeling when they are involved in everyday affairs. They may even have a dream of a future event that comes true.

Of course, I truly believe that everything in life happens for a reason. *Everything is connected,* as Vanessa said, and that includes everyone we meet in life. A person doesn't have to be psychic to relay a message to you. Some people are like Heidi, who uses her empathic abilities to connect with psychic energies, **angel energy**, as she calls it, to impart messages or Michelle, who while she is conducting a physical healing on someone, continually hears messages by her guides (at least when she worked on me she did).

Physical Signs

As mentioned, things like license plates and bumper stickers on cars often talk to me. On a walk with Dr. Dave I saw a car go pass us with a sticker that said, "We Stand by You." Without missing a beat, the next car coming towards us had a license plate with "Angels" on it.

Frequently, I see "TV" on a license plate, telling me, "Yes, TV is talking to me," reminding me when signs started to come through to me on the TV. Its as if the Universe is saying, "God is here, always talking to me!"

Oftentimes, it is as if the Universe is truly reading your mind. One afternoon, I was inspired after one of our Concordia services with Rev. Ian and was driving, thinking, "There is no, "no," only "yes," in my consciousness." As I pulled up to a stop sign, the car in front of me had "No No" on its license plate!

Jane and her twin sister run a health clinic in Hartford, CT, and told me of a divine happening one day when we were discussing signs. Their father had passed away a few months before and she and her sister were going out to lunch together to celebrate their fiftieth birthdays. On the way to the restaurant, Jane told her sister, "I know we are going to see a sign from Dad today." As they pulled into the restaurant parking lot, a large white SUV pulled in beside them with "Phil-50" on its license plate. Their father's name was Phil.

Another *Divine Happening* occurred to Dr. Dave's two nephews, during a very trying time in their lives. They had lost their brother through a violent accident the week before Christmas. After the wake, they were at a drive-through, and they noticed the car in front of them had a license plate that said "Scott," their brother's name. If that wasn't enough, under the plate there was a bumper sticker that said, *"See ya, gone to Heaven."* They knew it was a clear sign from their brother.

Numbers continually talk to me as well. They could be in print, on signs or billboards, on a digital clock or a license plate. Sometimes seeing the same number over and over may be a sign of things to come, as Dr. Dave's father did in seeing his wife's cemetery plot number in advance. Oftentimes, for me, it is in seeing a consecutive triple number that gives me a messages.

Doreen Virtue, Ph.D. in *Healing with the Angels* (1999) describes the meanings of triple numbers:

111 ~ Your thoughts are manifesting at a rapid pace. Keep them positive lest you manifest the negative.

222 ~ Your newly planted ideas are beginning to grow into reality.

333 ~ The ascended masters are with you and aiding you.

444 ~ The angels are all around you, surrounding you with love and help.

555 ~ Major life change is upon you. Also represents Christ consciousness.

666 ~ Your thoughts are out of balance, focusing too much on the material world. Angels are asking you to focus more on service and spirit.

777 ~ Angels are applauding you that you are on the right track. Miracles are about to occur.

888 ~ You are nearing completion in a phase of your life. Great financial abundance is yours now and in the future.

999 ~ Completion. This is an end to a big phase in your life.

000 ~ A situation has gone full circle. You are one with God.

Knowing the meaning of triple numbers, I see them everywhere, continually, usually not just by themselves, and often in succession. My car's clock turns to 1:11, a car passes me with 111 on its license plate, then a truck goes by with the last 3 digits of a telephone number on its side ending in 111.

Once, when I was doing a radio show with Greg, I noticed some triple numbers in his studio. On a wall he had a flyer with his phone number ending in 555 and on the opposite wall he a had a poster with 777 printed on its top and bottom. I asked Greg if he knew what those numbers meant. He said he didn't so I explained the meaning of triple numbers to him and those two sequences. On the way home, as we pulled into our driveway Dr. Dave told me to look at our odometer. Just as we drove into our driveway the last three digits turned to 555.

Sometimes signs just keep recurring, as if to get your attention. One day I got a letter in the mail with the saying on it:

> **"The will of God will never take you, where the Grace of God will not protect you."**

Of course, I loved that and cut it out to put on my refrigerator. The next day I was in a store to buy some paper plates, and I saw the exact same saying on a poster. That, of course, I bought as well.

Another time, when I was driving, trying to relax a little, because I was in so much pain again, I was praying to God to give me a sign that everything would be okay. As I turned the corner, a car came toward me with *"DIVINE"* on its license plate. My tears then turned to ones of joy and relief.

Media Signs

Signs continue to come to me through the TV or radio. During my spiritual awakening the signs were blatant. The TV was outright talking to me, and, as I previously noted, the signs were often talking back and forth. Good was being answered by evil. Since then, the conflicts have gone, but I still get tuned into the TV or radio. Often I will be reading a passage that says, "We have to work as one." Then a commercial comes on the TV saying, "We have to work as one."

Once, when we were in the car discussing signs, Dr. Dave mentioned that he often sees a street light go out (or go on) as he drives by it. It just so happened the next day I was reading *Beyond the Flower of Life* (2009), by Maureen St. Germain, and she stated that, when you go by a street light that goes on or off, at that instant the *"Universe"* is confirming your thoughts. When I told Dr. Dave this as we happened to be driving, he said, "That's great, but I would still feel better if the lights went on when I went by; I'll have to work on that." Sure enough, a few minutes later we drove under a street light that was off and it went on. Dr. Dave said, "Did you see that?" I commented, "See what happens when you put your mind to it?"

It should certainly become evident by now that music really talks to my soul. Songs and song lyrics have inspired me, encouraged me when I was down and they connected me to Spirit throughout my life. I believe that most musicians, and song writers are *divinely* inspired. Ken Carey who channels Native American spirits in *Return of the Bird Tribes* (1988), states that they have, "… guided those that have been open to us, such as musicians."

To say that music speaks to me would be an incredible understatement. I'd be thinking of a song, and I'd get in my car, and that song would be playing on the radio. Songs and song lyrics continue to talk to me daily.

One time, Dr. Dave and I went to a Kenny Rogers concert and I in so much pain sitting there I thought to myself, "How am I going to get through the night?" Then his warm-up group, *Savannah Jack,* a trio of young men that are all incredible vocalists came on. One song they sang, that really touched me as I was sitting there in incredible pain, was "I Feel Your Pain." The song was about Jesus feeling our pain, and it also gave me such comfort at the time. After the concert, we had the opportunity to buy their CD and meet them as they all signed it for us.

People Signs

Often a stranger can bring you a message. Granted, I am very observant when it comes to signs. Rarely, when I'm out, I don't see something that has special meaning to me. Often, someone is either wearing something or says something to me. It may not mean anything to them, but it certainly does to me. I might be at a store, and a woman with butterflies on her shirt will make a passing comment to me that resonates with me.

One time, I went into a gift store that specialized in delivering balloons to send Dr. Dave one for our anniversary. The clerk, a young man, had a tee shirt on that had "Trust Me" on it. On the counter, I noticed a large transformer toy. I placed my order and left. Rather than having them deliver what I had ordered, I decided to go and pick it up the next day. When I arrived at the store, the same clerk had a tee shirt with one large word printed across it, "SPIRIT." At that point I thought to myself, "It all makes perfect sense, the Spirit was telling me to trust it, in my transformation."

Another time I was on my way to a favorite card store to get some cards and was thinking of a line from Kryon:

> *"You will be in the driver's seat, you will be the pilot, and your guides will be your passengers, your co-pilots."*

Just as that thought crossed my mind, a truck passed with me with, "How's my driving?" written across the back of it. I answered to myself, "Excellent. I love it. Thank you. Keep it coming." After I had gotten a few cards, I was in line at the register behind two men, when one turned to the other and asked, "How's my driving?" I couldn't believe it. In a matter of minutes, the same message had come to me three times.

Remember, everything happens for a reason. This includes people you "bump" into. Some may carry a special message. Others may teach you something. If you have ever had that *déjà vu* feeling when meeting someone for the first time, it may be for a reason. It is quite possible you knew that person in a previous life. Be open to what they are openly, or not so openly, telling you.

Animal Signs

Just as people can bring you a sign, so it is with animals. Every culture appears to have meaningful symbolism with animals. The Chinese have their zodiac based on animals, Native Americans have all types of power animals, and many of their native names are animals names, symbolizing its attributes. Even the United States embraced the characteristics of the bald eagle as their national symbol.

People often identify intentionally as well as unintentionally (by Spirit) with specific animals. They may have a love of butterflies, dragonflies, hummingbirds, cardinals, frogs, cats, a certain breed of dogs, dolphins, tigers, horses (or unicorns), or even elephants, and surround themselves with statues, artwork, or even the animal. These feelings maybe out of the connection one is making to the animal, or perhaps they are soul memories, a memory from a previous life of a special connection with a certain animal. An individual may have been saved by a St. Bernard (dog) in a previous life and in this life feels a strong bond with that animal. Or, conversely, one may have died by a snake bite in a previous life, and now has a tremendous fear of snakes in this life.

Many animals have sharper senses than we do and may, in fact, be seeing or sensing energy that we do not. Such was case with my beagle, Felicia, when she was barking at entities attacking me. Animals possess an extraordinary consciousness (see Chapter VI: Divine Consciousness; Animal Consciousness). So when your pet dog or cat is acting unusual, it may be that it is sensing something you cannot, trying to give you a direct message.

When animals appear they may be bringing a special message from the Divine. Such was the case with my butterfly appearing to me "out of thin air" and in continuing to come to me (at times everywhere I looked) in my cracked kitchen window, hitting me in the chest on Mt. Shasta, and it seems whenever I am out. I don't have to look far to see someone wearing a butterfly imprinted on his or her clothing, or have a piece of butterfly jewelry on, or see a picture of one on a sign, or, even see a real butterfly flying past me. All continue to say to me, "You have been transformed!"

Another example of an animal bringing a message from Spirit to me was from a praying (of course) mantis. At a time when I was just getting started in my healing work, and business was slow in developing, I started having trouble with my basement apartment tenant. She decided that she wasn't going to pay me, and called the city Inspection and Code Department to complain. Subsequently, a number of inspectors descended on my house and told her that she had to leave that night and told us that there were a number of code violations we had to correct in the house. It appeared that a number of renovations in the house were done without the necessary permits. So, Dr. Dave and I had to correct them, and at one point, the city even turned our heat off for a month (no hot water). We had to go to a gym to take showers. The whole ordeal cost us thousands, when funds were very tight to begin with.

In the middle of all the turmoil in our house, Dr. Dave called me outside one day and said, "Mary, look at this. This is unbelievable. It's a praying mantis." I had no idea what a praying mantis was, and I don't believe I had even ever seen one before. It looked to me like a very strange and large grasshopper, it must have been eight inches long, and it had a funny looking head. Dr. Dave continued, "You know what they represent?" "No, what?" "They mean 'good luck'!" I thought, "Well, we certainly need it now." Seeing a praying mantis may not be that unusual for many, although they are rare, but we live in the city. Our back "yard" is a paved parking lot. We didn't have any trees or even grass there. The other thing that was extraordinary about this praying mantis is that it stayed on the back side of our house for a month. This was in October when it was quite cold at night, through all our troubles in the house. It was in fact, reassuring us daily, saying to us, "I am here, everything will be alright!" When our gas (the source of our heat and hot water) was finally turned back on, he was gone!

Some "power" animals and their meanings that have "spoken" to me:

Butterfly:	Transformation, metamorphosis, freedom, spiritual growth.
Cardinal:	Holiness.
Dolphin:	Communication, telepathy.
Dragonfly:	Rebirth, living in the present.
Dove:	Purity, love.
Eagle:	Nobility, discrimination. Highest expression of spirit.
Frog:	Transformation and metamorphosis, respect, reincarnation. Acronym: *Forever Rely On God.*
Geese:	Stand by each other. Working together.
Hawk:	Clarity, great vision, illumination.
Humming bird:	Magic is in the air.
Lioness:	Self-assuredness, action, authority, courage and divine strength.
Owl:	Wisdom, alchemy, brings light into dark places.
Peacock:	Magic, graciousness, and generosity.
Pelican:	Nurturing and protection of your inner child.
Praying Mantis:	Good luck, fortune is upon you.
Raven:	Sorcery and magic.
Swan:	Love, beauty, grace, courtship.
Turtle:	Longevity, patience, persistence (you need

	to stick your neck out to get anywhere). Its not about the speed; its about getting there!
White Buffalo:	Reverence and sacredness.
Wolf:	Wise teacher, guide, and leader.

The next time an animal shows up either physically or symbolically, it may be carrying a special meaning from Spirit. If a certain animal continues to show up look into its meaning.

"Believe in yourself! Have faith in your abilities! Without a humble but reasonable confidence in your own powers you cannot be successful or happy."

~ Norman Vincent Peale

Intuitive Signs

Clairsentience is derived from a French word meaning "clear feeling." It is described as the extrasensory ability to feel, sense, taste or smell through inner sensing. It's that "feeling" you get about something. It differs from clairvoyance, "clear seeing" that is having a vision, and clairaudience, "clear hearing," hearing inner voices. I have had experiences of clairsentience frequently and have had numerous stories of people getting a "feeling" about something that turned out to be a connection with higher consciousness and the spirit realm.

One day, while walking to a local pizzeria, Tommy's Pizza, I was thinking of calling Ann for a wrap (they often made the bloating in my abdomen feel better). I hadn't seen or talked to her in over a year. Just then, who drove up beside me, but Ann! She pulled over and said, "Mary, I was just thinking of calling you. I've been seeing you everywhere (referring to my ads or articles on me). I wanted to call you for a healing." A little later, while sitting at Tommy's, I got a call from Dr. Dave to tell me he was on his way home and he asked me if I want to go to Tommy's for dinner.

As I mentioned in My Divine Journey chapter, the day I met Heidi, I had a feeling that I needed to go in the opposite direction from what I had set out to go in. It became very evident why I went to the White Light Bookstore that day after I met Heidi. She was instrumental in sending me on my divine journey. Heidi has the ability to be physically and psychically empathic and she can receive messages from guides and angels. She was one of the first lightworkers I had met that told me how special I was. At our first meeting she was being told that it was important to meet me, and that I had the "light of God" inside of me and that I have a very "**high vibrational energy**" in me. But, what really blew me away was when she told me that she could feel the pressure in my abdomen.

People get signs, feelings, and intuitions all the time. One day, my mother said she wanted me to do a healing on a friend of hers that was having the beginnings of Alzheimer's, but, my mother wasn't sure she would go for an "energy healing" by me and was wondering how to approach her friend. The next day, my mom got a call from her friend, telling her that she had been very depressed yesterday and started praying to Padro Pio and she got a vision of me and her depression left. I hadn't seen her in years, and my mom had not told her what I was doing now. I believe, through my mother's intent, she connected with the spirit world that gave her friend a divine message.

My good friend Claudia told me of a great clairsentience experience. She briefly had a business partner who was a girlfriend she had known since high school, but the partnership didn't work out. They parted company and never spoke to each other again. One day, about five years later, when Claudia was typing away at her computer, she got a feeling "out of the blue" that her friend and former business partner had died. She stopped her typing, went to the obituary archives on the Internet, and found that she had in fact, died the month before.

The next week Claudia was walking in a cemetery and had another feeling come over her about her girlfriend. She had no idea where she was buried or if she was even in this cemetery. When she stopped and looked down, she saw that she was standing in front of her girlfriend's gravesite. If that wasn't enough, a few weeks later, she was thinking of going back to her girlfriend's gravesite, but couldn't remember where it was. As she walked around a bend, she came to the gravesite again and saw that her parents where there visiting their daughter's gravesite.

Dreams

Dreams are a way Spirit connects with you. Guardian angels that are often deceased relatives can talk to you in a dream telling you of future events. Dr. Dave tells the story of the night his mother died that illustrates how one's dreams can make that connection. His mother was in the late stages of Alzheimer's disease and was totally bedridden and dependant on his stepfather for everything. By all accounts, everyone thought she would be like that for years to come.

One night, Dr. Dave had a dream that he and his family were walking through the woods. His stepfather, brother, and sisters were walking on a dirt path ahead of him when he turned to look behind him and saw that his mother was twenty or so yards behind them. He said, "Come on Mom; you'll get lost!" Her reply was, "You go on without me; I'll be O.K." That morning, Dr. Dave woke up to his stepfather calling to tell him that his mother had died that night.

Calling for Signs

"Take out the trash; learn to throw out everything you don't need in your mind.
"When you are truly in the now you will be amazed at what you can do!"

~ The Peaceful Warrior

Many psychics are average people that have just become very attuned to the signs they feel and/or see. They listen to those feelings/voices and aren't afraid to tell you about them. I don't know how many times I heard someone with psychic abilities tell me, "I don't know why I'm telling you this but…" or "You might think I'm crazy, but I'm being told…." and, what they came up with was right on the money.

The first time I met Michelle at the Colonics Institute in West Hartford, Connecticut, she told me, "They are telling me you need to finish your book, the world needs it." Now, I had just entered her office, had never met her before, had never told her anything about my background, and had never mentioned, that Dr. Dave and I were planning to write a book. But, she "knew" that Dr. Dave and I were writing my story.

There are many techniques you can use and practice to help you see and feel signs:

Observation:

As the song says, there are signs everywhere. All we have to do is to be aware of them. Are you seeing the same numbers recurring? Find out what they mean. Are you hearing the same song over and over again; playing almost every time you get in your car? Listen to the lyrics. Are you hearing the same message from the TV or a radio? Be aware of what the universe is trying to tell you. There is something going on around you all the time. Be more aware.

When the Universe gives you a Sign, Never ignore it!

Body Kinetics

As discussed above use the wisdom of your body to get answers. Use a pendulum or simply hold an object to your heart and feel your body moving forward or backward. Or, use dowsing rods to get answers. People use this technique to determine things such as, whether a particular herb or vitamin is what they need, or even if they should purchase something like an article of clothing. Your body knows!

Open a Book

Close your eyes and randomly open a book, like a Bible or a dictionary, and point somewhere on a page; open your eyes and read what you have placed your finger on. This was one of the techniques Denise Linn talked about in *The Secret Language of Signs.*

After reading her book when we were on a vacation, Dr. Dave did it, and his finger landed on the word "fat." He remarked, "Well that's certainly the right sign I'd better get back to my diet."

Divination

Divination is the practice of seeing divine or supernatural signs or omens that often may foretell future events. It is using your body's wisdom as well as being open to what the universe is telling you (or trying to tell you).

Healers have used the body's wisdom for thousands of years to diagnose health problems and even make simple decisions. **Kinesiology** is the scientific study of the body's muscles and their movements. **Applied kinesiology** is a technique developed by chiropractors in the 1960's based upon the theory that every organ dysfunction in the body is accompanied by a weakness in a specific corresponding muscle. By using manual muscle testing and conventional diagnostic methods, the chiropractor can evaluate structural, chemical and mental aspects of health.

A typical applied kinesiology test would involve having a patient resist a force applied by the therapist such as holding an arm out. By measuring the strength of the patient's resistance, a weak or strong muscle response can be observed. A weak muscle response would be indicative of stresses or imbalances in the body.

This is the technique Glen used on me the first time I went to see him. He called it, "Using the wisdom of the body's cells." By having me hold my arm out and asking me questions and measuring my resistance, or lack thereof, he was able to determine what was making me sick, which, in my case, was demonic possession.

Another technique that uses the body's wisdom to answer questions is a form of **body kinesiology**. Believing the body's cellular wisdom knows what's best for the body, it can help you make decisions. This technique is done by the individual. Standing up, you would hold something in your hands, clutching it toward your heart, and then close your eyes, asking yourself if your body needs it (such as a bottle of certain herbs). You then feel either a pull forward, meaning yes, or backwards, meaning no.

A simple diagnostic test many lightworkers use is with a **pendulum.** By, again, using the wisdom of the body, the lightworker either suspends a pendulum on a chain or has the client do so and asks questions with known answers, and observing which way the pendulum rotates. Once the directions of the rotation for yes and no responses are established, other questions can be asked and answered by the pendulum's rotation, reflecting the wisdom of the body. Usually, a clockwise rotation indicates a yes, and a counterclockwise rotation means no. A back-and-forth motion indicates a neutral response.

In the book, *People Who Don't Know They're Dead* by Gary Leon Hill, one of the lightworkers, Ruth Johnston, a psychiatric nurse, worked extensively with a pendulum. She would use it not only to get answers on entity possession and how to clear it, but also for everyday decisions in her life. When she and her colleagues encountered earthbound spirits that would not leave after asking them politely, she would ask the pendulum if Archangel Michael was needed. If she got a yes from the pendulum, she would call upon his assistance to help the entity move on.

Dr. Dave used this technique on me when I was experiencing a build-up of negative energy again. At the time, my eyes were red, tearing, and swollen, the lips and skin on my face dry and peeling, and I felt as if I was ten months pregnant again. Dr. Dave used the pendulum to ask if I was having an allergic reaction to something. The pendulum swung counterclockwise, saying "no." Should I go to my family doctor for medication? The pendulum swung counterclockwise again, "no." Are my symptoms from entity possession? The pendulum swung in a clockwise rotation, saying "yes." Should I go to a shaman for a clearing? The pendulum said, "no." Should I see Grace for a healing? The pendulum said, "yes."

Should I call upon Archangel Michael for help and protection? As Dr. Dave held the pendulum over me it began to swing in a clockwise motion even faster. For the other questions it would make a rotational arch of some six inches. But when we asked about Archangel Michael, it began to swing so fast it was almost horizontal. We took that as a BIG "YES." We couldn't believe it!

Dowsing

Prior to a Kriya yoga session with Rev. Ram Smith, he measured our energy fields with dowsing rods. He said he wanted to measure our aura fields before and after the session. He held two cylindrical handles to his chest that had two freely rotating L-shaped metal rods resting on their tops. He asked that I stand at the far wall and slowly walk toward him. When I was about nine feet from him, the rods rapidly spread apart. He commented that I had an unusually large aura field.

As Dr. Dave did the same, only one rod moved when he was about five feet from him. Ram stated that Dr. Dave must have a block on one side. After our yoga session Ram had us repeat the dowsing exercise. The room we were in was over twenty feet wide yet, after the session, the rods quickly spread apart when I was against the far wall. Dr. Dave's field also doubled and was balanced after the session as both rods spread apart for him.

The technique of dowsing has been documented going back thousands of years. It has also been called divining, doodlebugging, and water witching. Traditionally, a Y or L-shaped twig or rod is used to find water, precious metals, gems or even lost objects. Records of dowsing have been found in the Tassili Caves in Northern Africa, dating back eight thousand years, etchings in the pyramids over four thousand years old, in China twenty-five hundred years ago, in historical records from Greece as early as 400 BC, and in the Bible's Old Testament.

The modern practice of dowsing is believed to have originated in Germany during the fifteenth century when it was used to find metals. The 1550 edition of Sebastian Munster's *Cosmorgraphia* contained a woodcut of a man with a dowsing rod in hand, in a mining operation. The rod is labeled *"Virgula Divina"* meaning, in Latin, "divine rod." During the Middle Ages, dowsing became associated with superstition and it was thought that the "devil" was responsible for the rod's movement. In 1701, the Inquisition stopped the use of dowsing in trials. However, it was still used in mining operations, and the technique was discussed extensively in a *1747 Mining Dictionary* and in *The 1831 Quarterly Mining Review*. By the end of the twentieth century, there were an estimated thirty-five hundred books and articles on the ancient art of dowsing.

Trying to explain how dowsing works often leads to it's controversy. Supporters and skeptics of dowsing believe that the dowsing apparatus has no special powers, but merely amplifies the small imperceptible movements of the dowser's hands. This psychological phenomenon is known as the ideomotor effect. The evidence is highly disputed about whether or not the dowser has subliminal sensitivity to the environment or has paranormal powers.

The idiomatic effect may have some influence on a pendulum's swing or even the downward movement of a Y-shaped twig, but when the dowser is holding handles with free-swinging L rods atop of them, as Ram did with us, it would not matter how hard he squeezed the handles, as the rods simply rested on top of them, and each time he did it the rods reacted differently.

Dreams

Your dreams can be packed with signs. The key is to remember them. Our mind, conscious and subconscious, are always going, always thinking. Most people have five or six dreams a night and, usually, only recall the last one before waking up. That's why you could be having a great dream, wake-up in the middle of it to go to the bathroom, fall back to sleep and totally forget what it was about when you wake-up.

Keep a journal next to your bed. The next time you wake-up in the middle of the night, immediately write down what you where dreaming about. You can also do it in the morning when you wake up as well. By paying more attention to your dreams, you may receive more signs, more messages from Spirit.

Intuition

> *"In the still small voice, listen for an answer.*
> *It may be a whisper, sounding like a dream*
> *...It is the voice of God."*
>
> **~In the Still Small Voice**
> **By Mark Stanton Welch**

Your guides and angels are talking to you all the time. You just have to learn to "hear" what they are saying That feeling you have in your "gut", that twinge in the back of your neck, or that chill you get down your spine, all can be feelings you get from your guides (*clairsentience*). Remember, people with psychic gifts get positive messages. Guides and angels are here to help you. They will never hurt you. True intuitions, feelings or voices you get are always positive messages. Even if they are a warning not to do something, this is a positive, protective message.

Once, when with Michelle Sutton, I asked her how she gets talked to by her guides, as she always told me amazing things when I was with her. She said that she had learned to hear her messages through her yoga breaths. Having practiced yoga for years, she had learned to pause between breaths, and in that void she gets a message. The key is to start trusting your inner feelings.

Divine Connections

Just like the *"My Name is I AM"* poster I had gotten twenty years before my battles with Gordan, when I look around my house, the things I surrounded myself with all have meaning. My "Amazing Grace" song poster, butterflies, beacons (lighthouses), purple curtains, all have special meaning to me now.

Once when Dr. Dave was looking for a book in our night stand by our bed, he found a small book of one hundred affirmations given to me by an ex-boyfriend. As he was looking through it (he loves positive affirmations), he saw that the very first one was *"My Name Is I Am."*

Once you start investigating phenomenon like numerology, astrology, the significance of colors, or power animals, it becomes clear why you are drawn to things in your life. These are *Divine Connections* in your life. They often don't become clear until you look into the meaning of them.

Sometimes, you may feel you are drawn to a particular object, and you do not know why. These feelings are "soul feelings." Feelings you have deep in your soul, your essence that are coming through. It may be from a previous life, or it may be that God or the divine consciousness is forewarning you of things to come, like my butterfly!

Why do we get DIVINE HAPPENINGS?

- **They are messages from your guardian angels, your spirit guides, or from even higher spirit dimensions such as ascended masters or the Universal One/God/ Source!**
- **They are messages from the Universe; telling you to pay attention; stop and look.**
- **They are messages telling you that you are not alone in this life; that there is a spirit dimension out there; saying "Wake up we are here with you; protecting and guiding you always!"**

"The Divine is all around you, always!"

COCOON

By Cindy Curran

*Like a butterfly, you may be in the stage of a cocoon
If nothing seems to happen from full moon to full moon.
And your faithfully doing all your spiritual, positive living work
However, nothing is changing and bad luck still seems to lerk.
Don't give up or panic and think something is wrong
Know that your desires need time to develop and grow strong.
A cocoon appears to be doing nothing as it is hanging on a tree.
But a beautiful butterfly is transforming inside,
waiting for the right time to break free.*

A caterpillar is grounded until it turns into a butterfly
And when we see the butterfly, its beauty
and its wonderment makes us sigh.
Now the butterfly is free it can go places and do things never before.
In my opinion, its life is better now that the butterfly can do more.
Just about everything in life needs time to incubate.
Therefore, the waiting period you should never rush or hate.
A baby lives in the cocoon of the womb as many months as nine.
The baby takes time to develop and we think that's just fine.
An elephant is pregnant for twenty two months long.
When its calf is born, in elephant talk, I bet it sings a happy song.
In the cocoon of an egg, waiting to hatch, is a baby chick.
If it doesn't have time to develop properly, it won't hatch or hatch sick.
Even in the extremely tiny cocoon of a mustard seed.
A huge tree needs time to be freed.
We don't expect these things to develop faster
than what they are supposed to do.
Because we expect that everything happens according to a
Divine plan and right on cue.
The most amazing transformation happens
when a caterpillar is in a cocoon.
An amazing transformation in your life will
also happen to you very soon.
Just keep your thoughts, mental pictures and
emotions as positive as can be.
And you will see that the things in your mind,
in your outer world, you will soon see.
Never let yourself down because you haven't seen your desires yet.
Just keep your energy positive through the darkest times,
and you will see your desires met.
There are some things in life that do get worse before they get better.
To cheer yourself up try reading positive books or write a positive letter.
Remember the old adage, which states that
it is always darkest before dawn.

This is also true of your desires, before being born.
It's interesting to note the baby, butterfly, chick and the mustard tree,
They all have to struggle out of their
personalized cocoon before we can see.
And when we see, we marvel at the beauty
and magnificence of them all.
And we know that the power of creation is not something small.
And so it is the same with your positive thinking,
Therefore, don't give up on your desires, even if they seem to be sinking.
Because when your positive thinking cocoon is full it will burst open.
therefore, no matter how long your desires are taking to manifest,
stop all your mopin'.
Know that, when your desires are freed, you will say, "Wow!"
So say, "Wow!" to what you want manifested in your life right now.
Sometimes the insight and resulting happiness happens
when a challenge is big.
And when your desires manifest, like the elephant,
you'll be singing plus doing a jig.
Have faith that everything will happen
according to plan that is Divine.
And look to the cocoon stage as a very good sign.
Because to everything in life, each has their own season.
And after every thing is said and done, things do happen for a reason.
Therefore, if nothing seems to happen from full moon to full moon,
Know that amazing transformation is happening inside of a cocoon.

"To effectively communicate, we must realize that we are
all different in the way we perceive the world, and use this
understanding as a guide to our communication with others."
~ Anthony Robbins

VI ~ Divine Consciousness

*"...Seeking out completion, searching for the whole,...Oh, the one you seek, the one you seek is you. Go within to greet I Am, **I Am**."*
~The One You Seek
By Mark Stanton Welch

Where does our consciousness come from? Science can explain how the brain works. It can map out regions of the brain and tell us what they do and what they control in the body. It can explain how electrical impulses activate neurons in the brain and how different waking states produce different brain waves, even where memories are located. But to take a step further and try to explain what consciousness is, science falls short. And, if we asked a typical scientist or medical doctor to try to explain how consciousness can leave the body, he or she may try to dismiss the idea by saying that there is no "scientific" proof that it can.

However, Dr. Dave has done considerable research on the subject of "proving" that consciousness can leave the body. This research can explain how out-of-body experiences, astral projection, near-death-experiences, psychic energy, and reincarnation all work, even how our consciousness, our very essence, is eternal.

Being basically a scientist, Dr. Dave explained to me how science works, and how scientific principles are formed. He told me that, when other scientists repeatedly replicate an experiment's results, they start formulating a principle or theory, like the theory of gravity. You can be pretty certain, no matter who drops something, or where someone drops it (on earth), that it will go down. This replicated observation forms the principle of gravity, that the earth exerts a downward pull on anything (with mass) that is dropped. So even though you can't see it, *IT* exists.

Dr. Dave explains that before we can discuss or attempt to prove that phenomena like out-of-body experiences, psychic energy or reincarnation exist, we must first prove that our consciousness can exist outside of our body. Using the scientific method, we must first explore, and answer, the question, "Are there documented and replicated reports of consciousness existing outside of the body?"

"The trouble with the world is not that people know so little, but, that they know so many things that ain't so!   ~ **Mark Twain**

Out-of-Body Experiences

Dr. Dave believes existence of independent consciousness can be proven in a number of ways. One such way is usually referred to as an *Out-of-Body Experience* (OBE). OBE's are reported cases of human consciousness leaving and returning to the body. When the experience is a voluntary act it is called *astral projection* or *spirit walking*. When it is not, it is often called a *"near-death-experience"* or NDE. The term "out-of-body experience" was first introduced in 1943 by G.N.M. Tyrrell in his book, *Apparitions.*

Reports of people being able to leave their bodies and return date back to the ancient Greeks with Aristotle. Aristotle believed that the spirit could leave the body, converse with other spirits and return to the body. Researcher Dean Sheils found that out of sixty cultures he surveyed world-wide, fifty-seven of them reported belief and documented instances of people having out-of-body experiences. A report in *Science Daily* (August 24, 2007), states that one in ten people have had an OBE at some time in their life.

An ancient school of thought called *"Animism"* developed from primitive societies' belief that everything has a soul. Plants, animals, humans and even geological forms such as mountains, lakes, rivers, oceans, the moon, the sun, stars, and natural phenomenon like thunder, lightning, wind and rain, all have souls. Indigenous societies all over the world developed rituals to honor these souls. Some of these beliefs evolved into Greek mythology, and then into various religions across the world. All religions have the common belief that the soul, the unseen life force within everyone, can leave the physical body and transcend into the spirit world. Another animistic belief is that death occurs when the out-of-body soul does not return to the body.

The ancient religious scriptures of India, the Vedas, that influenced modern Hinduism and Buddhism, described humans as having seven different "bodies." The lowest energy body is the physical body. The rest they describe are nonphysical and invisible to normal human sight, corresponding to different planes and levels of reality, each vibrating at a higher frequency than the one below it. The energy body outside of the physical body is the etheric body. This is what is often seen by those with psychic abilities as a glowing halo around the body.

Outside the etheric body is the astral or emotional body. It is a layer of emotional energy that changes colors, based on one's emotional state of mind. Clairvoyants and psychics may be able to see these colors, and giving them insights to other's feelings. Outside the astral body, vibrating at a finer or higher vibration, is the mental body. Beyond the mental energy body lies the spiritual body, connecting the individual to the spiritual plane. Still higher energy bodies outside the spiritual body are called casual energy fields or planes.

In the Indian philosophy, there is an entire world, the astral plane, that exists between the physical and the highest spiritual worlds. This world is composed of an incalculable number of planes and subplanes that rise in an ascending scale based on increasing vibrational frequencies. Lower astral planes are where earthbound spirits reside. In the higher planes more spiritually evolved beings like masters, guides and teachers exist.

The Vedas describe that during sleep we can travel through the astral plane. During death, one leaves the physical body and continues to journey into higher planes of existence, bringing along memories. After staying in the astral plane the soul continues to rise to the mental plane, leaving behind the astral energy body as well. The soul continues upward awaiting rebirth into a physical body.

A religious philosophy that was influenced by ancient Greece and Renaissance philosophers that promotes metaphysics is *Theosophy*. Theosophy in Greek means *"God wisdom"* and it was established as a religion in 1875. Theosophists trace the origins of their religion to the universal striving for spiritual knowledge that existed in all cultures. From the writings of Plato to Renaissance philosophers like Paracelsus, Robert Fludd, and Jacob Boehme, Theosophists believe that consciousness exists everywhere. Spiritual units of consciousness called *Monads* can manifest as angels, human beings or other forms, and are the reincarnating parts of the human soul. They also believe that out-of-body experiences happen when the astral body separates from the physical body.

Also during the mid 1800's, a movement called *"Spiritism"* promoted the belief in consciousness outside of the body. A French educator, Allan Kardec (1804-1869) wrote a number of books promoting a philosophical doctrine that endorsed the belief in the existence of spirits, non-physical beings that live in the invisible or spirit world, and the possibility of communication between these spirits and living people through mediumship. Five main points of the Spiritist doctrine are:

1. There is a God as "the Supreme Intelligence and Primary Cause of everything."
2. There are Spirits, all of whom are created simple and

ignorant, but own the power to gradually perfect themselves.

3. The natural method of this perfection process is reincarnation, through which the Spirit faces countless different situations, problems and obstacles, and needs to learn how to deal with them.

4. As part of nature, Spirits can naturally communicate with living people, as well as interfere in their lives.

5. Many planets in the universe are inhabited.

The central tenet of Spiritism is the belief that the spirit is eternal. It evolves through a series of incarnations in the material world. The true life is the spiritual one; life in the physical world is just a short-term stage where the spirit has the opportunity to learn and evolve. Reincarnation is the process where the spirit, once free in the spiritual world, comes back to the world for further learning.

A type of *New Age* religion that attempts to connect the West with many of the religious philosophies of the East is *Eckankar*. Eckankar means "Co-worker with God" and was founded by spiritual leader Paul Twitchell in 1965. Eckankar teaches that there is one Supreme Being, the Holy Spirit or God, that the soul is eternal, and that it is on a journey of self and God-realization. Adherents believe that the soul unfolds via karma and reincarnation, and you can learn to explore spiritual worlds through soul travel (similar to astral projection). Eckankar today operates throughout the United States and is world-wide (see www.eckankar.org).

Astral Projection

Another way consciousness can leave the body is through astral projection This involves willingly projecting one's consciousness out of his or her body while in a meditative state. The experience, unlike a dream, occurs in real time, and the individual projecting reports observations of events going on that the meditating body could not possibly be aware of. For example, a person lying and meditating on the East Coast that astrally projects her consciousness to her brother's house on the West Coast is able to tell her brother who he had over for dinner that night and what they were saying at the dinner table.

Astral projection is also a premise in Theosophy. Theosophists believe that the human body consists of several energy bodies around the physical body. The outer energy body is called the etheric double and is constant, in that it does not change as the physical body ages or dies. When the body does die, the etheric double becomes reabsorbed into the elements of which it was composed. Outside the etheric double body is the astral body.

The astral body is also a replica of the physical body, but supersensitive and vibrating at a higher frequency. It is believed that everything in the physical world has an astral counterpart, and there are things in the astral world that have no counterpart in the physical world, such as just thought entities. These entities may be used in ritual magic, healings, and in carrying messages or information.

People with the ability to see energy, such as psychics, are able to see a change in a person's thoughts or moods by seeing the different colors projected by their astral body. The astral body can be seen as a bright shinning glow around the physical body that is referred to as the astral aura. The aura can be multi-colored and brilliant, or dull according to the individual's character, mood, or energy.

During astral projection, consciousness can travel without limit in the astral realm. It interacts with astral things, not physical things. It is believed that during sleep the astral body can separate from the physical body. Since it is the astral body that is the vehicle of consciousness, it is the astral body, not the physical body, that is aware of what is happening when outside the body. For most of us that do not remember astral experiences, our travels during sleep are vague, directionless, and without purpose. But, for the trained astral traveler, the journey can be controlled, allowing the individual to travel limitless distances recall all details of his or her travels.

Theosophy believes that the astral body is connected to the physical body with a silver cord that can stretch endlessly. The cord must remain attached or death will occur. When one does approach death the astral body lifts up and away from the physical body and the silver cord breaks to allow the astral and higher energy bodies to leave. Death is seen as a type of permanent astral projection.

In the early 1900s, Sylvan Muldoon, with the help of psychic researcher Hereward Carrington described his experiences of willful astral projection in *The Projection of the Astral Body* (1929). Along with Muldoon's astral journeys they documented a number of other accounts of spontaneous OBEs or astral projections.

Baird T. Spalding described encounters with Masters that could at will, astrally project. In *Life and Teaching of the Masters of the Far East* (1964), he states that a Master named Emil was able to transport himself instantaneously over hundreds of miles. During their journey through the Himalayans Emil stayed behind in a village with a member of Spalding's party, while Spalding and the rest of the group traveled for five days to another village. When they arrived at the village, Emil told them he would meet them, to their amazement, he was there waiting for them. When the member that was left behind joined Spalding he told them he had been with Emil until four o'clock in the afternoon when Emil lay down to take a nap. At that same time, he appeared at Spalding's village ninety miles away.

Robert Crookall, in the 1960's, reported accounts of astral projection in several books: *The Study and Practice of Astral Projection* (1961), *More Astral Projections* (1964), *The Mechanisms of Astral Projection* (1969), *Out-of-the-Body Experiences* (1970), and *What Happens When You Die* (1978). He documents hundreds of cases of astral projection, and describes techniques on how to do it.

Celia Green in her book, *Out-of-the-Body Experiences* (1968), collected written and first hand accounts of four hundred subjects that reported having OBE's. Less than 4 percent of her subjects reported being attached by a silver cord. Most (80 percent) stated that they felt that they were a "disembodied consciousness."

Near-Death-Experiences

The most documented cases of human consciousness leaving the physical body, observing what is going on and returning to the body is in what are called *near-death-experiences* (NDE's). In a NDE, a person is "clinically dead" (no heart beat or brainwave function) for a number of minutes (usually). During that time, the NDE person experiences his or her consciousness leaving the body and can see what is going on. Often, the person sees doctors or paramedics working on his or her body on an operating table or at a scene of an accident. Or, the person reports moving through a tunnel or toward a bright light or, even, seeing and talking to deceased loved ones and family members. Then the individual abruptly, often against his or her wishes, return to the body and regains consciousness.

Researchers Raymond Moody and Kenneth Ring spent years interviewing cases of people who had NDE's and have documented hundreds of such reports. What they believed to be happening in the NDEs was that individuals' consciousness was ejected from their physical body into their astral body. Being outside their physical body, they are not only able to observe their body and what is going on, but they also often feel a link to the spirit dimension. NDE individuals often report a feeling of extreme peace and calmness when touching the spirit world. Sometimes there is a feeling of remorse when turning away from the "bright, loving light" they are sensing, to return to their physical body.

In another study, Dutch cardiologist Dr. Pim van Lommel reports and documents cases of 344 patients that had been resuscitated after suffering cardiac arrest. Of the 344 patients, 18 percent reported NDE's that included an out-of-body experience. They remembered details of their cardiac arrest, despite being clinically dead with flat-lined brain wave activity. Dr. Van Lommel concluded that consciousness continued despite the lack of neuronal activity in the brain. He stated, "At that moment these people are not only conscious; their consciousness is more expansive than ever. They can think extremely clearly, have memories going back to their earliest childhood and experience an intense connection with everything and everyone around them, and yet, the brain shows no activity at all!"

Dr. Van Lommel believes that the brain may be acting like a receiver of information that is generated by memories and consciousness. The brain exists independently of consciousness and tunes into consciousness as a radio or TV picks-up radio waves in order to operate.

The most comprehensive study to date on NDE's was complied by Dr. Jeffrey Long. With the aid of his Website, *www.NDERF. org* (Near Death Experience Research Foundation) he collected and documented sixteen hundred cases of NDE's in his book, *Evidence of the Afterlife* (2010). Dr. Long reports that the cases he collected represent every age group from cultures from around the world. Through his findings and by looking into research by other investigators such as Moody and Ring, he found that those having had NDE's reported a number of similar experiences: They reported an out-of-body experience, heightened senses, emotions, and feelings, passing through a tunnel and seeing a brilliant light, encountering other beings such as deceased relatives, friends or mystical beings, loss of the sense of time and space, encountering or learning special knowledge, and either a voluntary or involuntary return to the body.

Dr. Long believes that his research proves with more than 99 percent certainty that life after death exists, based on his nine lines of evidence. Similar to Van Lommel's assertion, his first line of evidence reports that consciousness is fully functional, even heightened when the individual is clinically dead. They report witnessing events happening that are later verified, even when under anesthesia, unconscious or blind from birth. The NDE's are consistent around the world, independent of the individual's religious, cultural, or ethnic backgrounds. And all report seeing similar phenomenon during their NDE, such as deceased relatives and having powerful and lasting life changing effects after the event.

The International Association for Near-Death Studies, Inc. (IANDS) has a Website that answers questions and continues to document near-death-experiences.

> *"A Human being is a part of a whole, called by us universe,' a part limited in time and space. He experiences himself, his thoughts and feelings as something separated from the rest...a kind of optical delusion of his consciousness. This delusion is a kind of prison for us, restricting us to our personal desires and to affection to a few persons nearest to us. Our task must be to free ourselves from this prison by widening our circle of compassion to embrace all living creatures and the whole of nature in its beauty."*
>
> **~ Albert Einstein**

Animal Consciousness

Some may doubt that human consciousness may leave the body, or that psychics are, in fact, psychic. However, when we observe the psychic abilities of the animal kingdom even more questions of traveling consciousness can be raised. It's often been observed that wild animals can "sense" impending danger. They flee areas before a earthquake, tidal wave, tornado, or hurricane occurs.

Pet owners know that their pets often show signs of "animal telepathy." Pets "know" when someone is coming home. They often sense what their owner is going to do before he or she does it. Today it is not uncommon for doctors to recommend to their patients with significant health problems like epilepsy to have a pet dog that will alert them before they have a seizure. Biologists would rationalize these behaviors as examples that animals simply have sharper senses, but their behavior often goes far beyond what they can sense in their immediate environment.

A British biologist, Rupert Sheldrake, developed a controlled study to see if, in fact, dogs and cats could read their owners' minds. In one study, he simply contacted sixty-five veterinarians in London and asked them if it was common that cat owners would cancel their appointments because they couldn't find their cats the day of the appointment. All sixty-five reported that it was quite common.

In another study, Sheldrake performed with dogs, he questioned whether dogs got excited to go for a walk out of routine or if they could really pick up "vibes" from their owners when their owners were just thinking of taking them for a walk. So, to test the dog's telepathy, he placed them in isolated outbuildings, and videotaped them there. He had the owners start concentrating on taking their pets out for a walk at different times during the day. In over half of the dogs in the study, when their owners were thinking of taking them for a walk, the dogs started wagging their tails and circling restlessly by the doors until their owners appeared. No dog showed anticipatory behavior when their owners were not thinking about taking them for a walk. Sheldrake suggested that his studies showed that the bond between a pet and its owner creates a subtle connection at the level of thought.

A doctor that makes rounds in a nursing home in Providence, Rhode Island also questions whether an animal knows more than he. In this case, a cat named Oscar that resides in the nursing home has the uncanny ability of predicting when a resident will die. David Dosa, M.D., in his book, *Making Rounds with Oscar: The Extraordinary Gift of an Ordinary Cat* (2009), documents how Oscar would go to a resident's room and sit by his or her side until the person died. In the past two years, Oscar has sat watch next to fifty patients until they died. Dosa says that Oscar is not the only cat in the nursing home. There are five others, and they do not exhibit this behavior. And it's not that Oscar is a social cat either; he is rarely seen in patients' rooms until they are about to die. Then he will keep watch from a few hours to a couple of days before the patient passes on.

Dr. Dosa, who is also an assistant professor of medicine at Brown University's Medical School, believes that Oscar's "sixth sense" may be due to his ability to detect a chemical the dying patient may be emitting before dying called ketones. These are biochemicals that cells emit when they begin to degenerate. If Oscar's keen sense of smell is picking up these ketones and is the reason he is visiting dying patients, it is still a mystery why he is the only cat with this ability.

Several times during my ordeals with negative entities, my pet beagle, Felicia, would growl and bark continuously at the air. This behavior was very unusual for her. Occasionally she would bark when another dog walked down the street past the house, but would stop when the other dog went by. But in the cases when I was physically sick, being attacked again by these negative entities, she would stand in the middle of the living room barking at what seemed like thin air for hours at a time. I knew she was sensing energies I couldn't see (but certainly felt) at that time.

This sixth sense of animal telepathy so often witnessed, along with countless examples of human consciousness leaving and returning in OBEs, constitutes clinical evidence of the existence of consciousness outside of the body.

How consciousness travels outside the body is another matter. Does it travel in waves, where psychics tune them in? Or, is psychic energy and traveling consciousness instantaneous as Professor Tiller suggests (see Chapter VII: Energy Healing)? And, can consciousness travel through dimensions? To take a look at how consciousness can continue through time we must look into evidence that reincarnation exists.

Proving Reincarnation

When Dr. Dave talks about reincarnation he also does so from a scientific premise. He says that the problem skeptics raise with reincarnation, particularly when revealed during hypnotherapy, is: How do you prove it? He could regress a patient into a past life and that patient would tell him of living in Medieval times as a princess, and then dying in child birth. How do you prove that person really once lived that life hundreds of years ago? Even if they came up with a name and location that could be verified in historical records, how do we know that that patient didn't read about it at some time in her life, buried in her subconscious, and simply remembered the story while under hypnosis? This is the problem with proving reincarnation experiences.

The belief in reincarnation dates back thousands of years and is a global concept. It sprang up independently all over the world, and it is believed by millions today. It is the cornerstone of religions such as Buddhism, Hinduism, and the Sufi sects of Islam.

Reincarnation was also a belief in Christianity until the Roman emperor, Constantine, who, at the Council of Nicaea, in 325 ACE, declared it heretical. At the time, the church felt the belief in multiple lives would give people too much time to "redeem" their sins, so all references to reincarnation were removed from all religious publications.

Once when meeting with shaman Joey Stann, he told Dr. Dave and I of visions he has had of being a shamanic healer for the past sixty thousand years. He said that through drumming circles and going into deep meditation, he visualized himself living in ancient Atlantis. During one ceremony of drumming and deep breathing with a group, he found that they all had experienced the same past life. After the ceremony was over, each participant was asked to write down what he or she experienced. Then they went around the circle, telling what they had written down. Joey said he was amazed that they reported being in the same place and seeing the same things.

Joey also said that we travel with the same soul groups from lifetime to lifetime. Often master teachers are reincarnated. For example, Abraham (Earth Incarnation: 1,812 to 1,637 BC), Buddha (E.I: 563 to 483 BC), Jesus (E.I: 0 to 35 AC), Saint Germain (E.I:

496 to 576 AC) and the Dali Lama (E.I: 1391 to 1474 AC) are all the same soul.

Joey then took a deep breath and seemed to look through me and said, "You were Pocahontas, an Indian princess in a previous life." Then he turned to Dr. Dave and said, "I see you were Geronimo in a previous life, and you are also a master teacher. I see why you are with Mary. You are here to help her." Now, unknown to Joey, Dr. Dave had a large portrait of Geronimo in his den. He thought that Geronimo looked like his great grandmother; that's why he had brought a picture of him years before ever meeting Joey.

It seems that the West has more difficulty believing in past lives than the East. Deepak Chopra, in *Life After Death; The Burden of Proof* (2006) states that the East has been able to embrace the concepts of reincarnation for several reasons. People in Eastern cultures embrace the idea of energy conservation, that the energy in the universe is constant. Energy just changes; it does not die; it gets re-created in different forms. Our life essence (soul) continues from life to life.

So, why would our conscious-soul-energy be any different? They also believe that if we can come back into a new body, in a new life, we can fulfill desires and ambitions that were unfinished in a previous lifetime. Being with loved ones again in the next life is consoling. Reincarnation also gives hope for social advancement. A slave in one life can return to be a master in the next. This belief in social, evolutionary, and soul advancement from one lifetime to the next, until one approaches enlightenment, is a fundamental principle of Buddhism.

Edgar Cayce (1877 to 1945), a psychic who would put himself in a trace to connect with psychic energies, reluctantly promoted reincarnation. Being a devout Christian, he did not believe his own readings, initially, when he uncovered clients' past lives. What he discovered after thousands of readings was that reincarnation was God's plan to help us evolve through life lessons. Animals, he reported, have their own path and humans do not reincarnate as animals.

A number of more recent researchers in the West have "proven" that reincarnation exists. Among them are Ian Stevenson, M.D., Michael Newton, Ph.D. and Brian Weiss, M.D.

Dr. Stevenson, professor of psychiatry at the University of Virginia, researched claims primarily from children that were recalling reincarnation-type memories. He documented over two thousand cases where children would describe places where they had lived before.

The children Dr. Stevenson interviewed were able to describe the house they lived in, the town they lived in, and even who they lived with. Some were able to speak languages that they were never exposed to in their present life. Dr. Stevenson researched these claims and verified that the information recalled by the children was true. He concluded that the only explanation is that these children had, in fact, lived in these places in a previous life.

Dr. Newton and Dr. Weiss both documented in several books, thousands of cases of reincarnation experiences/past lives, using hypnosis. Dr. Newton, author of *Destiny of Souls* (2004), *Life Between Lives* (2006), and *Journey of Souls* (2006), not only regressed people into past lives, but he also had them talk of the time between lives, where they were before they were born, their time in the spirit realm.

Dr. Weiss was chief resident in psychiatry at Yale University School of Medicine, and later chairman of the Department of Psychiatry at Mount Sinai Medical Center in Miami, Florida. He is author of best selling books, such as *Many Lives, Many Masters* (1988), and *Messages from the Masters* (2000). Like Dr. Newton, Dr. Weiss was able to regress patients into past lives and the time between lives.

Perhaps, if you regress one or two or six people into that time between lives, and they tell you similar stories, it could be considered coincidence. Or, even expected, in terms of popular beliefs of what the spirit world might be like. However, when thousands of people from all different walks of life, all different cultural and religious backgrounds, all tell of the same experiences and what the spirit world is like, you have what is considered "clinically significant" evidence. And, when several researchers come up with the same results, we can develop a universal principle or theory, just as in any other scientific principle or theory. These researchers have, without a doubt, proven that reincarnation exists. They describe **facts** like:

- *We plan the life we come into based on what we want and need to learn.*
- *We travel from life to life with many of the same people that make up our soul-group, including our soul-mate.*
- *Our souls are immortal; we do not die; our loved ones do not die; We merely transition into the spirit world when we leave our physical bodies, being reunited with our loved ones.*
- *The challenges in our life are often predestined by us in order to "grow our souls."*
- *There is no "heaven or hell," only the spirit realm that exists in another dimension.*
- *The purpose of our life on earth is to learn and grow spiritually.*
- *We do have spirit guides that are with us and help us all the time.*
- *We are eternal spiritual beings, simply having a brief, physical experience on this Earth.*

"*...Better recognize your brothers, ev'ryone you meet.*
Why in the world are we here? Surely
not to live in pain and fear!
...Well we all shine on, like the moon
and the stars and the sun

...On and on and on and on
~Instant Karma
By John Lennon

Soul Memories

"The Universe itself is a thought, a thought from which was born a dream, which is partially visible as matter. You are infinite, you are eternal; within in you are your dreams of creation."

~ Anastasia

Ever have a feeling of having done something before when you were doing it for the first time? Been to a new place and know you have been there before? Met someone for the first time and instantly felt connected to him or her? These are soul memories. Memories coming to you from a previous life. This is often called a *Déjà vu* experience that comes from the French phrase that means "already seen."

Children are often much more open to these experiences than adults, perhaps because they haven't lost as many memories as adults have of their previous lives. Or, perhaps, they haven't been as conditioned by this life yet, as adults have.

Do you prefer mountains to the ocean? The ocean rather than a drier climate? Do you like walking through the country, or, are you are drawn to the city life? Do you feel drawn to a certain type of house architecture? Are you drawn to music or art? To a certain profession? To certain people in your life (friends or relatives)? We are not consciously aware of why, but our soul knows and compels us to do certain things. These are often memories coming into our subconscious from a previous life, soul memories.

Clarissa Pinkola Estes, Ph.D., in *Women Who Run with the Wolves* (1992) states that our soul has a memory, a homing device: "...Even when it is our own dismal choices that have blown us off course, too far from what we need, hold faith, for within the soul is the homing device. We all can find our way back."

When I think of things I have been drawn to all my life and then I've had psychics tell me who I was in previous lives, it makes uncanny, perfect sense to me now. Several psychics told me that Jesus is my guardian angel, and it turned out to be quite a *Divine Happening* that twenty years ago I bought a house on Sharon Street (off of Pleasant Valley Parkway), in God's *"Providence."* And, I recently found out that Jesus was also called the *"Rose of Sharon."* Of all the places I could be living in, Rhode Island also has towns of Galilee and Jerusalem, as in a **New Jerusalem!**

"You do not have to imitate or compete, for you are a special creation of God, as everyone else, and you have full access to the unlimited potential of infinite Intelligences." - **Dr. Ernest Holmes**

Ancient Wisdom

"The ancient new, because the ancients knew!"

Regression therapist Andy Tomlinson, in his book *Healing The Eternal Soul,* describes four universal principles of **Ancient Wisdom**. The first principle is **The Law of Correspondence**. This principle explains how the spirit dimension operates. Just as the *Big Bang* theory explains how the physical universe may have started, the Law of Correspondence explains how the universal spirit energy started from a single source and then smaller pieces broke off to start creating souls.

Every person has a soul that is pure spirit energy. This soul energy body contains all our memories and experiences gathered from each physical life lived. Our soul energy body grows with each life when lessons are learned, until physical incarnations are not needed. We can then stay in the spirit dimension as a guide or teacher unless we would like to be born again to do the same on earth.

The second principle is ***The Law of Karma***. Karma is usually thought of as *"what goes around comes around"* or, as the Bible put it, *"as you sow, so shall you reap."* But, in Ancient Wisdom terms, it goes a lot deeper. Karma is the spiritual payback that your soul has to ***learn*** in order to grow and move up the "spiritual ladder" so-to-speak. It is where the abuser learns how the abused feels when in a subsequent life he or she becomes the abused, the victim. The robber gets robbed, and the killer gets killed in the next life. It is where forgiveness is learned for the deeds we have done and what others have done to us. If lessons are not resolved and learned they are repeated in the next life until they are.

The third ancient principle is ***Reincarnation***. Our souls are eternal. Only the physical body dies. What makes up us, our essence, continues on and on, continually evolving through life lessons learned in each lifetime.

The fourth principle is the ***Law of Attraction***. This principle is the concept that we travel in soul groups. The same people appear in instrumental roles in our lives to help us with life lessons. In a past life, your mother may have been your sister or your daughter. When in the spirit dimension, we plan the roles we will play in each others' lives to help us learn and grow spiritually.

This was what Jackie (see Chapter IV: My Divine Journey) was talking about when she saw (without having ever met Dr. Dave) that he and I had been together in several lifetimes, in many different roles. She saw that we were brother and sister, best friends in the military and husband and wife in the past. And, she saw us as true soul-mates continuing into the future.

> *"The only way I will be great to myself it is not what I do to my body; it is what I do to my mind…. We are here to be creators we are here to infiltrate space with mansions of thought, to make something of this life."*
>
> ~ **Ramtha (J.Z. Knight)**
> ***What The Bleep Do We Know!?***

Psychic Consciousness

It appears that when consciousness leaves the body it can travel like radio waves. Dr. Ernest Holmes, author of *The Science of Mind: A Philosophy, A Faith, A Way of Life* (1938) and founder of the Science of Mind religion, makes the same assertion about consciousness:

> *"Recognizing that we are surrounded by a Universal Mind, it does not seem strange that certain people should sense our thoughts even when we are not aware of the fact, because thought operates through a medium which is Universal…always present.*
>
> *"This all leads to the conclusion that what we call our subjective mind is really the use that we, as individuals, make of a Universal Subjectivity. Just as radio messages are operative through a universal medium, so our thoughts are operative through a Universal Medium."*

When psychics tune in, when people have premonitions, or when dreams foretell the future, all may be using the ability to pick up on these thought waves that are continuously traveling through space (in this dimension and others) and time, the Universal Medium, that Dr. Ernest Holmes describes.

In a famous controlled experiment by the University of Stanford, psychic abilities were confirmed. In 1972, a sensing device called a SQUID (Superconducting Quantum Interference Device) was installed in the basement of a physics lab at the university. The SQUID recorded the magnetic field of the earth on a graph that produced a continuous S-curve.

A New York artist and gifted psychic, Ingo Swann, was flown in for the experiment. He was asked to project his consciousness into the SQUID. When he did this, the SQUID started to record a straight line, something it had never done before. When Swann stopped concentrating on it, the SQUID resumed its S-curve graph. When asked to concentrate again on the SQUID the same straight-line graph was produced for the forty-five seconds Swann concentrated on it. Swann then drew an accurate diagram of the inner workings of the SQUID, having never seen the device before.

An extremely thorough investigation of the existence of consciousness outside of the body can be found in Dr. Dean Radin's book, *The Conscious Universe: The Scientific Truth of Psychic Phenomena* (1997). Dr. Radin states that even with tens of thousands reports from around the world for centuries, of psychic phenomena such as telepathy, clairvoyance, psychokinesis, and precognition, the scientific community states that there is no "scientific proof" that such phenomena is real. Dr. Radin explains that science is always built upon replicated experimental results. He states that typically psychic phenomena is not replicated, and therein lies the problem the scientific community has with it all. However, natural phenomena such as meteor showers or ball lightning can be difficult to replicate as well, yet science accepts them as real.

Dr. Radin uses "scientific" methods, such as statistical analysis, to prove the existence of psychic phenomena he refers to as *"psi."* He states that the replicated results that verifies scientific experiments is acceptable at 50 percent, meaning that a successfully replicated result is considered acceptable if you get the same results at least half of the time. The most widely accepted method of statistical analysis today in science is called *"meta-analysis."* This is the statistical analysis of all studies conducted on a subject, rather than looking at individual trials of one study or experiment.

Using meta-analysis, Dr. Radin reports that from 1880 through 1995 there have been over three hundred studies of psi (ESP, telepathy, remote-viewing, dream-telepathy) with over 5.6 million participants that shows a successful "hit" rate of theses studies in excess of 50 percent. The meta-analysis reports that the overall odds of chance that this meta-analysis is *incorrect* is ten million to one. Dr. Radin concludes "What psi offers to the puzzle about consciousness is the observation that information can be obtained in ways that bypass the ordinary sensory system altogether, and there may be ways of directly influencing the outer world by mental means alone."

His investigation of scientific research of the past one hundred-plus years confirms the existence of psychic phenomena. He also states, "Much of the awe and wonder of traditional religions comes from stories of miracles, which are dramatic illustrations of divine power. From a parapsychological point of view, the great religious scriptures are encyclopedic repositories of stories about psi effects; telepathy, clairvoyance, precognition, mental healing, and mind-matter interactions."

Eternal Consciousness

Unseen forces affect us all the time. Few can discount the important role that gravity or even air plays in our physical lives. And where would our technology be without radio waves that operate our radios, TVs, and wireless devices? Yet, when it comes to psychic abilities or OBE's, people often have trouble with these concepts because they are "unseen."

Deepak Chopra points out that our visible universe comprises only 4 percent of the total mass and energy in the universe. That means that 96 percent of the universe is unseen energy. This unseen energy is in and all around our "physical" dimension.

The small band of energy we can see is called visible light. All the other frequencies of wave energy that greatly affect our lives, like radio waves, microwaves, infrared radiation, ultraviolet radiation, X-rays, and gamma rays, are unseen.

Consciousness is the same. Just because we cannot see it doesn't mean it does not exist. Science has even confirmed the existence of psychic phenomena, through quantum physics. Quantum physics asserts that information can "jump" from particle to particle, even through dimensions. This information, or consciousness, is thought to be energy traveling outside the body. Consciousness can enter into different dimensions and times. And, it is eternal.

"...The heart and brain have access to a field of information not bound by time or space..... The body is constantly connecting with information in the fields around it....When you correct the distorted information coming into the body you can heal the body....Our body is controlled by our mind not our genes."

~ The Living Matrix

Consciousness, therefore, is the "me" part of the soul. It is the ego, the sense of I that is eternal, that part of you that stays with you from lifetime to lifetime. It may travel in a present life, in an OBE, or as an astral projection that can witness other places, maybe even other times. Or, it may leave the body temporarily in a near-death-experience. It may travel like radio waves, or it may move instantaneously through space and time. Our consciousness-soul-energy is part of the 96 percent of the universe that is unseen energy. It goes on and on and on!

I Am Consciousness

"Life is a mirror and will reflect back to the thinker what he thinks into it."

~ Dr. Ernest Holmes

Sometimes when you look back at various things that have shaped your life and then you find out what they mean, it all makes perfect sense. As described above in the previous section, *Soul Memories*, such was the case with the power of "I Am." I never gave the words much thought when I framed the poster of *"My Name Is I Am"* that I hung in my den twenty years ago. Nor did I pay much attention to them, even in my battle with Gordan when I blurted out *"I Am"* for some reason.

I don't know how many times when I was growing up that I had seen *The Ten Commandments* on TV, and never took note of one particular part, until one day Dr. Dave called to me when it was on and said, "Mary, look at this." It was at the part when Moses was talking to the burning bush, that God was talking through, and he asked, "By what name should I call you?" God answered, "Simply call me, *I Am*!"

Susan Shumsky, Ph.D., in *Divine Revelation* (1996) describes the *I Am* consciousness quite nicely. She states, "The I Am presence is the indwelling of God at the core of your being. It is your divine self, the aspect of yourself that is one with God. It is your divine consciousness. It is God's perfect image of you, your perfect self, the oneness of Spirit within you." She says it is the "*OM*," the creative word of God. "I Am" means "I exist and know myself to be." When you say "I Am" you are connecting with the God-source within yourself, as well as to the universal energies of God.

Dr. Shumsky describes Jesus as a great example of the creative use of the "I AM," consciousness. The miracles he performed were the practical use of God's law of "I Am" in action. She reminds us that Jesus said:

> "*I AM* the way, the truth and the life…
> *I AM* the light of the world…
> *I AM* the resurrection, and the life."

Godfre' Ray King, who channels ascended master Saint Germain, devotes an entire book to the power of the I AM presence in *The I AM Discourses* (1940). In it, Saint Germain describes "I AM as the mighty presence of God in you-in action." When you recognize it, "You will have taken one of the greatest steps to liberation."

Through my awakening I have learned the power of *I AM*. When you say "*I AM*" you are connecting to Universal energies, for good or bad. If you say something like, "I AM depressed." You attract those negative energies to you. You become what you think, what you say to yourself. I find it amazing that so many people still do not realize the power of their own words and how they continually attract exactly what they do not want in life.

It is not uncommon to hear people say things like; "I AM; anxious, scared, depressed, unable to do this, broke, unattractive, too fat, too stupid, not good enough." By saying such things, they are attracting Universal energies to them, giving them just what they are saying. By saying what you want, you do the same. You start connecting with the Universal energies, connecting with the God-source within and attracting what you want in life.

> *"Change your thoughts and change your world!"*
> ~ **Norman Vincent Peale**

Bruce Lipton, Ph.D., author of *Biology of Belief: Unleashing the Power of Consciousness, Matter and Miracles* (2005) and *Spontaneous Evolution: Our Positive Future* (2009), describes the new science of epigenetics. Epigenetics is how your beliefs influence your genes. They can turn things like cancer cells on or off. He says that your beliefs are energy fields that shape your genetic expression. Extensive documentation shows that the placebo effect greatly influences the individual. By taking something as innocuous as a sugar pill, but believing it has a specific effect on the body, a person experiences that expected effect.

Dr. Lipton describes that the reverse is just as possible. This is the *"Nocebo Effect,"* that negatives beliefs can make you physically sick. He states, "Your positive and negative beliefs are equally positive. If you think you are powerless then that thought will manifest, you will become a 'victim' of your predispositions."

> *"Whether you think you can or think you can't, you're right!"*
> ~ **Henry Ford**

Use the power of *I AM* to start transforming your life! Make a list of what you want to change. Put it in *I AM* positive statements and put it on your bathroom mirror. Recite it when you get up in the morning and before you go to bed at night. Start attracting what you want in life. As Jesus said:

"You can renew your life through your beliefs!"

I now know the power of my thoughts, my beliefs. Psychologists tell us that when you do something differently, and daily for twenty-one consecutive days, it becomes a habit. By using the power of *I AM,* it will change how you think and start *transforming* your life. Say:

"I AM Prosperity."
"I AM Happy."
"I AM Attractive."
"I Am Smart and Resourceful."
"I Am Loved."

Turn the word IMPOSSIBLE to I'M POSSIBLE to *I AM POSSIBLE!* The power of I AM consciousness can change your life. Perhaps, learning about it was one of your soul's purpose in this life. Perhaps, using the power of I AM consciousness will lead you to your spiritual awakening!

"You don't get what you want; you get what you can take, and the taking is all mental."

~ Dr. Ernest Holmes

I Am
By Dona Oxford

Sheila Sinapi, Exe. Producer

I am stronger than a willow tree in winter
I am beautiful because my mother told me so
I'm patient like a flower awaiting springtime
I'm as graceful as a new born baby doe
I am taller than the pyramids of Egypt

I am worth more than the diamond on your hand
I am gentler than a summer breeze in August
I am all these things, just because
I AM

"We create our own reality; we only see what our minds
believe we see."
~ What The Bleep Do We Know!?

" Our beliefs about what we are and what we can be,
precisely determine what we will be."
~ Anthony Robbins

"If you complain you will remain.
But, if you praise you will be raised."
~ Joel Osteen

VII ~ Energy Healing: Connecting with the Divine

"There are no miracles, but, just the natural byproducts of proper use of God's Universal Laws in action."

~ Dr. Joshua David Stone

At our first Divinely Touched conference, Dr. Dave discussed how energy healing works. He explained that just as consciousness is unseen, the invisible energy within the body, and around the body has been used for healing long before records of healing were ever kept.

Throughout history, different cultures determined that the human body is composed of various energy layers, and by manipulating these energy layers, or points, healing can be affected. In this century, science is "getting in on the act." It is trying to explain how these unseen healing forces operate through quantum physics. However, we believe all energy healing occurs through connecting with *Divine Energies!*

Ancient Energy Healing

"Way back in ancient times people living on the Earth had the capacity to use wisdom and intelligence far surpassing the abilities of modern Man. People at the time of the Earth's

pristine origins enjoyed ready access to all the information in the entire database of the Universe."

~ Anastasia

In Dr. Dave's brief history of energy healing, he described how the ancient Chinese were the first to document it some five thousand years ago. The Chinese discovered the body's life force, vital energy, *Qi* or *Ch'i* flowed through the body in meridian systems.. Stimulation of these *acupuncture* points produces changes in the nervous system and promotes healing.

Acupressure works in a similar fashion. By applying pressure with one's hands rather than using needles, as in acupuncture, healing is also promoted. The points stimulated may have healing effects on other parts of the body. For example in treating vascular headaches points between the thumb and palm of the hand are stimulated relieving the pain of the headache.

Reflexology is very similar to Chinese acupressure, but the healing stimulation is restricted to the hands or the feet. It is believed in reflexology that the healing meridians that correspond to all areas of the body end in the hands or feet. The practice of reflexology may actually predate acupuncture using needles. Historical records in China and Egypt describe healing techniques using the hands and feet. Even the Cherokee Indians of North America practice a form of reflexology that has been passed down from generation to generation.

Thousands of years ago in ancient India, *Chakras* were discovered. Chakra is a Sanskrit word meaning "wheels." A chakra is believed to be a whirling vortex of subtle energy in and around the body called *"Prana"* by the Hindus. There are seven major chakras that are associated with major nerve centers and endocrine glands in the body.

Some two thousand years ago, a very well know "energy healer" named Jesus used a technique called "laying-on-of-hands." What he was quoted as saying about his miraculous healings was:

> ***"These things that I do, also you can do and greater."***
> ~John 14:12

And:

> ***"With God All Things Are Possible."***
> ~ Matthew 19:26

Unfortunately, the healing ministry of the church declined over the next few centuries. In Europe the healing ministry was carried on by the royal touch of kings. Kings of several European countries were allegedly able to cure diseases such as tuberculosis through the laying-on-of-hands technique. In England, this method of healing began with Edward the Confessor (1003-1066) and lasted for seven centuries, ending with the reign of a skeptical William IV (1765-1837).

A Medieval Swiss physician, botanist, alchemist, astrologer, and occultist, Paracelsus (1493-1541), made a number of connections in his research into human health. Paracelsus is credited with founding the sympathetic system of medicine, that is, the belief that celestial bodies and magnetic forces influence the human body. He proposed a link between humans and the heavens through a subtle pervasive fluid, and attributed magnetic qualities to this healing substance. Paracelsus stated that this vital healing force was not in an individual, but radiated around him like a "*luminous sphere.*" By utilizing this outside healing force he believed health could be restored.

An English physician, astrologer, and mystic, Robert Fludd (1574-1637) continued Paracelsus' magnetic healing tradition. He believed that the human being possessed the qualities of a magnet. Dr. Fludd also emphasized the role of the sun in health as a source of light and life. He considered the sun as the purveyor of life beams required for all living creatures on earth and believed that the subtle energy of the sun entered the body through the breath, similar to the Indian concept of *prana.*

A German physician and astrologist, Franz Anton Mesmer

(1734-1815), credited his miraculous healings with using a universal energy called "*fluidum.*" Mesmer claimed that fluidum was a subtle physical fluid that filled the universe and was the connecting medium between living things on the earth and heavenly bodies. Early in his medical career he discovered that by placing a magnet over areas of the body afflicted with disease, it would promote a cure. He believed that the magnets he used in healing where conductors of an ethereal fluid from his own body that created the subtle healing effects in his patients. He considered this force to be magnetic in nature and referred to it as "animal magnetism." He felt this force was concentrated in the palms of his hands and developed his own technique of laying-on-of-hands.

However, the medical community of the time investigated Mesmer's claims and, although they did not dispute his healing abilities, they attributed it to a type of hypnotic suggestion. He was widely discredited and his name became synonymous with being hypnotized or "mesmerized."

This division between the medical community and energy healers only widened in the next couple of centuries. As physicians learned more about the human body and developed better medicines, they relied less on healing techniques they could not explain. The belief, or even stigma, that energy healing is the result of the patient's belief in the therapy, is called the "placebo effect." This belief is still prevalent today not only with the medical community but in the lay community as well.

Reiki Healing

Reiki comes from the Japanese words "*rei,*" meaning "*God's wisdom*" or "*higher power,*" and "ki" meaning "*life force energy.*" It is a method of energy healing using the ancient art of laying-on-of-hands that also can increase and balance life force energy to allow for emotional, spiritual, and/or physical healing.

There are two main "schools" of Reiki, Shamballa, and Ursi.

Shamballa Reiki is believed to have been used in ancient Atlantis and was renewed by the ascended master St. Germain in the 1700's. Shamballa Reiki heals the body, mind and spirit by connecting one to the "Universal Source." Shamballa teaches that, as we become attuned to Shamballa energy, it raises our vibration and aids our spiritual evolution.

Legend has the origins of Shamballa Reiki beginning in the lost continent of Atlantis. Atlantean Reiki used 22 healing symbols during treatments. St. Germain reintroduced Shamballa Reiki with 352 symbols that are considered to be healing energy frequencies. During treatment these symbols and multi-dimensional energies are absorbed directly into the individual's energy field.

Ursi Reiki was introduced in the mid 1800's by Mikao Ursi, a minister. As the story goes, Mikao was asked to show how Jesus did his healings, and, not being able to answer it, he went on a ten year quest to learn how. His search led him to study Buddhism, as he believed the life of Buddha greatly resembled that of Jesus. He was told by Buddhist monks that the ancient spiritual healing methods had been lost, but, if he attained enlightenment, he might be able to regain them.

Mikao then, reportedly, traveled to the United States where he studied at the University of Chicago Divinity School and received a Doctor of Theology degree. He then returned to Japan and began studying at a Zen Buddhist monastery. There he found ancient texts written in their original Sanskrit. In them he discovered a "test" he had to go through in order to be able heal like Jesus.

The test was a twenty-one day period of meditation, prayer and fasting that Mikao undertook on Mt. Koriyama in Japan. On the final day of the meditation, Mikao saw a beam of light come at him, hit his third eye (forehead area) and then lost consciousness. While unconscious he saw millions of rainbow colored bubbles and, finally, Reiki symbols as if on a screen. Mikao came down the mountain, knowing how to heal like Buddha and Jesus.

Mikao took his healing abilities to the slums where he healed a great number of beggars. He expected them to be able to get honest jobs after being healed. However, he was disappointed to see many of them return to begging and even become angry with him because they had no more excuses for not earning an honest living. Mikao left the slums and began healing and teaching people all over Japan about Reiki. He also began charging for his healings and trainings, feeling that people valued Reiki more when they paid for it. Mikao trained somewhere between sixteen and eighteen Reiki Masters before he died in 1930.

Regardless of whether Reiki started in Atlantis thousands of years ago, with Buddha in 600 B.C.E, or with Mikao Ursi in the late 1800's, it has spread throughout the world today. It may be the most recognized form of energy healing.

Qigong

Qigong is a Chinese meditative practice that uses slow graceful movements and controlled breathing techniques in order to promote the circulation of "*Qi*" within the body. In Chinese, Qi means "air," and "gong" means "discipline" or "skill." The practice of Qigong is believed to have evolved as a spiritual branch of Chinese medicine over a thousand years ago. In the late 1900's it expanded to where hundreds and even groups of thousands of people would gather in public places in China to perform Qigong movements.

During the "Qigong wave" of the 1970's, groups of ten thousand to forty thousand people regularly gathered in inside Chinese stadiums or parks to practice together. Practitioners of Chinese medicine view Qigong as being therapeutic in stress reduction through its movements and breathing exercises. Some believe Qigong effects are more metaphysical, claiming that *Qi* can be felt as a vibration or electrical current that physically circulates through the body in energy channels called meridians. Many testify the energy they get through Qigong reduces or eliminates pain.

Medical Qigong was officially recognized as a standard medical technique in 1989 in Chinese hospitals. It was also included in the curriculum of major universities in China as part of Chinese medicine. The Chinese government decided to regulate it in 1996 and made it part of their National Health Plan. However, the Chinese government became concerned that Qigong could be used as a political weapon, and they banned large Qigong gatherings in 1999.

Today there are over ten thousand styles of Qigong with over two hundred million people practicing it world-wide. They mainly practice it to:

* Gain strength and conditioning
* Improve health or reverse a disease
* Reduce stress
* Gain skill in working with Qi to become a healer
* Become more connected with the *Tao, God, Source, or Great Spirit*, for a more meaningful connection with the universe.

Ancient "New" Energy Healing

Electro-Magnetic Effect

In the mid twentieth century, an orthopedic surgeon, Dr. Robert Becker, found that electro-magnetic currents could increase healing in the body. He first experimented with amphibians and reptiles and observed that weak electric currents would increase limb regeneration. Through repeated experimentation, he added magnetism to the current and noticed more rapid healing.

By applying these techniques to patients with bone fractures, he was able to promote faster and more complete healing. In some instances, patients regenerated lost bone tissue and healed fractures that would not have otherwise healed.

Therapeutic Touch

A professor of nursing at New York University, Dr. Dolores Krieger, reasoned that the magnetic effects in energy healing might have to do with blood hemoglobin levels. The hemoglobin in the blood is mainly composed of iron, and Dr. Krieger believed that patients treated by an energy healer might show an increase in blood hemoglobin levels.

In 1971, Dr. Krieger along with Otelia Bengssten, M.D., and Dora Kunz, a clairvoyant, conducted a research study with the energy healer, Oscar Estebany who participated in many of Dr. Bernard Grad's experiments (see The Placebo Effect and Energy Healing). In this experiment a large number of medically referred patients with various illnesses were used. There were nineteen patients in the experimental group and 9 patients with similar illnesses in a control group.

The experimental group received energy healing from Oscar and were also given "magnetically charged" cotton batting by him as well. The control group received no treatment. Dr. Krieger measured hemoglobin levels in all the patients at the beginning and after several healing treatments. She found that there was a significant increase in hemoglobin levels in the healer-treated group.

This study was repeated in 1973 with a larger group of patients. In this study Dr. Krieger had forty-six ill patients in the experimental group receiving healings, and thirty-three patients in the control group. She obtained similar results. Patients that received laying-on-of-hands treatments from Oscar showed elevated hemoglobin levels. From her hemoglobin experiments, Dr. Krieger reasoned that the application of healing energies through techniques like energy healing (laying-on-of-hands) produces true bioenergetic and physiologic changes in the body. This indicated that belief had nothing to do with the healings, they where physiological.

After confirming that energy healing does, in fact, promote physical-biochemical changes, Dr. Krieger had another question.

Can the techniques of energy healing be learned, or does one have to be born with "special gifts"? Oscar Estebany believed that his abilities could not be taught, and you had to be born with healing powers. However, Dr. Krieger's associate, Dora Kunz felt differently.

Dora Kunz was a clairvoyant that could also see and diagnose energy blockages in individual's subtle energy fields. Using her intuitive abilities and knowledge of the healing arts, she began a workshop on instructing others in the art of energy healing. Dr. Krieger was one of Dora's first students. Following the workshop, Dr. Krieger developed a curriculum to teach the laying-on-of-hands techniques to nurses. Concerned with negative connotations energy or psychic healing might have with the medical community, she called her technique *Therapeutic Touch.*

Dr. Krieger believed that the healer in the process of laying-on-of-hands, or Therapeutic Touch acted as conduit in transferring energy to the sick individual. The healer's energetic system represents a charged battery, at a high potential, that is used to jump start the subtle energy system of a sick individual that is at a low potential of energy. The flow of healing energy from high to low potential appears to be similar to the flow of electricity, and has been termed "*paraelectricity.*"

Dr. Krieger's first class in Therapeutic Touch was taught as a master's level course to nurses at New York University. The nurse's she taught slowly became proficient in her hands-on techniques of energy healing. Dr. Krieger observed that the more a nurse practiced the technique, the better he or she became at it.

Being a researcher, Dr. Krieger designed a study to see if her nurses trained in Therapeutic Touch could produce similar results to that of Oscar Estebany. In this study, she had sixteen registered nurses that had been trained in Therapeutic Touch work with thirty-two ill patients. In a control group, sixteen nurses without Therapeutic Touch training worked with similarly ill patients. Dr. Krieger had the hemoglobin levels measured in both groups of patients before and at the conclusion of the study. The control group showed no change in hemoglobin levels at the end of the study. However, in the nurse-healer treated group, there were significant increases in hemoglobin levels in the patients. Her statistical analysis showed that the odds of the results obtained in this study attributed to chance were one in a thousand.

In contrast to what Oscar Estebany believed, Dr. Krieger proved that energy healing could be learned. Since the 1970's, thousands of nurses have been trained and have implemented Therapeutic Touch to promote healing in their patients throughout the world.

The Reconnection

In 2003, Dr. Eric Pearl, a successful L.A. chiropractor, published *The Reconnection: Heal Others, Heal Yourself.* In his book, he documented his discovery of a new type of energy healing, that he called *"Reconnective Healing."*

While working as a chiropractor, Dr. Pearl's patients told him about miraculous healings they experienced from him. They reported that they felt his hands on them when he, in fact, was far away from them. Later, they reported being healed from a variety of illnesses, such as cancer, cerebral palsy, chronic fatigue syndrome, AIDS-related diseases, and even birth disfigurements.

Dr. Pearl described these healing energies used in Reconnective Healing as a new bandwidth of healing frequencies that connects one with Universal energies and the very essence of who we are. He believes these healing frequencies are here for the very first time. He explains that these healing frequencies are here due to the cosmic shift the earth is going through. This shift was predicted by the ancient Mayans, the Incas, the Hopi, Nostradamus, Edgar Cayce, and the Kabbalah. The shift is a state of evolutionary change through which the earth is accelerating. It is as if time is speeding up because of this acceleration. And, as our "Earth dimension" expands it encompasses this new healing frequency.

Dr. Pearl explains that is why Reconnective Healing is different from other healing modalities. He states that:

> *"Each of our bodies contains its own set of energetic lines and points. Although only remnants of what they once were, these lines and points continue to serve as our interface with the universe: a channel that facilitates our communication of energy, light and information between large and small, macrocosm and microcosm, the universe and humankind. At one point in time we became disconnected from these lines and we lost the fullness of our inherent connection to the universe, distancing us from our previously rapid and expansive rate of evolution. The Reconnection brings in "new" axiatonal lines that reconnect us on a more powerful and evolved level than ever before. These lines are part of a timeless network of intelligence, a parallel-dimensional system that draws the basic energy for renewal functions of the human body."*

The new bandwidth of energy, light, and information is unlike anything else reported in energy healing. Dr. Pearl teaches practitioners of Reconnective Healing that this healing energy connects with Universal energies and the distance between the healer and the patient is not a factor. The Reconnective practitioner uses a hands off technique on patients, and its effect can actually increase the further the practitioner is from the patient. Since 2001, Dr. Pearl has taught the Reconnection to over seventy thousand practitioners in seventy-one countries world-wide.

EMF Balancing Technique

The EMF Balancing Technique uses one's electromagnetic field (EMF), Tai Chi-like movements, and Reiki-like symbols to facilitate healing. It was developed by Peggy Phoenix Dubro who discovered the Universal Calibration Lattice (UCL) during a period of spiritual awakening.

Dubro describes the UCL as a complex electromagnetic energy field surrounding the body. It is a system in our energy anatomy that is an extension of our sympathetic and parasympathetic nervous system. Through balancing the electrical field in the UCL, the EMF practitioner helps the client reach greater physical, mental and spiritual health and peace.

During an EMF balancing session, the practitioner uses specific movements, usually without touching the client who lies fully clothed on a massage table. Specific intents of encouragement are also spoken by the practitioner to the client. There are twelve phases of treatment a client can receive starting with balancing and alignment of ones energy field, through mastery and moving toward enlightenment in Phase 12.

Dubro, along with physicist David P. Lapierre, describe how the UCL functions and EMF healing works in their 2002 book, *Elegant Empowerment, Evolution of Consciousness.* Their book describes in detail how the UCL and electromagnetic energy healing works through quantum physics theories. Currently thousands of practitioners have been trained in the EMF Balancing Technique in seventy countries world-wide.

ASYRA

ASYRA testing combines the body's wisdom, *Homeopathy* and computerized technology. Homeopathy is based on the principle "like cures like." This is how vaccines work. A little bit of the virus is injected into the body causing the body's immune system to produce antibodies to protect against the virus if it is encountered again.

Homeopathy was first theorized by Paracelsus (1493-1541), who was a Renaissance physician, botanist, alchemist, and astrologer. It was put into practice by Samuel Christian Hahnemann, M.D. (1755-1843). He found that by administering minute doses of a pathogen similar to the one causing the illness, it would cause the body to build resistance to the original disease. Homeopathy differs from a vaccine in that the homeopathic remedy given is extremely diluted and rarely produces any side effects that a vaccine might produce. The diluted homeopathic solution carries vibrational energy that stimulates the body to counteract or correct disease symptoms.

In ASYRA therapy a computerized system called CEDSA (Computerized Electro-Dermal Screening) is used. This computer measures imbalances in the body's meridian paths (as in acupuncture), in various organs in the body, and in the body's nutritional requirements. The therapy was developed by Dr. Reinhold Vol in the 1950's. He found that, by measuring the amount of current going through a body tissue, organ, or system he could detect the health of that tissue, organ, or bodily system.

During an ASYRA test, the patient holds two probes that are attached to the CEDSA computer. The CEDSA measures balances and imbalances throughout the body. Specific frequencies of the imbalances are measured by the CEDSA system and a homeopathic dilute is produced. When the dilute is taken, the specific healing frequencies enter the body and are distributed through the nervous system and stimulate cells to respond. The cells and tissues respond to their natural optimum pattern of health.

Energy Bodies

"Luminous beings, are we. Not this matter!"

~ Yoda,
Stars Wars V:
The Empire Strikes Back

The energy paths that circulate through the body that were observed by ancient cultures and modern medicine in the past hundred years have also been observed to transcend the physical body. In the 1940's, Semyon Kirlian a Russian researcher, proved "scientifically" what psychics who can see energy have known for thousands of years. By using high voltage applied to a photographic plate, an energy corona or aura is produced. This type of photography is also called electrography, electro-photography, and/or corona discharge photography. The exact mechanism of what is being shown may be controversial but it relates to what many psychics describe.

The word "*clairvoyance*" comes from the French word meaning "clear seeing," referring to the ability to see beyond known human senses. It is believed that such psychic clairvoyant abilities is that of seeing these subtle energy fields. The aura or corona around one's body observed in Kirlian photography is also observed by psychics when they describe energy shells around the human body. There are even reports of psychics seeing the whirling colors of chakras around the body.

Carlos Casteneda, in *The Teachings of Don Juan* series, reports that Indian shaman Don Juan Matus could see people as luminous egg-shaped balls of energy. By manipulating these energy fields, Don Juan was able to alter his physical and mental states and those of individuals he worked with.

Clairaudience is the ability to hear a voice in your mind. Just as those that start developing clairvoyant abilities may initially question what they are seeing (is it real?), those that have clairaudience initially have a difficult time believing the inner voices they hear. The same subtle energy fields are being picked up, but in the case of those with clairaudience abilities, they hear the information.

In *A Practical Guide to Vibrational Medicine* (2000), Dr. Richard Gerber discusses various energy shells outside the body. He describes the *etheric body* is an invisible duplicate of the physical body around the outside of the body. This is the first layer of what is called the higher spiritual bodies. The etheric body has a higher vibratory rate or energy frequency than the physical body. This etheric energy body covering the physical bodies is again visible to psychics and clairvoyants. It may also be what Don Juan was describing when he spoke of the luminous eggs he saw surrounding people. The etheric body is what is manipulated when energy healers use hands off techniques to heal the body such as in Reiki, Therapeutic Touch, EMF Balancing, or Reconnective Healing.

The Astral Body

Outside of the etheric energy body lies the astral or the emotional body. While the etheric body is closely associated with the physical body, the astral energy layer appears to be more mobile. This is the layer that leaves the body when individuals astrally project, have an out-of-body experience (OBE), or near-death experience (NDE), and leaves their body. Medical literature documents thousands of cases of people leaving their bodies when "clinically" dead or in a coma and they later describe what was going around them in detail. They report a feeling of leaving their physical body, often looking down at their non-responsive bodies, and observing all that was happening.

Astral projection is being able to project one's consciousness outside the body at will. Throughout history, there have been documented cases of people doing this; projecting their consciousness to another location and recalling exactly what happened there (see Chapter VI: Divine Consciousness).

The Mental Energy Body

Surrounding the astral body is the mental energy body. This layer is composed of subtle magnetic energy that vibrates at a higher frequency than the astral body layer. The mental energy body is believed to contain the energy of thought, creativity, invention and inspiration.

This is the energy layer clairvoyants and psychics may "tune into" when they start telling someone things about the person. They may see personality traits, hobbies, interests, relationships, even the person's past or future. By seeing or sensing the vibrations from the mental body layer, they are able to psychically connect with someone.

The Causal Field

The outer most energy layer is called the causal body, causal field, or spirit energy field. This layer connects the soul to the spirit dimension. The causal field also contains all of the soul's past life memories. While our physical body is born, ages and dies in each lifetime, the causal body remains intact through each reincarnation. This explains how traumas, conflicts and soul memories can be carried from lifetime to lifetime. This can even influence the health of the physical body. An imprinted trauma or illness can manifest itself in the next lifetime. A conflict that was incurred in a previous life may be an issue in this life.

This is the law of *Karma*. Karma is the concept where deeds (bad or good) in one life are paid for in the next one. Sometimes it is a life lesson one has to learn to fulfill his or her karmic debt. For instance, if one was a thief or a rapist in a previous life, in the next life, he or she is stolen from or raped.

Sometimes an imprint of an issue or trauma on the causal field greatly affects your current life. If in a previous life you had drowned, or were attacked by dogs, in this life you might have a fear of the water, or of dogs. If in a previous life you were shot or stabbed, in this life you may have chronic "unexplained" pains where you were previously wounded. This is why such issues, traumas, and unexplained pains are healed and released through regression hypnosis. When the individual is made aware of how these things have happened to them, the fears, anxieties, or symptoms they were experiencing are then released from their causal energy field.

The causal field can be observed in several ways. It can be sensed by psychics that may describe people's past lives or by hypnosis where the hypnotherapist can regress patients into their subconscious, uncovering imprints in the casual field of past lives. It can be observed through deep meditation or dreams. Through deep meditation, people often get visions of past or future events. The same is often true when dreaming. One's dreams may connect all the energy layers and certainly, the causal field to the spirit dimension. You don't usually have to venture too far to find someone that has a story of a dream coming true.

Dr. Dave had a couple of great examples of connecting to higher energy fields through one's dreams. His mother had a dream of a fire in her mother's house, when they lived over a hundred miles away, and, sure enough, when she called her mother the next day a fire in her house had destroyed the second floor. Also, as described in the *Divine Signs* Chapter, Dr. Dave had a vivid dream of his mother saying goodbye the night she transitioned to the spirit dimension. It is not uncommon for people to connect to these higher energy fields while dreaming.

To explain, as far as science can, how causal field energy can connect with the spiritual dimension, that transcends space and time, we have to look into theories of quantum physics theories. But first we need to answer the question: Does energy healing work because the patient expects it to work? Or, is the energy healer, in fact, healing the patient by using these higher energy fields?

The Placebo Effect and Energy Healing

As described earlier, many physicians believe any positive effects achieved through energy healing can be attributed only to the patient's belief system in what is called the placebo effect. The results of experiments that Dr. Bernard Grad of McGill University in Montreal, made on energy healing in the 1960's *should* silence critics. Dr. Grad, also concerned with the placebo's effect on energy healing, set out to develop an experiment that would be free of the patient's belief in the process.

Dr. Grad devised experiments with mice and induced them with thyroid goiters by placing the mice on special diets. The mice were then separated into groups of mice treated with energy healers and ones that were not treated, which served as a control group. Further sub-control groups were set-up. To simulate the heat of healer's hands, a group of mice was kept in a cage that had been wrapped with electro thermal tape. A third sub-control group of mice was handled by people that were not healers.

The experiment lasted for forty days, and at the end, all the mice were examined to determine which had the largest goiters. While all the mice in all four groups had an increase in goiter size, the mice in the healer treated group had significantly smaller goiters and slower rates of growth of the goiters, than the non-healer treated groups.

In another set of experiments, Dr. Grad took out the human element entirely. Again using goiter induced mice, he had one group exposed to healer treated cotton balls twice a day and another group was "treated" with untreated cotton balls. After performing statistical analysis on the two groups, Dr. Grad found that the group exposed to the healer treated cotton balls had a significantly slower rate of goiter growth.

In a third study by Dr. Grad on energy healers, he measured their effect on healing wounds on mice. Coin-size pieces of skin wee removed from the backs of forty-eight mice. They were divided into three groups of sixteen. The first group was a control group and no special treatment was given. The second group was treated by energy healers that were able only to wave their hands over the mice, no physical contact was allowed. The third group of sixteen mice were in special cages that were exposed to heat similar to that of the healer's hands.

When Dr. Grad examined the mice after thirty days he found the mice in the healer-treated group were either completely healed or nearly completely healed. The other two groups showed significantly less healing than the healer-treated mice.

Dr. Grad's results were replicated in another study by Dr. Remi Cadoret and G.I. Paul at the University of Manitoba. They used a larger group of three hundred mice in their study, and added another control variable. They had another control group of mice treated by people that claimed no special healing abilities. Dr. Cadoret and Paul's results were similar to Dr. Grad's, indicating that the mice treated by healers had significantly faster rates of wound healing than those that were not.

These studies suggested that energy healers did, in fact, have a bioenergentic influence on healing that was above and beyond anything that could be attributed to belief, faith in the healer, or the placebo effect.

Connecting Science and Spirituality

"God does not play dice with the universe."
~ Albert Einstein

The field of quantum physics began in the early 1900's. It is a set of principles that describe the behavior of subatomic particles. Quantum theory provides accurate descriptions for many previously unexplained phenomena such as black body radiation and stable electron orbits. In the development of quantum theory, physicist Max Planck (1858-1947), considered the founder of quantum theory, proposed that energy waves could be described as consisting of small packets or quanta.

Albert Einstein (1879-1955) further postulated that an electromagnetic wave such as light was composed of particles called photons. This led to a theory of unity between subatomic particles and electromagnetic waves called wave-particle duality in which particles and waves were neither one nor the other, but had properties of both. Quantum mechanics led to the development of the transistor, electron microscope, magnetic resonance imaging, the laser and semiconductors.

An interesting discovery of quantum physics is that of nonlocality, the phenomenon that when two particles interact, they continue to influence each other and transfer information between them instantly, no matter how distantly separated they become. They can be separated by inches, feet, or millions of miles, and the transfer of information is immediate, indicating instant communication. This transfer of information is not bound by the laws of the physical universe, such as traveling at the speed of light (186,282.4 miles per second). It is believed this nonlocal transfer of information operates in an unseen reality, one that connects all physical events with the universe.

Using theories in quantum physics, we can explain how energy healing, clairvoyance, etheric energy, and the casual energy field functions:

- Light is composed of electromagnetic energy that has properties of both particles and waves.
- These subatomic particles can transfer information as well and are not bound by properties of space or time.
- Human thought/consciousness produces energy similar to that of light-energy with the same properties; consciousness is not bound by space and time.
- Consciousness/thought is composed of energy that can affect matter near or far.

Science is now explaining how energy can leave the body and affect its surroundings, be it near or far (energy particles are nonlocal). Professor William Tiller, Ph.D., Chairman of the Department of Materials Engineering at Stanford University, summarizes how medical science has evolved in the past two hundred years.

Two hundred years ago, science was driven by Newtonian physics. The body was viewed as a biological-mechanical system: If a bone breaks, you splint it; if an organ fails, cut it out, repair, or replace it; chemicals kill bacteria that cause disease, reduce fever, or swelling; and the discovery that vitamins and minerals can restore what is lacking in the body and promote health.

In the 1900's, with the discovery of quantum theory, electro-magnetic energy was added to the equation of what affects the human body. As Einstein put it in $E = mc^2$ (where E is energy, m is mass, and c is a constant number, the speed of light), matter and energy are related and interchangeable. If we can convert matter into energy, we should be able to take energy and produce matter.

Dr. Tiller evolves the biological-mechanical-energy system further in what is known as the Tiller-Einstein Model (see table VII-1). He states that the human energy field is additionally affected by electro-magnectical energy that affects the subtle and etheric energy fields outside the body. Dr. Tiller concurs that there are energy fields surrounding the body. These energies inwardly affect the health of the individual and outwardly connect with universal energy fields. Dr. Tiller theorizes that these astral energies outside the body travel at speeds between 10^{10} to 10^{20} times the speed of light (over 10 billion times). In other words, when someone astrally projects his or her consciousness from New York to Paris, it is done instantaneously.

Table VII-1 Tiller-Einstein Model:

< 1900's *Function ⇔ Structure ⇔ Chemistry*
1900's *Function ⇔ Structure ⇔ Chemistry ⇔ Electromagnetic Energy Fields*
2000 > *Function ⇔ Structure ⇔ Chemistry ⇔ Electromagnetic Energy Fields ⇔ Subtle Energy Fields*

Ancients Knew

It seems ironic that the discipline that has caused such a division between faith, the unseen, and the unexplainable is now *explaining* how energy can leave the body. Science has always dismissed concepts like psychic phenomenon. However, through quantum physics, the unexplainable, is being explained!

Quantum physics is explaining how energy is composed of matter and can leave the body, affecting various energy layers around it. The scientific-medical community that for centuries hardly believed in the healings of Jesus, was mystified in how Paracelsus, Dr. Fudd, or exiled Franz Anton Mesmer healed patients; and could not explain how acupuncture, Qi gong, Reiki, Therapeutic Touch, EMF Balancing or Reconnective Healing worked, now enlightens us all "scientifically" through quantum physics!

Science is now explaining what sages, mystics, and religious leaders have professed for thousands of years, that energy travels in waves and can effect the physical world. That our consciousness does not die when the physical body does. Our consciousness is energy that continues on when the body does not. What has been observed during NDE's and in past life regressions is being explained by "science." Perhaps we are now learning what the ***ancients knew***.

"The body is only 'thought.' It is only what we imagine it to be. It has no density when the current of the Divine is running through it."

~ Shirley MacLaine

VIII ~ Spiritual Healing

"You must unlearn, all that you have learned!"

~ Yoda,
Star Wars V

Divine Interventions

Through the *Grace* of God I was led on a divine healing journey. I hate to think where I would be if I had not met the people I had met. They saved my life in so many ways. Several sources told me that I should have died from what I went through, but through my faith, their physical, and spiritual healings, and through their writings, I was saved (and I'm sure my guardian angels were working overtime!).

My first encounter with such an extraordinary healer, was when I met Grace Avila. She verified what I had been feeling inside, and through her, I began the understanding side of my spiritual awakening. When doctors had no idea of what was going on inside of my body, energy healers and lightworkers saved my life. In the process, they opened worlds to me about which I had never known existed, or even dreamed of.

The question of whether our consciousness can live outside of our body was discussed earlier in Chapter VI, *Divine Consciousness*. Researchers Ring and Moody thoroughly investigated how our consciousness can leave and return to our body when having *near-death-experiences,* but, what I have experienced and came to learn from those who can see spirits, is that sometimes when people die their souls do not "go to the light." In other words, their souls do not transition to the spirit dimension as it should. They become trapped in the physical-earth realm. Perhaps death was too sudden and these spirits or entities did not know they had died. They then become drawn to the life-energy of a living person. Several psychics, and those that can see spirits/entities have told me that, due to my high vibrational energy, that these entities were attracted to me, thinking I was the light.

I've come to believe that not only my physical ailments (for which doctors could offer no explanations), but my psychological issues were caused by these entity attachments as well. It became evident to me when I felt that bloating in my abdomen, which felt as if a ball of energy was moving around inside me, that it was entity energy within me. I also believe now, that these same entities were doing whatever they could to keep me from my true purpose in this life; of helping others and helping to awaken humanity to the real world (all that is going on in both the physical and the spirit dimension and how they affect each other).

Entities were responsible for my waves of depression, my insecurities, and self-abusive and destructive behaviors, but through the *Grace of God*, and some amazing healers like Grace, Heidi, Judy, Joey, Michelle, Vanessa, Quan Yin, Mark, and Anthony, and getting back together with my soul mate, Dr. Dave, I was truly *saved.*

William Baldwin, Ph.D. in *Healing Lost Souls* (2003) believes that many of the mental, emotional and even physical pains can be attributed to entity attachments. Throughout his over twenty years of practice and research in regression therapy, he has been able to heal patients by releasing what he calls "earthbound entities."

He states that an earthbound entity (EB) is the soul of a newly deceased person that fails to reach the "Light" or fully transition into the spirit dimension. The EB can become attached to a living person, causing all types of problems. This is different from spirit possession where an EB will totally take over the individual, causing a total personality change.

Dr. Baldwin believes that these earthbound entities, "…can interfere with any aspect of human life." He has found that entities can even influence a living person's attitudes, beliefs, and behaviors, causing phobias, emotional upsets, relationship problems and addictions. When someone undergoes a sudden change in behavior, often following an accident, illness, surgery and even a death in their family, it could indicate a new entity attachment. A misguided earthbound entity he calls a "dark force entity" can cause its host anger, rage, violence, and criminal behavior.

Susan Shumsky, Ph.D., in *Divine Revelation* (1996) states, "The Entity World consists of astral beings invisible to the outer eye. These beings have a slower, denser vibration than spiritual beings. The entity world is often experienced by those sensitive to subtle vibrations. The entity world has been ignored by countless religions and philosophies that deny its existence out of fear. People don't often want to give energy or credence to the negative side of life."

Entity/Spirit Possession ~ Historical Perspective

Entity and spirit possession belief goes beyond recorded time. Tribal medicine men and shamans cast out evil spirits and passed down rituals of doing so from generation to generation. Archeologists believe that the circular holes drilled into skulls of uncovered ancient skeletons were methods early medicine men performed to release evil spirits within the afflicted. Many of the skulls showed healing around the edges of the holes indicating that the "afflicted" lived for years after the procedures.

Records left by the ancient Chinese, Greeks, Romans, and Hebrews described exorcism rituals. Stone tablets dating back to 2,500 B.C.E. by the Assyrians depicted prayers to tribal gods to release demons. In ancient Egypt, exorcisms were performed by a team consisting of a physician to heal the patient and a priest to drive out the demon.

In Persia in the sixth century B.C.E. a religious leader named Zoroaster developed exorcism rituals that used prayer and "holy" water to drive out demons. Around the same period of time in India, Buddha's mother was considered to be a great exorcist. A few centuries later, King Solomon was known for his exorcism skills as well.

In the New Testament, one fourth of all of Jesus's healings involved casting out "unclean spirits." The Bible has some twenty-six references to Jesus speaking of exorcising spirits, such as:

"Jesus preached and cast out devils." (Mark 1:39)

"A certain man which had devils a long time…Jesus had commanded the unclean spirit to come out of the man…He that was possessed of the devils was healed." (Luke 8:27-33)

"Master, I have brought unto thee my son, which hath a dumb spirit…and he asked his father, how long is it ago since this came to him? And he said, of a child…Jesus rebuked the foul spirit, saying unto him, thou dumb and deaf spirit, I charge thee, come out of him, and enter no more into him. And the spirit cried, and rent him sore, and came out of him; and he was as one dead; insomuch that many said he is dead. But Jesus took him by the hand, and lifted him up; and he arose." (Mark 9:17-27)

"Jesus gave his twelve disciples power against unclean spirits, to cast them out." (Matthew 10:1)

The Catholic Church developed rituals of "casting out devils" over the next couple of centuries into their own exorcism rituals. The ability to learn how to cast out unclean spirits was viewed as a sign of true discipleship by the church, based on the teachings of Jesus.

During the Middle Ages (500 to 1,500 A.CE.), treatment of mental illness was mostly conducted by the clergy, believing the cause of mental illness was due to evil spirit possession. During the next couple of centuries, however, the clinical-scientific method developed and greatly influenced the medical community. As described in the Chapter VII: Energy Healing, we entered into the Newtonian scientific era.

Sir Isaac Newton (1643-1727) is considered one of the most influential scientists in history. He was an English physicist, mathematician, astronomer, alchemist, philosopher, and theologian. He developed the laws of thermodynamics that describe the physical laws of motion and gravity, invented the first practical reflecting telescope, and helped develop calculus. His world was that of the practical, observable, measurable one and belief in supernatural forces that might make people sick had no bearing.

Newton's scientific methods developed into the scientific age of the 1800's and casting out evil spirits and exorcisms were relegated to medieval religious beliefs and left to priests and indigenous peoples. As the scientific/medical community techniques evolved in the twentieth century to clinical trials and scientific evidence, the spilt between believing in what could be identified with the five senses and the unseen, and immeasurable forces widened.

Dr. Baldwin makes the observation that up to 1900 three subjects; multiple personality disorders, hypnosis, and spirit possession were quite acceptable in the medical/science communities, but in the early 1900's, all three quickly faded into obscurity.

Multiple personality disorder came into the forefront again with the publishing of *The Three Faces of Eve* (1957). Hypnotherapy began to regain its standing in the medical community with the founding of the American Society of Clinical Hypnosis (1957), and its acceptance by The American Medical Association (1958), the American Psychiatric Association (1962). However, belief in spirit possession continued outside of the medical/science community.

Although, not as "mainstream" as in the Middle Ages, it was still prevalent in religious sects and in in followers of the occult.

William James (1842-1910), who is considered to be the father of American psychology, had his feet in both worlds. He was highly involved in developing the clinical side of human thought and personality, yet he still believed in unseen and spiritual influences on the individual. He stated:

> *"That the demon-theory will have its inning again is to my mind absolutely certain. One day to be scientific indeed to be blind and ignorant enough to suspect no such possibility. If there are devils, if there are supernormal powers, it is through the cracked and fragmented self they enter."*

A psychiatrist, Dr. Carl Wickland, documents in *Thirty Years Among the Dead* (1924) his technique of releasing spirits that were afflicting his patients. Dr. Wickland describes how in working with his wife, Anna, a psychic, they were able to identify trapped earthbound spirits and direct them to the *Light,* releasing their negative influences on their patients.

Psychotherapist Annabel Chaplin, in her book, *The Bright Light of Death* (1977), describes cases where she was able to help her patients by releasing entities into the *Light* during her therapy sessions. She reported that the results were often miraculous.

Clinical psychologist, Dr. Edith Fiore, documents that spirit possession is responsible for 70 percent of her patients' problems in *The Unquiet Dead; A Psychologist Treats Spirit Possession* (1987). While regressing her patients, often into past lives, she would uncover entities responsible for causing their hosts a variety of difficulties from physical pains, to mental disorders and obsessive behaviors. By releasing these displaced spirits through depossessions, she was able cure them when psychotherapy could not.

Richard Jackson, who has been releasing EB's from his clients and performing exorcisms for over thirty years, believes that many of the dark force entities that Dr. Baldwin talks about have been created through the collective human consciousness. He states that, due to religious beliefs that date back thousands of years, human thought has created these negative EB's. Belief in entities like the devil, Satan and demons has lead to their existence in the earthbound spirit dimension. He states that media attention such as movies and TV shows that sensationalize Satan, demons, and possessions continue to promote such beliefs and make them realities.

Why Are There Spirits Harming Us?

Two questions that bothered me for years, come to mind when discussing entity possession: Why are these earthbound spirits harming the living? And, if we all have guardian angels, why do they not protect us?

All of the spirit releasement practitioners I have met and read appear to agree that the trapped earthbound entities are trapped because they do not know they are dead. They may have met a tragic or unexpected death, such as in a car accident, and they did not transition into the spirit world as they should have. They may have seen the "Light" and then turned away from it, not realizing they were dead, or they may have died not believing in an afterlife. They may have turned away from the Light due to erroneous religious beliefs, thinking that because they had sinned they were going to hell. They then become confused and trapped in the lower astral energy fields.

Dr. Susan Shumsky states that there are a number of reasons why entities do not go to the Light and become earthbound:

1. The person is very attached to the body, to the earth, or to people on earth.
2. The person's loved ones are very attached to him or her and won't let go.
3. The person does not believe in God or in life after death.

4. The person does not know that he or she is dead due to an accident or a violent death.
5. The person committed suicide.
6. The person cannot let go of unfinished business on earth.
7. The person is confused and refuses to accept help from loved ones.

Reverend Eugene Maurey in *Exorcism: How to Clear at a Distance a Spirit Possessed Person* (1988) states that these earthbound spirits are stuck here, not knowing they are dead. They are often wanderers with no place to rest. They may inhabit familiar places, like their home, a church, their place of business, even a familiar bar. Most that inhibit these places cause no problems; they simply like it there. However, Maurey asserts that their presence here delays their spiritual and intellectual growth. They may be trapped in this dimension for years, even a hundred years, as time is irrelevant to earthbound entities. They are not moving on with their destiny.

They are trapped in the astral plane, the plane of energy just outside the human body. Being in that plane they have not ascended into the mental, causal, or spiritual planes. The earthbound spirits still act as they did when they were alive. They have the same personality, feelings and intellect as they did, but may be more confused as to where they are and what is happening. If they had problems with substance abuse, which may even have led to their deaths, such as alcoholism or drug abuse, they are still having those desires. If they had anger issues, a low self-esteem, depression, fears, or anxieties, they carry these feelings with them in their astral plane existence.

Maurey explains that there are two primary ways an entity invades, or possesses a living person, voluntary and involuntary possession. Voluntary possession occurs when an individual has a strong bond to the deceased and does not want to let go. Sorrow strengthens this often unhealthy attachment by both the grieving person and the earthbound entity. This mutual attachment allows the entity to enter the living person. This may initially comfort the living; however, it can eventually lead the possessed person to be controlled by feelings or negative habits of the deceased.

Involuntary possession can occur when a living person is in a weakened state of consciousness. This can happen when one is ill, unconscious during an operation, intoxicated, or weakened during a prolonged illness. A strong entity can invade the individual and start to take over the individual's personality.

Sonia Choquette, in her book, *Ask Your Guides* (2006), makes the distinction between positive and negative entities. She states that positive entities are of a high vibrational nature and are guides that are subtle, patient, calm, and loving, and won't tell you what to do. They will certainly never tell you to harm yourself or anyone else.

However, an entity of a lower vibrational nature is negative and can distort things. They are lost and confused light beings that can try to harm living beings by suggesting things that will bring someone down, such as through substance abuse. Sonia believes that negative thoughts, behaviors and habits can attract these low vibrational entities. If someone has self-defeating thoughts, is prone to being anxious, afraid or depressed, or has a substance abuse problem, the person can attract a similar entity. Like attracts like, and the low vibrational entities amplify the negative feelings and behaviors in the living beings they invade.

I have the most difficulty with the second question: *"If we all have guardian angels, why do they not protect us?"* I have had a number of psychics tell me that I am protected by the Holy Family, Jesus, Avalon, and thousands of angels. So, if I'm so protected, why was I so often attacked by harmful earthbound entities or even more harmful forces? Where was all of my "protection"? Why did my guardian angels not protect me?

According to Maurey, the answer to the above questions has to do with why we are here. Because we have free will, we may be in some way responsible for our own possession. If the purpose of this life is to learn and grow our souls, then challenges in life help us to those ends. Whether our challenges are from the physical world or the supernatural world it makes no difference. He believes that our spirit guides will not intervene unless asked, but once asked, your spiritual guides will seldom refuse to help.

When I look at all the wonderful people I have met on my spiritual awakening, all the amazing authors and the knowledge I have been led to, it certainly makes it all seem as if it was truly a *divine plan*. Whether it was by my design or a higher power's design it certainly changed my life and gave it a whole new direction, a whole new meaning. Maybe that was the plan all along!

Symptoms of Possession

Have you ever felt a sudden chill down your spine, or a tap on your shoulder when no one was there? Looked into a mirror and felt someone else was looking back? Felt a strange sensation come over you that made you say or do something very unlike your self?

I, like most, have had these experiences and didn't give them much thought until my spiritual awakening. Now I don't second guess any unusual feeling or happenings. Possible entity/spirit influence could include:

- Unusual physical sensations in your body.
- Looking into a mirror and seeing someone else.
- Doing or saying something completely out of character for yourself.
- Hearing inner voices that are not yours.
- Having a feeling "come over" you like a wave of depression.
- Sudden character shifts or mood swings.
- Physical difficulties that have no medical answers.
- Sudden physical pains not experienced before, or that have no normal cause.

- Low energy, poor concentration, poor memory.
- Sudden compulsions or addictions to things like alcohol, drugs, or sex.
- Unexplained noises in your house.
- Unexplained energy in your house.

I have experienced many of the above at one time or another (see Divine Journey). From the physical trauma that seemed to intensify with my battles with Gordan, to seeing energy in other forms to unexplained events with energy. I never could have dreamed of what I experienced.

When doctors had no idea what was going on in my body, but energy healers did, when energy cracked windows and windshields, when I saw people's faces change, when house alarms continually went off, when Divine Happenings occurred all day long around me, I had no choice but to believe in other "realities." It was as if the spirit dimension was continually saying to me, "***Here we are. Pay attention! Wake up!***"

If all that wasn't convincing enough, I was led to so many different lightworkers, energy healers, and shamans that told me the same thing. They saw what was trying to tear me down physically, and they told me who I was and where I was going in this life. I'm not talking about one or two card readers. A dozen different lightworkers from all over the country told me my energy was amazing, and that I was on a *"Divine"* path.

Mental Illness

Ever have a sudden feeling come over you, like a wave of depression, unexpected anxiety, or a chilling fear? Ever wonder where did that come from? All of the lightworkers, shamans, exorcists, and authors described above could tell you what was causing these disorders. Common problems such as depression, anxiety, phobias, compulsions, and even addictions can be due to entity possession.

Dr. William Baldwin states that many aberrant behaviors such as emotional problems, phobias, and addictions are all caused by dark force entities. Dr. Susan Shumsky believes that highly sensitive people can be possessed if they leave their auras open, which could result in personality changes. Psychiatrist Dr. Carl Wickland, psychologist Dr. Edith Fiore, and psychotherapist Annabel Chaplin, all have seen miraculous personality changes when releasing these dark force entities from their patients.

Disorders such as schizophrenia, bi-polar disorder, and multiple personality disorder are all believed to be caused by one or more entities taking over someone's personality. What do most psychiatrists and MD's treat these disorders with? Mind-numbing drugs. Our society has become so dependant on drugs/medications to treat everything, that doctors rarely seemed to be concerned with the causes of such disorders. They just search for which medication to give, depending on how much of the side-effects the patient can tolerate. The patient is told to take this drug for life, and if the person still hears voices or sees images/visions, then doctor can always "up" their dosage.

Dr. Dave had a bumper sticker in his office from a conference that said, *"Change Your Mind About Mental Illness."* He often told me during our spiritual awakening and journey together that, that sticker certainly became meaningful to him. He was never in favor of giving medications for mental disorders, which is why he had written a book, *Holistic Mental Health-Revised* (2009), on alternatives to medications. However, through my experiences and all the healers and authors I have been led to, he has changed his mind on the cause of most mental disorders. When he revised and updated his book in 2009, he even added a chapter, *Spiritual Healing.*

Entity Removal

As I described in The Divine Journey, the lightworkers, psychics, and shamans that worked with me had different techniques of releasing earthbound entities and dark forces.

Dr. William Baldwin's technique, as he describes in *Healing Lost Souls,* is to place his client in an altered state first. When the client is relaxed, such as in a hypnotic trance he is able to talk to the possessing entities in his client. He is able to find out who they are and why they are there. He is able to tell the earthbound entities that they are deceased, and harming their hosts. Then he convinces them to leave, and to go "to the Light" in order to continue their evolutionary journey. This is done by calling upon the entities' spirit guides to come forth and assist them in their transition into the *Light* or spirit dimension.

Dr. Baldwin's final releasement technique, which is important to protect his clients from further attachments, is to seal them in light. He has clients envision a light starting in their center and growing and extending outward to where it creates a protective bubble of light around them.

Dr. Baldwin states that often his clients have layers of entity attachments in them. When he releases more dominant ones, others come up in further sessions. He found that some clients had hundreds and even thousands of entity attachments in layers and layers. This is what Grace had told me I had when she first began working with me. As she began releasing entities into the Light, similar to Dr. Baldwin's technique, she found layer upon layer in me. She told me that she had released hundreds of attached entities in her sessions with me.

Eugene Maurey, in his book, *Exorcism, How to Clear at a Distance a Spirit Possessed Person,* strongly suggests that any clearing and releasing of entities be done at a distance. He believes if an exorcism is done in person, the exorcist (the one conducting the releasement) runs a risk of having the releasing entity invade him or her. In his technique, Maurey holds the image of his client in his mind and then uses a pendulum to get answers to his questions. He asks, if the person is possessed, how many are attached to the person, if the person has any entities in his or her house or at work, and if these negative energies are affecting the person's health. His final question is directed to his client's higher spiritual self and he asks permission to clear this person.

Maurey begins his clearing process by calling upon his guardian angel to assist him. He asks his guardian angel to talk to any possessing entities, to tell them that they are dead, that they do not belong here and are causing trouble to the person they are with, as well as themselves, and that they must leave. He continues to speak to the entities through his guardian angel, telling them how to leave, and that they have a guide that will take them into the spirit dimension to their next level of development. They can join their loved ones who have already crossed over to the Light.

If an earthbound spirit is reluctant to leave, Maurey will threaten them by telling the entity he will trap it in a small black box that has nails piercing it, and that that they will be in that black box forever without any human contact if they do not leave at once.

Reverend Maurey states that he has cleared, released, and exorcised thousands of earthbound entities using these techniques. It doesn't matter where the possessed person lives, as he has conducted distance exorcisms from his home in Chicago on possessed people all over the world. This is similar to what Joanna Neff did for me with her distance clearing from her home in Colorado.

Dr. Edith Fiore conducted her exorcisms in person, working with patients that exhibited mental disorders such as depression, anxiety, phobias, or addictions. She was not as concerned with her being exposed to the demonic earthbound entities as Rev. Maurey was.

In her "depossession" technique, she does, however, begin by protecting herself. She recommends placing a white light around yourself by imagining a miniature sun around your body. It extends around your body at arm's length in a brilliant aura that protects you from any negativity or harm.

Dr. Fiore, as in the other techniques, starts by telling the entities that they are not alive, that they joined the body of another live person, and that they are harming them. She continues that the entity is not fulfilling its own destiny of transitioning to the spirit world where it will be with its deceased loved ones and that there is nothing to fear; there is only heaven, no hell. When it goes into the Light, into the spirit dimension, it will have a wonderful, peaceful life, and there are guides and guardian angels here to help and guide it in its transition.

Example of a Clearing Prayer

The individual you are working with should be lying down or in a relaxed position such as in a reclining chair. Have the person close his or her eyes and take a number of deep breaths. We find using a pendulum can help answer questions in the process of how to proceed. By holding a pendulum over your subject with your free hand resting on the person's arm or leg, do the following:

1. Say, "Show me yes," and note which way the pendulum swings.
2. Say, "Show me no," note which way the pendulum swings It should swing in the opposite direction.
3. Ask, "Are there earthbound entities causing (name)'s problems, illness, condition?" See which way the pendulum swings. If you receive a "no," you might try and ask for other causes of the problem(s). If you get a "yes" then continue.
4. *Ask for guardian angel help*. Ask, and get a "yes" or "no" from the pendulum for each, such as: "Can I call upon Jesus to assist us?" "Can I call upon Archangel Michael to assist us?" "Can I call upon Archangel Raphael to assist us?" "Can I call upon my or (name)'s spirit guide to assist us?" You may get several yes's, so be sure to use all the help you can invoke.

Once you have the protection and help you will need, set the pendulum aside and remove your hand from the person. Begin the cleansing:

1. ***Protect yourself and your client***: Say, "I am placing a protecting and purifying light around me. Nothing can penetrate it. My guardian angel and St.____ and Archangel _____ are standing by, protecting me from any and all harm."

2. Say, "A ball of purifying light is forming and growing and expanding in your abdomen. With each breath you take, the ball of light is growing larger, purifying your every cell, every fiber, expanding outward, and pushing any and all darkness out of you."

3. ***Explain to the entity or entities***: "All earthbound spirits and entities I need to tell you that you are no longer alive, you no longer have a body. You have joined a living being and your presence is harming (name).You may not have realized that you died, and, at the time of your death instead of moving toward the light, you became frightened or disoriented and turned away. You may have been attracted to (name) thinking that by joining with (name) it will make you feel better, but you are harming (name)."

4. ***Ask them to leave:*** "You are harming yourself by not moving on. You have trapped yourself in a lifeless, futile existence. It does not have to be this way. By leaving (name) you can go to the **Light** where there is infinite love, infinite bliss, heaven, and be with your deceased loved ones again. You have nothing to fear, there is no **hell**, only infinite **love**. Your loved ones and your own spirit guide are waiting for you, waiting for you to join them. To even return in another life, another body of your own, if that is was you desire. You are not fulfilling

your destiny, your soul's purpose, by staying here with (name)."

5. ***Send them on their way***: "I am calling (name)'s guardian angels and your spirit guide and your guardian angels to assist you in your transition now. It is time to leave! As you look out you will see a growing white light. Feel the love radiating from it. You may see someone familiar coming towards you. This is your spirit guide here to help you transition to your next phase of existence. An existence of ***love***, ***light*** and ***laughter*** with your loved ones, your soul group. They are all waiting for you. Go now and live in eternal and after-lasting bliss as you are supposed to. You have nothing to fear. Your guides are here to help you. Go now and fulfill your true destiny. Leave (name) NOW!"

Shaman Techniques

The shamans, like Joey, Judy, and Gerry that worked on me did very little talking to the entities. Their techniques involved more physical techniques with background ritual music. They used herbs, like sage and frankincense, or tobacco from the Amazon. They had power animals as helpers, such as eagles and hawks, and used feathers from them in their healing rituals. They had healing crystals and rocks from sacred places. They used drums and special toning bells with sounds or vibrations that they said entities didn't like. During their sessions, they played background music that was drumming and ritual chanting by their shaman teachers.

As they worked on me, sometimes I was naked on the floor, or in a chair, or on a massage table while they danced, chanted, sprayed liquids on me, and blew smoke on me in efforts to get these negative entities to leave. In all cases, they were able to see these entities in me.

I didn't have to tell any of them that I had extreme bloating and discomfort in my abdomen or back. They described what they looked like to me (often before I could protest that I didn't want to know), and where they were in my body. All three of them described dark reptilian like entities with long tentacles wrapped around my stomach or down my back, exactly where I was having pain.

All my shamans were able to pull these entities out of me, making my pain go away. The bloating in my stomach also subsided over the next few days after their rituals. Of course, after each healing they all thought all my problems were over, and all were quite surprised when they saw me again with similar attachments.

Protection From Harmful Entities

My divine journey was my apprenticeship in entity releasement and spiritual cleansing. Each lightworker taught me more and more about releasing these earthbound entity attachments and how to protect myself. Each healer I met gave me another piece to the puzzle.

2: Samuel: 9:

I have been with you where ever you went
I have destroyed your enemies before you
I will make you famous
Like the great ones of the earth
I will give you rest from your enemies
Fear not I will surely be kind to you.

Every lightworker, shaman, and psychic I have met seemed to have his or her own techniques of entity removal, and all appeared to help somewhat. There were physical, as well as psychological/spiritual interventions. Physical interventions that helped release entities and protect against future possession included the use of sage, crystals, salt baths, herbs, and castor oil wraps:

Sage (*Salvia officinalis*) is an herb that is a member of the mint family. It has been used for its medicinal and culinary properties for thousands of years. Its Latin name, *Salvia* means "to heal." Due to its aromatic properties, it has been used to ward off evil since ancient times. In the Middle Ages, it was cultivated in monasteries and used for both medicinal and spiritual properties.

I believe it was Dr. Bob that first recommended sage to me. He used it to purify rooms when he did clearings and house exorcisms, and he suggested that I do the same in my home. The sage, as an essential oil, is diluted into water and put into a spray bottle and then sprayed in the air in each room. He also suggested that I bring a small bottle with me and use it in hotel rooms when traveling, as hotel rooms are very susceptible to lingering entities. Sage in an essential oil form can be found in most health food and herb stores or can be ordered from *www.medicineflower.com*.

Crystals, like sage, have been used for healing and protection since ancient times as well. Many of the psychics and shamans I have met used various crystals for their healing, protection and connection-to-the-divine properties. It was recommended that I use quartz to help protect me from negative energies. Judy Hall's *The Crystal Bible: A Definitive Guide to Crystals* (2004) is, a terrific guide to crystals. She gives a brief history of, and the healing properties of hundreds of crystals. An excellent Website that connects the healing properties of crystals to the chakras and astrological signs, and where you can purchase crystals is *www.healingcrystals.com.* Other excellent sites where you can purchase healing crystals include, *www.healingcrystals.net* and *www.celestialights.com*.

Salt has cleansing, energy releasing and healing properties. It was recommended that I take hot salt baths to help neutralize a lot of the energy that seemed to be burning me up on the inside. Initially I used Epsom salts and sea salt (coarse crystals from the Dead Sea), both easily purchased from a supermarket. However, when I was working with a shaman, Judy Lavine, she suggested that, because of my extraordinary internal energy, I use the large salt pellets that are used for water softeners. These pellets, about the size of a penny come in forty pound bags that we purchase in warehouse stores (like Sam's Club). Adding a couple of cups of the salt pellets to my bath water helped disperse some of the energy that was causing my abdominal bloating.

Castor oil wraps greatly helped to dissipate a lot of the abdominal bloating I felt. By soaking a cloth in castor oil, placing it on my abdomen, and then wrapping Saran Wrap around my body to keep it all in place, I was able to reduce the bloating and get some relief. After spending the night "wrapped," I would get up and take a hot salt bath that would allow me a few hours of relief from the feeling that I was about to explode.

"Canker-Be-Gone": One recurring symptom I had, along with my abdomen bloating, dry and flaking skin, and exhaustion, when the dark forces where attacking was canker sores on my tongue. I had never experienced cankers on my tongue before. However, all three times I ended up in the hospital my tongue was filled with them. Doctors had no explanation for them and couldn't offer me anything to relieve the soreness and pain from them. Interestingly enough, I found a remedy to relieve the pain and actually cure them in a New Age bookstore. It is called "Canker Sores Begone." I guess the bottle caught my eye because it had a wizard on it. The one I used to get rid of my canker sores is distributed by Robin Bar Enterprises, Laguna Niguel, CA, 92677 (phone: 888-877-6315).

House Clearing: Judy Lavine also suggested that I keep negative earthbound entities out of my house and offered a number of suggestions, all of which I did. To clear a room, in addition to spraying sage, she recommended using a large toning bell. She said that entities are very attuned to, and dislike, the higher vibrations that are produced from a metal toning bell. She gave me a special bell that I could ring in each room, especially my bedroom, to cast out any negative entities. She told me that as I went to each room in my house, ringing the bell, also to take a flashlight and make a sign of the cross on a wall in each room.

Judy gave me clear quartz crystals to put in the four corners of my house that would also prevent entities from entering. She also told me to how to make and bury a special glass jar outside on the north side of my house. This would also help prevent harmful earthbound entities from entering. The last measure she had me do to protect myself was to place blank CDs, shiny side out, on the inside of all the windows in my house. Judy explained this would also help to keep entities from entering.

In severe cases of entity house possession, a house exorcism may be necessary. Maurey stated that most earthbound entities that are trapped simply seek familiar places, such as their homes or places of business, and they wander about in their own dimension, paying little attention to other live inhabitants of the same spaces. Occasionally, this is not the case. The entity is upset and confused over its astral plane existence, and intruders in "its" space are not welcome.

Dr. Bob told me of a story of when he did a house exorcism that didn't go quite as well as he had planned. He said he was called in because of the usual unexplained noises and ill feelings that went beyond cold shivers when entering certain rooms in this house. The new occupants were actually getting sick. They had intense feelings of anxiety and depression and nauseous feelings in their stomachs.

Dr. Bob said that when he started to clear the house through prayers, he could see the walls start to bleed. He felt several malevolent presences that he was able to clear by sending them into the Light. But, after a couple of hours, the angels told him to stop But he knew was not done; he wanted to finish. He didn't listen, and he continued, only to have a powerful entity stab him in the left eye, causing him to be permanently blind in that eye. He still regrets not listening to his inner voice that was telling him to stop; he had done enough for one day. He did finish the job the following week. He said he learned not to second guess that inner voice, which was most likely his guardian angel, ever again.

When talking about some of my health problems with Richard Jackson, an exorcist with over thirty years experience, he suggested that he should clear my house. I was grateful for this suggestion because he had told me he was somewhat retired from doing this type of work, and if he did it he would only do it locally. I lived three hours away from him, but for me he felt he should make an exception.

Richard began clearing my house by starting in my basement and systematically going through each room, saying prayers in English and Latin. As he said the prayers, he burned incense of myrrh and frankincense that he had gotten from the Vatican. He also left a number of rosaries with me telling me I should put them around my house in different rooms. Not wanting to exclude any Native American influences, he also left me an eagle and hawk feather.

Belief: All of the above techniques and interventions require some degree of belief. As my knowledge and exposure to these unseen worlds evolved, so did my belief in myself. Belief in my ability to clear myself of negative influences, and to heal myself.

Using things like crystals for protection against negative forces is fine as long as one doesn't become overly obsessed with the things. When you can't leave your house because you misplaced your protection crystal you have become too dependant on things. I had to get to the point where belief in myself and my ability to visualize protection is what protected me.

Many of the shamans I worked with over the years, and certainly many of the books I have been led to used and promoted the use of meditation and visualization. Similar to what Dr. Fiore promoted in her book *The Unquiet Dead*, I developed a protection prayer/visualization of covering myself with white light. Dr. Fiore's protection visualization was:

> *"Imagine you have a miniature sun, just like the sun in our solar system, deep in your solar plexus. This sun is radiating through every atom and cell in your being. It fills you with light to the tips of your fingers, the top of your head, and the soles of your feet. It shines through you and beyond you an arm's length in every direction, above your head, below your feet, out to the sides, creating an aura—a brilliant, dazzling, radiant White Light that completely surrounds and protects you from any negativity or harm."*

I also visualized the White Light in and around me to the point where I am standing in the sun. I am totally immersed in it, and I am one with the sun. There is no darkness anywhere within me, around me or near me. I am totally light, totally ***sunshine*** !

Judy Hall's book, *The Art of Psychic Protection* (1997), is an excellent resource as well. In addition to several meditations throughout her book she provides a resource section listing flower and gem essences, crystals, and aromatherapy that may also be used for protection against entities.

The Unity School of Christianity has a *Prayer of Protection,* and one of my favorite song writers, Mark Stanton Welch also turned it into a song:

> *The light of God surrounds me.*
> *The love of God enfolds me.*
> *The power of God protects me.*
> *The presence of God watches over me.*
> *Wherever I AM, God is.*

"Ghost Hunting"

After everything I have been through with earthbound entity possession, all of the years of pain and discomfort, the depression, the anxiety, the fear caused by these attachments, not only to me, but also most likely to millions of people world-wide for countless years, I find it unbelievable people will go out and "look" for ghosts. They think it might be exciting to try and find something from another dimension so to speak. They are playing with fire!

I find it mind-boggling to think people would go out and look for spirits that could significantly harm them, and if they did find an earthbound spirit or "ghost," how would they protect themselves against it? These people that are out hunting for ghosts are using specialized "ghost-hunting" equipment to find them, meaning they have no psychic abilities to see or sense the entities.

The psychics I have met do not need to use any equipment to see, hear or sense earthbound entities. The psychics and lightworkers I know certainly knew what they were dealing with and had a healthy respect for what these dark entities could do. They also knew how to protect themselves and how to send the entities to the "Light."

Chances are pretty good these "ghost hunters" have no idea how to protect themselves against an attack from these dark and misguided forces. It would be humorous to me if it were not such a serious subject, that people are using equipment to look for spirits, when there are so many genuine psychics out there that can, in fact, see these spirits.

All this ghost hunting business in the movies, on TV, and in the media, may make it look quite glamorous, but, to me it is like someone going tiger hunting without proper equipment, or protection. They are just running through the jungle *blindfolded*, trying to find a tiger, and when they do, they try to grab it with their bare hands! For people that have no psychic abilities, trying to find "ghosts" is just as crazy. I understand the excitement of it all. Its like watching horror movies, it can be exciting, *unless you have been a victim of something horrible.* In that case, you will be the last person to willingly sit through something that reminds you of what you have been through.

Throughout this book, I hope I have made my point. That entity possession is real! It has happened throughout history. It is happening today. Dr. Dave has explained how our consciousness can travel outside of our body, how our souls are our eternal consciousness. If our consciousness does not transition to the spirit realm correctly, it can get trapped in this dimension and misguidingly harm living beings.

When people start playing with things about which they have little understanding of, they can get burnt! Looking for entities and not knowing how to release them and send them on their way or how to protect oneself from them, is asking for trouble. It is pulling a tiger by its tail!

"God is the defender, ascender and finisher."

Spiritual Protection and Recommendations:

- When experiencing supernatural events as in, hearing voices, or seeing energy (images of people or faces changing), consult with a lightworker (spiritual healer, exorcist, shaman, or medium). Inquire as to if they can connect with spiritual energies, and their background and experience with releasing such energies.
- When experiencing chronic anxiety, depression or phobias that appear to have no origins seek out a spiritual healer.
- When experiencing chronic physical aliments that doctors have no diagnosis or cure for, seek out a spiritual healer.
- Use the above clearing prayers for entity releasement and protection.

- Use alternative therapies such as sage, crystals, salt and castor oil for healing and protection.
- DO NOT seek out, or try and attract entities.

* The above suggestions are not intended as a diagnosis, prescription, treatment, or prognosis, or substitute for medical care or licensed medical care. The reader should not modify, suspend, or stop any medical care or licensed health care he or she is now receiving without first consulting with appropriate medical or licensed health care professionals responsible for such care.

Spiritual Awakenings

> *"Light up the Darkness."*
>
> **~ Bob Marley**

Spiritual awakenings have occurred since the beginning of recorded time. When humankind realized that there are forces greater than they are, they began connecting to them. This connection, or spiritual awakening, is what changes someone's life. Spiritual awakenings come in all sizes and shapes. Some are immediately life changing. Some occur gradually by seeking inner peace and spiritual connections. Others occur like a head on collision.

Abraham Maslow (1908-1970), humanistic psychologist, and best know for developing the *Hierarchy of Needs*, describes a spiritual awakening as a "peak experience." He depicts a peak experience as one of profound moments of love, understanding, happiness, or rapture that leaves the individual more alive and self-sufficient and more aware of him or herself and his or her role in the universe. Maslow believed that people at the top of his Hierarchy of Needs, self-actualizing individuals, who are more spontaneous, creative, and not bound by social conventions, have many such peak experiences.

Wayne Dyer, Ph.D. psychologist and author, describes a peak experience as a "quantum moment." In his movie, *The Shift* (2009), he asserts that such an experience has four characteristics: a vivid experience, that is a surprise, is benevolent, and is enduring, lasting forever.

Barbara Harris Whitfield in her book, *Spiritual Awakenings* (1995), discusses several ways people have had spiritual awakenings. Barbara states that one-third to 40 percent report that they have had awakenings through near-death experiences. The NDE may have occurred in an accident as in a car accident or drowning, on an operating table, or even in childbirth. Many report feeling or seeing deceased relatives, guardian angels, heaven, and the loving Light of God. They report that the experience changed their lives by letting them know that they are eternal beings and there is a Universal/God consciousness. The experience gives them the realization that their consciousness is not bound by the physical body.

Another way people have awakenings, Whitfield explains, is through intense meditation or prayer. In meditation one may have an out-of-body experience, experiencing what people experience in near-death experiences. Prayer can give a sense of intense connectiveness to the Universal/God forces. In shamanic rituals using techniques such as holotrophic breathing (intense breathing), or in Kundalini exercises, where the Universal/God connection can occur, one can make that transformation as well.

Sometimes a vivid dream can create a lasting and spiritual connection. Whitfield tells stories of people telling her of a specific dream that awakened their souls. They may have gotten messages from deceased loved ones, spirit guides or even that the Holy Family told them something that turned their lives around.

A third of spiritual awakening experiences can come from a crisis according to Whitfield, such as during the loss of a loved one, or even through withdrawal from chemical dependence. She reminds us that the Chinese symbol for crisis also represents "opportunity," and often a crisis or suffering can cause liberation, a traumatic change in ones life and/or a spiritual awakening.

David R. Hawkins, M.D., Ph.D., in *Power vs. Force: The Hidden*

Determinants of Human Behavior (2002), describes an awakening as coming from Spirit. He states, "The agency of change in spiritual struggles of personal metamorphosis is always beyond the power of the seeker. Great saints, such as Francis of Assisi, have typically asserted that they were mere channels of a higher power-they've taken no credit for personal initiative in achieving their state, which they attributed to Grace." Dr. Hawkins believes that the spiritual awakening occurs when an individual of lesser awareness, is transformed by "osmosis" by being under the influence of one with higher awareness. He states that sometimes prayer and meditation can facilitate a rise from a lower energy field into a higher one.

When reviewing my journey Maureen St. Germain, one of my mentors, described how my awakening was similar to Margaret Starbird's. After reading Margaret's book, *The Goddess in the Gospels: Reclaiming the Sacred Feminine* (1998), I too, believe the similarities were remarkable. Margret also had a spiritual awakening while in a mental ward in a hospital, seeing and later making sense, of unbelievable synchronicities (***Divine Happenings)*** while there. She states:

> *"In the process of my transition, I was not less conscious; I was super conscious, accessing ways of knowing that were not in my usual mode. Synchronicities were pouring through me, showing me connections I could never have imagined. And I was given the gift of interpreting the symbols and the knowledge that I did not have to accept as final, but rather had the power to rewrite the script to suit myself. It was if I had been given antennae with which to pick up information from* ***unsuspected frequencies***. *My spiritual crisis was like that of a* ***butterfly*** *bursting its cocoon to enter a new phase. But at the time I had no inkling of the process of transformation that was occurring. It was an uncharted sea!*

> *"My task when I gradually returned to my normal conscious*

state was to sort through the events I had experienced and to make sense of them-to discover their meaning and purpose."

Sometimes people around you unknowingly play a role in your awakening, as if acting out roles. The *Divine Happenings* become uncanny, leading you into that super-conscious state. Margaret also found that at one point, "The doctors and hospital staff seemed to have been programmed like actors on a stage, speaking their lines so as to trigger my transformation. Their script managed to jolt me into looking at reality." Just like when I was in the hospital *Underworld,* and the doctors and staff were making statements about things that were said to me by Gordan, and they all acted liked they were playing a part in a very bad horror movie, that I was starring in! Even at times, Dr. Dave made statements to me or did things in ways that I now know are uncharacteristic that were influenced by malevolent spirits!

> *"When you have an awakening you start to view your life in a whole new reality; you may even think you are having a nervous breakdown because your life views change so much;…it changes you from the inside out!"*

~ What The Bleep Do We Know!?

In my case, my spiritual awakening occurred through a crisis of which I had no understanding at the time. It was as if I had been thrown into a fire and only began to make sense of it all when the flames subsided over the next four years. As Dr. Dyer described a quantum movement, it was vivid, certainly a surprise, benevolent, and enduring. And, like Margaret Starbird, during my spiritual transformations, I was super-conscious, and, only much later, began to make sense of all I had been through. Each psychic healer and shaman gave me a few more pieces of the puzzle of what happened and why it happened to me. I certainly felt the influences of a higher energy field, higher frequencies. It caused me to burst out of my cocoon and spread my wings, transformed forever! And, like all the others that have had spiritual awakenings, it totally turned my life upside down and changed it forever. But, I guess that is what a spiritual awakening is.

Am I Ready
By Kristine Wilbur

Who am I?
Am I ready for the laughter?
Am I ready for the joy........that's coming my way?
In my life,
I'm so used to feeling lonely
And it's normal to feel bad
and comfortable with pain.
But today I feel the lightness
today I feel the grace.
And the world and my imperfections
I embrace..
But now I've felt that joy of living
As my eyes become unblind
And this awesome change in perception
blows my mind!
So am I ready for the joy
that's coming my way?
Am I ready for the joy
that's coming my way?

"Without *Transformation* there would be no *Butterflies!*"

IX ~ The Divine Race

"Humanity is going to have to have a substantially new way of thinking if it is to survive."
~ Albert Einstein

"...There's a battle outside and it is ragin'
...And don't criticize what you can't understand
...Your old road is rapidly agin.'
*...The order is rapidly fadin' and the **first one now will***
later be last
For the times they are a changin'."
~The Times They Are A-Changin
By Bob Dylan

The Evolution of Consciousness

"Change your thinking, change your life!"
~ Dr. Ernest Holmes

For thousands of years this earth has been in 3-D consciousness. This is the consciousness of the physical world. Of ego, of greed, of man hurting man, of war, of domination. Scientists would describe the world as what you can only see with the five senses; the physical world of height, width and depth.

In the past one hundred years we have progressed to a 4-D world. One that adds the fourth dimension of time to the 3-D world. With that understanding consciousness began expanding. Quantum physics and the Theory of Relativity began connecting the physical world of the senses, the world without, to the subatomic world within and to time.

In the twentieth century we began renewing ancient healing methods and beliefs and combined them with modern understanding of the physical and subatomic worlds. We have begun expanding our consciousness from the world without, to the world within. We have come to understand that by controlling our thoughts, we can control not only our mental well being, but our physical one as well.

We have come to understand that unseen energy in and around us affects us in so many ways. We have come to realize that there are people on the planet that can see and use these energy fields. They can see, feel and read these energies. They can use them to heal, to tell the past, present or future. And, some can even use them to create.

As consciousness continues to develop in this century

HIS-tory will become *HER-story!*

The divine feminine will be the driving force of human consciousness. Love and light will overshadow man's ego that has kept the planet in pain and darkness for thousands of years.

The divine feminine will be the catalyst to evolve our human consciousness from 4-D consciousness to 5-D consciousness, which is connecting to the spirit dimension. In the near future, not the few, but, the majority of humankind will be able to connect with the spirit dimension. They will be able to see and feel energies around us, connect with the psychic energies to see into the future, understand our pasts, where we came from, and be able to heal themselves and others with their thoughts and a wave of their hands. They will be able to see and hear the unseen forces around us, the ones that help and guide us, not the ones that hold us down or keep us from our true destinies of a pain free, happy and fulfilling life.

"Remember, I'm pulling for you. We're all in this together!"

~ Red Green

The Age of Aquarius

Just as the Fifth Dimension's (great name) 1960's song, ***Aquarius*** states:

> *"When the moon is in the Seventh House*
> *and Jupiter aligns with Mars*
> *Then peace will guide the planets*
> *and love will steer the stars.*
> *…This is the dawning of the Age of Aquarius."*

We are in fact, entering into the *Age of Aquarius*. It takes the Earth approximately 2,160 years to pass through one sign of the twelve zodiac constellations. Astronomers believe that we entered into the Age of Pisces about two thousand years ago. This would place the earth entering into the Age of Aquarius in the next hundred years or so.

Caroline Myss describes that the Piscean Age is signified by its symbol; two fish swimming in opposite directions. This has been expressed in the past two thousand years in man's continual need to divide and conquer, separate and study, split the East and the West; in division of body and soul, male and female, and yin and yang.

She states that the Age of Aquarius is one of moving into unity and holism. We will move into an environment of a global community, where humanity will be drawn together. Body, mind and spirit will become unified.

Alice Howell in *The Heavens Declare: Astrological Ages and the*

Evolution of Consciousness (2006), states that the Age of Aquarius will bring about, "The discovery of the inner Self, the Divine Guest within us, and with it the need to recognize this in *all* people and in nature as well: it will be the dialectic of the individual and the cosmos. More simply stated, it could mean the discovery of the sacred in the commonplace, a reconciliation of the transcendence and immanence of spirit-a cosmic ecology, if you will-a deep understanding of the interdependence of all life."

> *"We need to go from a Me generation,*
> *to a WE generation."* ~ **Ed Lightfoot**

Many believe that this shift to a higher consciousness of unity, love and peace began in the 1980's with the Harmonic Convergence (1987), and is now flowing through 2012. The year 2012 has become popular due to the ending of the Mayan calendar. The Mayans had developed a 5,125 year calendar that began in the year 3,113 BC, and ends in 2012. Many authors and Hollywood are cashing in on the "end of time" scenario of 2012.

I could not disagree more with their interpretation of what 2012 signifies. Just as the world did not begin in 3,113 BC, it will not end in 2012. All the Mayans did, was to develop a calendar that had a 5,125 year cycle, just as we have decades and centuries. At the end of their cycle, their calendar begins again for the next 5,125 years. There is no record of the Mayans predicting the end of the world. All the "end of time predictions" are being promoted by irresponsible authors or movie makers in order to make money for themselves.

Daniel Pinchbeck in his book, *2012 The Return of Quetzalcoatl*, describes a shift in consciousness in the years to come. He states that the Mayan and Toltec civilizations of Mesoamerica described 2012 as the end of a "Great Cycle" of more than five thousand years and the conclusion of one world cycle and the beginning of the next one. He also says that the end of the Great Cycle is associated with the return of their deity Quetzalcoatl. Quetzalcoatl in the

Mesoamerican language, Nahuatl, means "feathered-serpent." It is believed that he was the patron god of priesthood and knowledge, and represents the fusion of spirit and matter.

Mayan and Aztec legend has it that at the end of the Great Cycle, when Quetzalcoatl returns, there will be a shift in the nature of the human psyche. Pinchbeck states that, "If this theory is correct, the transformation of consciousness will lead to the rapid creation, development, and dissemination of new institutions and social structures corresponding to our new level of mind. From the limits of our current chaotic and uneasy circumstances, this process may well resemble an advance toward a harmonic, perhaps even utopian, situation on the Earth." Pinchbeck believes, "human consciousness is rapidly transitioning to a new state, a new intensity of awareness that will manifest as a different understanding, a transformed realization, of time and space and self."

As we approach 2012 and beyond, Pinchbeck states a shift in consciousness will occur; "Human consciousness, the sentient element of this Earth, is the process of self-organizing to a more intensified state of being and knowing—what the Russian mystic G. I. Gurdjieff called a 'higher octave.' When the Hopi talk of a Fifth World, or the Aztecs anticipate a Sixth Sun, when St. John foresees the descent of the Heavenly City or New Jerusalem, they are describing the same thing: a shift in the nature of consciousness."

> *"The World will be saved by the Western women."*
> **~ The Dalai Lama**

What I see happening in the year 2012 and beyond, as we move into the Age of Aquarius, like Daniel Pinchbeck states, is a rise in the consciousness of the planet. As I stated above, **His**tory will become **Her**story, as the divine feminine energy will take over the planet. Love, unity, and peace will start to dominate the planet in 2012 and through the Age of Aquarius. I see humans, *Homo Sapiens* (Latin meaning "Wise Man") evolving into *"Homo Luminous"* (Beings of

Light). Earth will move from the Dark Ages (prior to the 1800's) and the New Age (1900's) to the Light Ages (2000 and beyond). This is the most exciting time to be alive!

> *"Resolve to Evolve and problems Dissolve!"*
> **~ Michael Beckwith**

> *"…No more backward thinkin' time to teach a new way.*
> *…The world won't get no better if we just let it be.*
> *…I know we can do it if we all lend a hand.*
> *…The only thing we have to do is put in our mind*
> *surely things will work out, they do every time."*
> **~Wake Up Everybody**
> **By Harold Melvin**

Crystal Children

Many of the psychics I have met have had their abilities since they were children. They were able to see or feel energy or have feelings about previous lives or future events. Some were encouraged by open and supportive parents. Others, were told not to talk of such things, or, even punished for "lying" when telling of what they were experiencing. Some where even taken to medical "professionals" and put on mind-numbing drugs.

A term for these special children being born in the 1960's and 1970's are "Indigo Children." This term was coined by Nancy Ann Tappe in her book, *Understanding Your Life Through Color: Metaphysical Concepts in Color and Aura* (1986). In it, she describes a new breed of children being born with "indigo" auras. That these children have special, unusual and/or supernatural abilities or traits. Lee Carroll and Jan Tober also wrote about these children in *The Indigo Children: The New Kids Have Arrived* (1998).

Crystal Children are gifted from an early age. They should

be listened to and encouraged to trust their feelings and express themselves. Parents can quickly tell fact from fiction. Is what they are saying coming true? Are they describing deceased relatives correctly? Are they telling of places that actually exist if talking about living somewhere else "before they were born"? (In a *Divine Happening,* Dr. Dave's daughter's name is Krystal, born in 1994).

Dr. Dave came home one day from work and told me about a student he was counseling at his high school. He said she was depressed and nearly suicidal. She had told him that she was hearing voices. Probing further, Dr. Dave determined they were not threatening or telling her to hurt herself. He found that she had had many other psychic experiences growing up, but, when she tried to tell family members what she was experiencing, they wouldn't believe her. When she told other doctors, they wanted to put her on medication. Dr. Dave told her about some of what I had been going through, and that he had met others with psychic abilities that could hear voices or see energy. She was nearly elated telling him, "You're the first doctor that I've talked to that doesn't think I'm crazy!"

Dr. Dave told me that, after that, her depression seemed to lift and she would often come by and see him. Dr. Dave gave her a copy of *Healing with the Angels* by Doreen Virtue, Ph.D. They had numerous talks on spirituality the rest of the school year. She graduated from high school and went on to college. She thanked Dr. Dave on graduation day, telling him, "I just want to thank you again for believing in me." Sometimes people just need someone else to believe in them.

Children are often so much more in tune with the spirit dimension. They are born in 4-D consciousness and, whether they are supported at an early age or not, will often determine how soon they progress to 5-D consciousness, where they open their gifts even more.

In *Healing with the Angels,* Doreen Virtue states that there is a "new breed" of children that were born in the 1980's and 1990's, that are often referred to as "Children of the Light," "Millennium Children," and "Crystal Children." They will come into adulthood around 2012. "Rainbow Children" are children born in this millennium. As children and teenagers, she states, are often misunderstood because they may be hearing voices, having visions, and be connecting to angel energies. They may even be frustrated in school over being forced to learn what they feel is meaningless information and subjects. Unfortunately, parents and doctors are often quick to put them on medications that presumably "help" them focus in school, or that quiet these voices and visions they have. These children often start to forget the connections that were coming to them, until many times, as young adults they have some type of an "awakening."

Oftentimes, Crystal Children are diagnosed with disorders such as ADD or ADHD, and even Bipolar Disorder. They are put on harmful pharmaceuticals in order to "focus" and "fit-in." Dr. Dave, in his book, *Holistic Mental Health-Revised,* (2009) discusses the controversy over such diagnosis and how harmful the "medications" they put children on are. They have a difficult time in school and rarely find adults that understand why they are different. But, their opening up to their gifts and their awakening as young adults may be a lot less traumatic than what others have gone through. Just as Dr. Michael Sharp described in *The Book of the Triumph of Spirit:*

> *"The third wave will struggle hardly at all. They will wake-up to emerging divine world order. They will not need to be convinced of the dying old. They will not need to be convinced of The Promise of Shambhala. They will see it with their own eyes."*

The Crystal and Rainbow Children will not have to struggle through the pain that I and others have gone through. They will awake, and help create a *"**New Divine World**"* order.

Divine Purpose

Why do so many people live in physical or psychological pain?
Why do people die of long, painful illnesses?
Why do children die?
Why are there so many obstacles in our life?
Why do "bad things" happen to good people?
Why does God allow so many bad things to happen in this world?
What is the purpose of this life?
Why are we here?

Like many, I have asked these questions so many times. So often, when I was in pain for months at a time, I asked what is the purpose of this all? I even begged God to take me to the spirit dimension and leave this world full of physical pain, addictions, vanity, hatred. Often, Dr. Dave had to reassure me this was all temporary, that my pain and turmoil were for a higher purpose. He said, if we were spirits, we would certainly be pain free and able to do anything, take any form, go anywhere just by our thoughts, but what would we learn?

We have come to believe, that we are here for a purpose, just as everyone is. The physical or psychological pain we go through in this life on Earth is so we grow and learn from these experiences. Sometimes we may become overwhelmed by these illnesses, these tragedies, even the circumstances of who we are and the family or the environment we are born into. We can be overwhelmed by our physical or mental addictions to things like alcohol, drugs, sex, food, mental compulsions, and habits. However, whether we learn our lesson in this life, or after it, when we are reviewing our life from the spirit dimension, we are always learning and moving our soul forward.

The purpose of life on earth is to learn and grow our soul! Earth is the school. Love is the Lesson!

Karma is always at work. Lessons we did not learn in a previous life may be learned and experienced in the next. If we hurt others in a previous life, we get hurt, and feel how it is to be a victim, in the next life. If we were a princess in a previous life we may be a pauper in the next.

We have come to learn and believe, that **we** choose our life lessons. What we need to learn in the next life to grow our souls, *we* decide before we come into that life.

So does God or do we choose our destiny? Most philosophers, psychics, shamans, and gurus would agree that we have free will. And our choices shape our destiny. Our free will determines our life on this planet, even before we get here.

We choose our life lesson, often with our soul group. We decide what lesson we need to learn in this life, and often our parents, children, soul-mates, close relatives and friends help us. When a parent loses a child to an illness or tragedy it was predetermined in the spirit dimension before he or she started this life. It was a contract between the parent and the child so that the parent may learn and grow from the experience. The pain and suffering we go through is predetermined before we start this life in order to grow our souls.

"…And in the end, the love you take, is equal to the love you make!"
~ The Beatles

The *free will* we experience may in fact, be predetermined before we enter this life by us! We choose our life experiences. The tragedies in our lives, the pain and suffering we go through, are all designed by us before we get here so that we may learn and grow.

The pain I have endured, the physical and psychological torment

I have encountered in this life from the people in my life, the illnesses I experienced and the unseen forces and entities attacking me, all were for a reason, that I might learn and grow and help others. It was my ***divine purpose!***

"Imagination is the true magic carpet."
~ Norman Vincent Peale

"…Imagine all the people living in peace
…Imagine all the people sharing all the world
…I hope someday you'll join us
*And the world will live as **ONE!**"*
~Imagine
By John Lennon

Suddenly I See "A New Amazing (awe and wonder of the Power and Presence of God) ***Race"***

"All that we are is the result of what we have thought."
~ Buddha

I see in the not-to-distant future:

A human race filled with enlightened, loving people.
A race of people that rely on the God/Source/Universe for everything, making God their constant partner, and best friend.
A race of people that can prove that nothing is ever irreversible,

incurable, or impossible. Knowing that all things are possible if you believe.

A race of people who are SET FREE from the robbers of the **TRUTH.**

A race of people where the power is in the hands of the **Just,** *who prove that the only true real power is* **LOVE.**

A race of people that choose to see impossible as **I'm possible** *(I Am possible) instead.*

A race of people that prove just as the Beatles song says:

> *"There's nothing you can do that can't be done,*
> *There's nothing you can sing that can't be sung.*
> *There's nothing you can see that isn't shown.*
> *There's no one you can save that can't be saved.*
> **It's Easy. All you need is love, Love is all you need."**

A race of people whose only fashion concern is the ONE that never goes out of style; **Caring and Love.**

A race of people with the ability to heal themselves with the power of their thoughts.

A race of people that never hates or harms anyone or anything.

A race of people celebrating ONENESS!

Parents that love and support their children. Who do not easily dismiss it as their child's imagination when they tell of hearing or seeing things that they don't.

Schools that teach children the power of positive thoughts, and how to believe in oneself.

People connecting with Universal energies. Connecting with the **God-Source.** *The* **I AM** *consciousness.*

People that are able to manifest their dreams into reality, through the power of belief.

People able to see all the wondrous signs in all their forms all around them.

People able to see energy in all its forms.

*People understanding that, "**What one person believes to be true is more powerful than what many accept as the truth**!"*

*People making everyday Christmas, in the **Spirit** of giving, and loving and promoting world peace.*

> **It's never to late to be what you could have been.**
> **Hope is not bound by age or time!**

When nobody believed me, I believed it was God leading me, and I listened to my heart. As Jesus said:

> **"Not as the world sees, do I see."** *And:*
> **"It will be done onto you according to your belief."**

I believe that your faith will always guide you!

> **"Vision is not what you see; it is**
> **what you see that will be."**

> *"As YOU believe, so YOU become!"*
> ~ **Unknown**

> *"The future belongs to those who BELIEVE*
> *in the beauty of their Dreams."*
> ~ **Eleanor Roosevelt**

"...Believe in what your heart is sayin.'
...Believe in what you feel inside.
...You have everything you need if you just believe."

~Just Believe
By Josh Grobin
Glen Silvestri / Alan Anthony

"Get a FAITH lift"

~ Lucille Hemond

Namaste

"We were born to thrive, not to strive."

~ Rev. Ian Taylor

The first time Reverend Ian Taylor spoke at Concordia Center for Spiritual Living, I knew he was special. He began with, *"Namaste, welcome home!"* He went on to say that he interprets Namaste to mean, "The divine in me salutes and honors the divine in you."

Namaste is a Sanskrit word used in India and Nepal as a greeting that can be translated as, "I honor the Spirit in you, which is also in me," "I salute the God within you," "That which is of God in me greets that which is God in you," "All that is best and highest in me greets/salutes all that is best and highest in you," or, "The Divinity within me perceives and adores the Divinity within you."

As I became to know Rev. Ian he certainly met all of the above. Each week Dr. Dave and I looked forward to hearing his sermons or as he calls them "lessons." He is so truly inspiring, connected and in 5-D consciousness that we believe he should be speaking in front of thousands each week. And, I know in the near future he will be.

Many of my friends started to call me Mary *"Divine"* as they got to know me. But, what I really feel and believe they are saying

307

is "Namaste." And, what I am saying when I say Mary *Divine* is just that.

The Divine in me blesses and honors the Divine in YOU!

NAMASTE!

"Always look for the God in others "
&
"Have a GOD Day, Everyday!"

" Make your destiny ONE with the Divine, and you'll have WON Divine Destiny!"

X Epilogue

*"Life is God's gift to you,
Living is your gift to God!"*
~ Rev. Ian Taylor

This has been the story of my spiritual awakening. As unbelievable (even to me) as a lot of it appears it all happened just as I have described. I feel so blessed to have met all the people I have met on my journey, and to have been led to the knowledge from the Masters throughout history.

I know now why I went through so much turmoil, bad relationships, and so much mental and physical pain. It was so that I could help others, and to help heal the Universe. It was my destiny, my karma, my mission, my *divine purpose* to go through what I went through. I now know that I have been blessed.

"Being lost was worth coming home."

Through all my experiences, it is my hope that others will gain new perspectives (as I did) about life, afterlife, and why we are here. That you will change your mind about mental illness. That you might see worlds you never knew existed.

Nothing is ever what it at first seems to be. Refuse to accept the *seemingly* negative appearance of a difficult situation or experience. Soon you will see things in a different way. It will have a new perspective on a different day. In time, time reveals. **Give time, time!** As my most beloved Rev. Ian says: ***"Maybe with slowness, but with sureness always."***

> *"It doesn't come to break you,*
> *it comes to make you, YOU!"*
> **~ Dr. Robert H. Schuller**

I could never have imagined how extraordinarily meaningful my life is today. It seems just a few years ago, before everything started happening, that all I had wanted, all I prayed for was to meet someone nice, stable and loving, that was perhaps a little older, so we could move to a seniors resort in Florida (I was in my early forties). But, God had other plans for me!

Don't ever underestimate God's plan for your life!

It reminds me of a song by Garth Brooks, "Unanswered Prayers." Where, in the chorus he says:

> *Sometimes I thank God for unanswered prayers.*
> *Remember when you're talkin' to the man upstairs*
> *That just because he doesn't answer,*
> *doesn't mean he don't care.*
> *Some of God's greatest gifts are unanswered prayers!*

I was **Divinely Touched** by God's grace, and by my guardian angels in the spirit and earth dimensions, *transforming* my life forever. Dr. Dave and I love Star Trek. The words from the theme song from the last TV series really summed-up how I feel about my journey.

"…*I've got faith to believe I can do anything, I can reach any star.*
I've got strength of the soul, no ones gonna bend or break me.
…*I've got faith, I've got faith, faith of the heart.*
Its been a long road!"
~Where My Heart Will Take Me
(Theme from Enterprise)
by Russell Watson

"We and they—all things and everything are a connected whole. That is the meaning of 'We are one.' The evolution of the Universe, then, is continuing not only around us , but within us. Our thoughts, our dreams, and our awareness are part of that Universe, the physical and spiritual, inextricably bound together."

~ Shirley MacLaine

"*The Source is always with you!*"

XI Divine Resources

Grace Avila

Spiritual Medium/Healer
Certified in Integrated Energy Therapy,
(IET), Reflexology,
Chakra Energizing
HEALING HEARTS CENTER
1542 Main St.
West Warwick, RI 02893
401-545-5295
www.healingheartsri.com
openheart323@gmail.com

Rita Marie Bryant

Spiritual Healer, Life Activations,
King Solomon Healing

203 Pickett District Road
New Milford, CT 06776
860-354-6457

www.pureheartscenter.blogspot.com
pureheartscenter@yahoo.com

*Christopher D.
Carlow, D. Ac.*

Doctor of Acupuncture
Certified in Tai Chi & Qigong
Instructor, Herbal Medicine

NATURES's HEALING
982 Tiogue Ave.
Coventry, RI 02816
401-219-6446
www.NaturesHealing.info
chris_carlow@yahoo.com

Jackie Eaton, RN

Spiritual Intuitive & Medium,
Reiki & Magnified Healing
Master Teacher,
Soul Life & Past Regression Facilitator,
Angel Therapy Practitioner

3240 Mendon Rd.
Cumberland, RI 02864
401-658-4417
www.angelights.net
angelights@cox.net

Ed Douzanis

Shamanic Teacher, Channeler,
& Reiki Master
19 Pierce Ave.
Lakeville, MA 02347
774-766-7427

Dr. Heidi Gabrilowitz

IET Master Instructor
Yoga Instructor
Sacred Space Blessing

401-258-6362

www.thelifebeatinstitute.com
hgabrilowitz@verizon.net

Pat Hastings

Author, Inspirational Speaker,
Spiritual Coach, Retreat Leader &
Radio Talk Show Host
Simply A Woman of Faith
PO Box 28844
Providence, RI 02908
(401) 521-6783

www.simplyawomanoffaith.com
pat@simplyawomanoffaith.com

Cora Hayward

EMF Balancing Practitioner,
Teacher of Teachers of Phases I-IV,
Teacher of Phases I-XII,
Practitioner of Phases I-XIII,
Massage Therapist
2 Spring Garden Ave.,
Norwich, CT 06360
860-639-1076 or 860-892-9299

www.emfbalancingtechnique.com
chayward01@snet.net

Linda Hogan

Energy Healer, Wisdom Teacher,
& Author of
Walk Gently Upon The Earth
& *The Shaman in Your Cupboard*

Salem, MA
401-949-0049
www.sacrednewearth.com
gaiahealer@yahoo.com

Richard Jackson

Spiritual Healer,
Exorcist

1211 Johnson Road
Woodbridge, CT 06525
203-387-7725

www.richardpjackson.com
rich22jack@yahoo.com

Judy Lavine

Shamanic Healer,
Medical Intuitive,
Teacher & Author

P.O. Box 16311
Rumford, RI, 02916
401-465-5438
www.JudyLavine.com
JudyLavine@gmail.com

Dr. Robert B. Marzilli Jr.,

Chiropractic Physician
Certified in ART, AMP, & CKTP

Marzilli Chiropractic Center
Suite 108A
1395 Atwood Ave.
Johnston, RI 02919
401-270-9595
drmarz@cox.net

Jerry Miller

Shamanic Healer:
Studied with Shamans in
the Amazon for 30 years

P.O. Box 126
East Haddam, CT 06423
860-873-8286

Stephanie Miller

Psychic Readings, Animal
Communication and Healing,
Channeling Spirits

West Warwick, RI
401-499-3525

atouchoflight@ymail.com

Joanna Neff

Soul Retrieval, Entity Removal,
Accelerated Healing

The Light Expansion Center
3250 O'Neal Circle #D13
Boulder, CO 80301
www.melora.org/soulclear
healinglightexp@infionline.net

Kerrie O'Connor

Medium, Intuitive Readings,
Metaphysical Workshops,
Energy Field Balancing
P.O. Box 2057
Salem, CT 06420
860-887-1201
www.kerrieoconnor.com
Union1111@yahoo.com

Amorah Quan Yin

Spiritual Teacher, Author, Healer

PO Box 1581
Mt. Shasta, CA
(530) 926-1122
www.amorahquanyin.com

Andrew Oser

Spiritual/Life Coach
Author, Retreat Leader
Workshop Facilitator
P.O. Box 232
Mt. Shasta, CA, 96067
760-525-4512
www.mtshastaretreat.net
adoser777@yahoo.com

Dr. Ysabel V. Reyes

Board Certified Internist
Nutritional Consultant
Past Life Therapy
Dream Interpretation
401-345-0896
401-615-0284
gaviotareyes@yahoo.com

Vanessa Riyasat

Intuitive Energy Master
& Intuitive Consultant
Classes, Workshops, Retreats
The Crystal Lotus
Healing Center LLC
203-232-7927
www.stairwaytohealing.com
Vanessa@stairwaytohealing.com

Marlene Robinson

BFA, LMT, NCTMB,
Reconnective Healing Practitioner
EARTH & OCEAN SPA
& Wellness Center
23 Brown Street
Wickford, RI 02852
401-397-3157 or 401-269-1301
mrobinsonlmt@yahoo.com

Maureen St. Germain

International Author and Lecturer
Certified Flower of Life &
Soul Retrieval Facilitator
Author of Beyond The Flower of Life
559 W. 183rd Bsmt 1
New York, NY, 10033
212-304-2123
www.maureenstgermain.com
info@maureenstgermain.com

Dr. Michael Sharp

International Author and lecturer
Author of The Great Awakening,
The Book of Light, The Book of Love,
The Dossier of Ascension,
The Song of Creation,
The Book of The Triumph of Spirit

www.michaelsharp.org

Rev. Robert "Ram" Smith

Minister, Musician
International Ananda Yoga &
Kriya Yoga Meditation Instructor

P.O. Box 676
Narragansett, RI
401-218-5858
anandarhodeisland.org
ramsmith108@gmail.com

318

Michelle Sutton

Spiritual Counselor, Reiki Master,
I-ACT Certified Colon
Hydrotherapist

COLONIC INSTITUTE of
West Hartford
43 North Main Street
West Hartford, CT, 06107
860-521-8831
www.heartsong-yoga.com
colonics4life@aol.com

"Chief" Joey Stann

Shaman &
Reiki Master

44 Winthrop Road
Edison, NJ 08817

www.joeystann.com
jstann@aol.com

Carol Stanton ND, RN

ASYRA Testing, Naturopathic
Consulting,
Ondamed Therapy, Reflexology

NATURE's WISDOM
WELLNESS CENTER
54 High Street
Westerly, RI 02891
401-596-5700
www.natureswisdomwelldom.com
natureswisdomwellness@yahoo.com

Reverend Ian Taylor

CONCORDIA Center for
Spiritual Living

292 West Shore Road
Warwick, RI 02889
401-732-1552

www.concordiachurchri.com

Dr. Kelley Taylor-Bentz
Holistic Chiropractor, Reiki
Master, IET Master, Life Coach

85 Sea Pine Road
Wellfleet, MA 02667
508-813-3881

www.emergewachingservices.com
drkelleyecs@hotmail.com

Fran Ganek M.Ed. ACHt
Angel Reader/ Angel Medium
Wellness Educator/ Presenter
Workshop Facilitator & Writer

774-641-5829

gracebyangels@gmail.com

**White Swan
(Cheryl Weeden)**

Reiki Master, Light Dancer
Medicine Wheel,
Certified Angelspeake, Spiritual
Intuitive Counselor

722 West Allenton Rd.
North Kingstown, RI
401-295-1277
whiteswansdream@yahoo.com

Terry Wildemann

Certified Coach, Writer, Trainer,
Workshop Facilitator,
and Intuitive. Holistic background as
a Reiki Master, EFT & Stress Coach .

Middletown, RI
401-849-5900
www.windsofchange.biz
Terry@TerryWildemann.com

320

XII A Divine Glossary

Acupuncture: Ancient Chinese medicine that uses manipulation, usually with needles, of meridian pathways in the body.

Akashic Records: Derived from the Sanskrit word *Akasha* meaning "sky" or "space." First used in Theosophy to describe records in nonphysical planes.

Ancient Wisdom: Wisdom passed down through the ages on subjects such as healing, life's purpose and the spirit world.

Applied Kinesiology: Chiropractic diagnostic method using manual muscle-strength testing for medical diagnosis and subsequent determination of prescribed therapy.

Ascended Master: A divine being who made a choice to return to serve humanity. They can return and travel anywhere at will, materialize objects and perform miracles such as miraculous healings.

Ascension: The attainment of enlightenment and immortality while an individual is still in a human-bodily form.

ASYRA therapy: Holistic diagnostic therapy that combines homeopathy with a computerized system called CEDSA.

Astral Beings: Beings that are trapped and dwell in the astral dimension.

Astral Body: Energy layer lying outside the etheric energy layer of the body.

Astral Plane: The world of the individual and collective subconscious mind.

Astral Projection: The ability to project ones consciousness outside of the body, and to be aware of events in other locations.

Astrology: A science of interpreting the position of the stars and planets at the time of one's birth, in order to predict one's life path and personality traits.

Atlantis: Legendary continent and ancient civilization in the Atlantic Ocean described by Plato, that sank 9,600 years ago.

Atman: The "I Am" self, the divine presence within, the aspect of individuality that is one with God. Derived from the Sanskrit meaning soul, often used in the Hindu religion.

Aura: The subtle energy field that encompasses an individual's physical body. Psychics often see this energy field in different colors.

Avatar: Sanskrit word meaning "He crosses over." An incarnation of God, and God embodied in human form.

Be-Attitudes: Attitudes of being in which one lives in God's Grace. These are true spiritual qualities such as unconditional love, compassion, forgiveness, kindness, etc.

Brahman: Sanskrit word meaning "Worship, prayer." The supreme, eternal Spirit of the universe, the impersonal God, the attribute less absolute wholeness.

Buddha: Sanskrit word meaning "The enlightened one." One who embodies divine wisdom and virtue. The first "Buddha" was

Siddhartha Gautama who lived in ancient India somewhere around 563 to 483 BC

Causal Field: Outer most energy layer around the human body that connects with the spiritual realm.

CEDSA: Computerized Electro-Dermal Screening device used in ASYRA therapy.

Chakras: Whirling energy points in the body, associated with specific colors. Sanskrit word meaning "wheel" or "turning."

Clairaudience: From the French word meaning "clear hearing." The ability to hear subtle sounds through sensing with the inner ear. Hearing through extrasensory perception.

Clairsentience: From the French word meaning "clear feeling." The ability to feel, sense, taste, or smell through inner sensing. Kinesthetic acuity beyond the range of normal bodily feeling. Feeling through extrasensory perception.

Clairvoyance: The ability to see beyond the five senses. Seeing with the "third eye," the eye of wisdom. Using extrasensory perception. From the French word meaning "clear seeing."

Consciousness: The higher identity, the intangible aspect of the individual that makes us aware of our self. The aspect of self that is changeless and immortal.

Crystal Children: Children born in the 1980's and 1990's that have unusual and/or special and psychic gifts.

De'ja' vu: From the French word meaning "already seen." A feeling of having been here before.

Dharma: From the Sanskrit word meaning "righteousness." One's true purpose, that which one has chosen to accomplish in this incarnation.

Divination: The art or practice that seeks to foresee or foretell future events, or discover hidden knowledge, usually by the interpretation of omens or by the aid of supernatural powers.

Divine: Of or pertaining to God, sacred, from God, heavenly, godlike.

Dowsing: The technique of using a tool such as a Y-shaped twig, L-shaped rod or pendulum to find things such as water or precious metals.

Earthbound Spirit: A human astral body or entity that is bound to the material plane after death.

Eckankar: A New Age religion established in the 1960's by Paul Twitchell. Eckankar means "Co-worker with God." It teaches that there is one Supreme Being, that the soul is eternal, and that it is on a journey of self and God-Realization.

Electro-Magnetic Effect: Applying electro-magnetic currents to the body that promotes tissue regeneration and healing.

EMF Balancing Technique: An energy healing technique that is primarily hands-off, developed by Peggy Phoenix Dubro in the 1990's.

Enlightenment: A higher state of consciousness, free from ignorance, judgment, and prejudice. Also known as *jivan mukti,* liberation of the soul, in which one is free from the need to reincarnate.

Entity: An individual, separate being. Usually referring to an earthbound spirit.

ESP: Extrasensory perception, a term popularized by J.B. Rhine in the 1930's. Referred to information perceived by clairvoyance, telepathy, or precognition.

Etheric body: Energy layer encompassing the physical body.

Exorcism: A Catholic ceremony in which usually a priest expels a possessing entity.

Grace: A state of awareness in which one is in contact with God's presence. In this state miracles can happen and divine blessings occur. With the Law of Grace, one can overcome the law of Karma, and annihilate the effect of past actions.

Guru: From the Sanskrit word meaning: Gu: "darkness" and Ru: "light." One who destroys darkness and illusion and brings forth the light. A spiritual guide or teacher, ultimately one's supreme self.

Harmonic Convergence: Celestial event that occurred on August 16, 1987, when eight out of the ten planets in our solar system formed an unusual configuration called a grand triangle where the Sun, Moon and six planets formed an equilateral triangle.

Hinduism: From the Sanskrit word "India, land of the Indus." A religious philosophy based upon the ancient Vedic texts and rituals. It teaches that one can gain union with God through meditation, devotion, and other disciplines.

Homeopathy: Holistic therapy that treats and cures illness by using dilutes that contain vibrational frequencies that stimulate the body to heal itself.

Indigo Children: Children born with special psychic gifts or abilities.

Ideomotor effect: Unconscious movements by the body, as in reflexive responses to pain.

Intuition: Inner listening, seeing or feeling. Direct inner perception or knowledge without the use of reasoning.

Karma: Sanskrit word meaning "act," "action" or "performance." In Indian religions it is the concept of action or deeds that causes a cycle of cause and effect often through lifetimes.

Kinesiology: The scientific study of human movement.

Kundalini: Sanskrit word meaning *coiled.* In Indian yoga it is referred to as corporeal energy that flows up from the base of the spine. Through yoga meditation one can evoke a *Kundalini* self-realization/awakening.

Labyrinth: A circular maze-like path made of stone or hedges used for walking meditation. Most common labyrinth is a 7 loop one that corresponds to the seven charkas.

Lama: In Tibetan Buddhism an enlightened master or saint that remains conscious during his previous death and rebirth, therefore remembers his past life.

Lemuria: Legendary continent in the Pacific Ocean that sank thousands of years ago.

Lightworker: An individual that practices alternative healing such as energy medicine, spiritual healing or psychic readings.

Lucid Dreaming: A vivid dream where you know you are dreaming and are able to take controls of events in the dream.

Kriya Yoga: A spiritual type of yoga that was revived by Mahavatar Babaji in the 1860's and made popular by Paramahansa Yogananda in his book, *Autobiography of a Yogi.*

Mantra: From the Sanskrit word meaning "Thinker." A phrase or word with special powers, either chanted aloud, or as a prayer, or thought during silent meditation.

Mayans: A Mesoamerican pre-civilization that thrived between 2600 BC and 1697 AD Their culture spread from Central America throughout the Yucatan Peninsula to Guatemala. Developed a 5,120 year calendar that started in 3114 BC and ended in 2012 AD

Mediumship: Also called channeling. When an invisible entity takes over one's body and mind in order to give messages as in a psychic reading or lecture. The medium often becomes unconscious during the process.

Mental Energy Body: Outer energy layer of body believed to contain the energy of thought, creativity, invention and inspiration.

Monads: Units of spiritual consciousness in Theosophy.

Namaste: Sanskrit word used as a greeting literally translated "I bow to you." As a modern greeting in India it often is interpreted as "the divine in me greets and salutes the divine in you."

Near-Death-Experience (NDE): An experience where consciousness leaves the body and is aware of events taking place during a time when the physical body is clinically dead, and then returns to the body.

New Age: Pertaining to a current cultural movement, characterized by interest in such topics and ideas of higher consciousness, holistic and alternative medicine, supernatural phenomena, occult sciences and Eastern spiritual philosophies.

New Thought: Non-sectarian metaphysical philosophy that teaches that the mind is primary and causative. God is indwelling Spirit, and metaphysical remedies, such as prayer and affirmation, correct thinking can heal all difficulties by connecting to universal energies within and without. Promoted in churches such as Unity Church and the Church of Religious Science.

Nirvana: Sanskrit word meaning "Blowing out." A Buddhist concept, meaning the cessation of all desires, the extinction of the ego identity, and the absorption of the individual soul. A Hindu concept, meaning blowing out the flame of life through supreme union with the absolute impersonal God.

Nocebo Effect: Negative beliefs that determine the outcome; can make the individual sick or even kill them.

Occult: Pertaining to psychic phenomena and sciences, such as alchemy, astrology, card-reading, divination, psychokinesis, mediumship, etc.

Out-of-Body Experience(OBE): When consciousness leaves the body, and one is aware of leaving the physical body such as in a Near-Death—Experience (NDE) or astral projection.

Paranormal: Psychic or mental phenomena beyond the average scope of experience. Sensory perception beyond the norm, such as clairvoyance, clairaudience, clairsentience, etc.

Parapsychology: A branch of psychology dealing with psychic phenomena, such as extrasensory perception, telepathy, mediumship, etc.

Placebo Effect: An improvement in a condition not from the treatment, but because the patient believes they will get better or a gain a specific result.

Precognition: Information perceived about future events, where the information could not be inferred by ordinary means. Also referred to as "premonition."

Psi: Referring to psychic phenomena, such as ESP, telepathy, clairvoyance, or psychokinesis.

Psychokinesis: Mental interaction with animate or inanimate matter. Also called "mind-matter interaction," "telekinesis," or "PK."

Psychometry: A psychic technique of receiving knowledge about a person by touching an object associated with that person.

Qigong: A Chinese meditative-exercising technique that uses slow graceful movements and control breathing that promotes health.

Quetzalcoatl: A Mesoamerican deity whose name in their Nahuatl language means "feathered-serpent." Dates back to 400 BC in the Aztec, Mayan and Toltec cultures.

Quickening: Vibrational lifting of the mind and body, often accompanied by rushes of energy, electrical currents, increased breathing or heart rate, ecstasy, or warmth in the body.

Rainbow Children: Children born with special and/or psychic gifts at the beginning of this millennium.

Reconnective Healing: A hands-off energy healing technique developed by Dr. Eric Pearl in the 1990's.

Reflexology: An energy healing technique that manipulates body meridian lines in the hands and feet to promote healing. Believed to have been developed in ancient China.

Reiki: An energy healing technique developed in Japan in the 1800's.

Reincarnation: The transmigration of a soul from one body to another, as in from lifetime to lifetime.

Rishi: Sanskrit word meaning "Sage." A seer, one who cognizes the truth. One who receives the hymns of the Vedas through direct mystical revelation.

Shaman: A medicine man or woman, healer, priest, and spiritual advisor for Native American tribes, and cultures in South America and Northeast Asia.

Shinto: In Japanese meaning "Way of Gods." A Japanese religion, originally a form of nature worship, now influenced by Confucianism and Buddhism.

Sikhism: Hindu word meaning "A Disciple." A Hindu sect whose tenets include the belief in one God, dismissal of idolatry, and the rejection of the caste system.

Spirit: A life energy or force that underlies and pervades the universe, a concept that is multicultural and interdenominational, not confined to any particular religious philosophy or lifestyle.

Subconscious: The aspect of one's mind responsible for the experience of one as an individual entity. The inner voice that comprises our personality and self-concept.

Sufism: A form of Islamic mysticism.

Supernatural: Beyond the normal range of human perception. Pertaining to the occult, ghosts, spirits, etc.

Synchronicity: Term coined by psychologist Carl Jung that describes an unusual happening that simply could not be a coincidence.

Tai Chi: Originated in China as a form of graceful movements for meditation and exercise.

Taoism: From the Chinese word meaning "The Way." A Chinese religious philosophy based upon the teachings of Lao-Tzu, emphasizing simplicity, truth, and wisdom.

Telepathy: Information exchanged between two or more minds without the use of ordinary senses.

Theosophy: A religious philosophy established in 1875 that embraces metaphysical concepts. Theosophy in Greek means *"God Wisdom."*

Therapeutic Touch: A hands-off energy healing technique developed by Dr. Dolores Krieger and Dora Kunz in the late 1960's.

Transcendental: Beyond the phenomenal relative world, not limited by boundaries of the physical universe, beyond causation.

Vedas: Ancient scriptures of India, that are the oldest known spiritual records, received as direct cognitions and revelations by ancient *rishis*.

Yoga: Sanskrit word meaning "Yoking." A discipline that help the practitioner to unify with supreme Spirit, often involving meditation (dhyan), postures (asanas), and breathing (pranayama).

Yogi: Sanskrit word meaning "One who is yoked." One who has achieved liberation of the soul and union with the supreme Spirit through East Indian spiritual disciplines that promote direct union with God.

Zen Buddhism: Sanskrit word meaning Zen: "Meditation." Buddha: "The enlightened one." A form of Buddhism, practiced primarily in Japan, Korea, and Vietnam, whose goal is to attain enlightenment through spiritual practices, especially meditation, intuition, and simplicity.

XIII Divine References

"Those who are meant to hear
will understand.
Those who are not
meant to understand
will not hear."
~ **Confucius**

Suggested Further Reading:

Andrews, Ted, *Psychic Protection*, (Dragon Hawk Publishing, Jackson, TN, 1998).

Arguelles, Jose, *The Arcturus Probe: Tales and Reports of an Ongoing Investigations*, (Light Technology Publishing, Sedona, AZ, 1996).

Armstrong, Jeffrey, *God Goddess the Astrologer: Soul, Karma and Reincarnation, How We Continually Create Our Own Destiny*, (Torchlight Publishing, Badger, CA, 2001).

Baldwin, William, *Healing Lost Souls, Releasing Unwanted Spirits from Your Energy Body*, (Hampton Roads Publishing Company, Inc., Charlottesville, VA, 2003).

Ban Breathnach, Sarah, *Something More: Excavating Your Authentic Self*, (Warner Books, Inc., New York, NY, 1998).

Beaconsfield, Hannah, *Welcome to Planet Earth: A Guide for Walk-ins and Starseeds*, (Light Technology Publishing, Flagstaff, AZ, 1997).

Becker, Robert O., & Gary Seldon, *The Body Electric, Electromagnetism and The Foundation of Life*, (William Morrow and Company, Inc., New York, NY, 1985).

Braden, Gregg, *The Spontaneous Healing of Belief, Shattering the Paradigm of False Limits*, (Hay House, Inc., Carsbad, CA, 2008).

Braden, Gregg, *The Divine Matrix, Bridging Time, Space, Miracles and Belief,* (Hay House, Inc., Carsbad, CA, 2007).

Braden, Gregg, *Walking Between Worlds, The Science of Compassion,* (Radio Bookstore Press, Bellevue, WA, 1997).

Bradley, Michael, *The Secrets of the Free Masons,* (Sterling Publishing, New York, NY, 2008).

Brennan, Barbara, *Hands of Light, A Guide to Healing Through the Human Energy Field,* (Bantam Books, New York, NY, 1987).

Bruce, Edith, *The Keys to the Kingdom,* (Light Technology Publishing, Sedona, AZ, 1997).

Bruce, Robert, *Astral Dynamics, A New Approach to Out-of-Body Experiences,* (Hampton Roads Publishing Co., Charlottesville, VA, 1999).

Brussat, Federie and Mary, *100 Ways to Keep Your Soul Alive,* (Harper Collins, New York, NY, 1994).

Burns, Barbara, *Channelling: Evolutionary Exercises for Channels,* (Light Technology Publishing, Sedona, AZ, 1992).

Burpo, Todd, *Heaven is for Real,* (Thomas Nelson, Inc., Nashville, TN, 2010).

Calabrese, Adrian, *How To Get Everything You Ever Wanted: Complete Guide to Using Your Psychic Common Sense,* (Llewellyn Publications, Woodbury, MN, 2000).

Calabrese, Adrian, *Sacred Signs: Hear, See & Believe Messages from the Universe,* (Llewellyn Publications, Woodbury, MN, 2008).

Campbell, T. Colin & Campbell, Thomas M., *The China Study: Startling Implications for Diet, Weight Loss and Long-Term Health,* (Benbella Books, Dallas, TX, 2006).

Carey, Ken, *Return of The Bird Tribes,* (Harper Collins Publishers, New York, NY, 1988).

Carey, Ken, *The Third Millennium; Living in the Posthistoric World,* (Harper Collins Publishers, New York, NY, 1991).

Carey, Ken, *Vision: A Personal Call to Create a New World,* (Harper Collins Publishers, New York, NY, 1985).

Carlson, Richard, Ph.D., *Don't Sweat the Small Stuff...And It's All Small Stuff* (Hyperion, New York, NY, 1997).

Carroll, Lee & Jan Tober, *The Indigo Children: The New Kids Have Arrived,* (Light Technology Publishing, Sedona, AZ, 1998).

Carroll, Lee/Kryon, *Don't Think Like a Human, Book II,* (The Kryon Writings Inc., Del Mar, CA, 1994).

Carroll, Lee/Kryon, *Letters From Home, Loving Messages from the Family, Book VII,* (The Kryon Writings Inc., Del Mar, CA, 1999).

Carroll, Lee/Kryon, *Lifting The Veil, The New Energy Apocalypse,* (The Kryon Writings Inc., Del Mar, CA, 2007).

Carroll, Lee/Kryon, *The Journey Home: The Story of Michael Thomas and the Seven Angels ,*(The Kryon Writings Inc., Del Mar, CA, 1997).

Charles, R.H., *The Book of Enoch,* (Dover Publications, Inc., Mineola, NY, 2007).

Chopra, Deepak, *Life After Death, The Burden of Proof,* (Harmony Books, New York, NY, 2006).

Chopra, Deepak, *The Seven Spiritual Laws of Success,* (Amber Allen Publishing, San Rafael, CA, 1994).

Choquette, Sonia, *Ask Your Guides,* (Hay House Inc., New York, NY, 2006).

Clark, Gladys Iris, *Forever Young; A Manual for Rejuvenation and Longevity,* (Light Technology Publishing, Sedona, AZ, 1987).

Coelho, Paul, *Aleph*, (Borzoi Publishing, Brazil, 2010).

Cramer, Cathleen M., *The Legend of the Eagle Clan,* (Light Technology Publishing, Sedona, AZ, 1995).

Crane, Patricia, *Ordering From The Cosmic Kitchen*, (The Crane's Nest, Bonsall, CA, 2002).

Crookall, Robert, *Out of the Body Experiences,* (Carol Publishing Group, New York, NY, 1992).

Curran, Cindy, *Cocoon,* reprinted with permission. chakrangel1@ yahoo.com

Deering, Hallie, *Light From the Angels,* (Light Technology Publishing, Sedona, AZ, 1995).

DiSano, Dr. Dave, *Holistic Mental Health-Revised,* (IUniverse, Bloomington, IN, 2009).

Doreal, *The Emerald Tablets of Thoth-The-Atlantean,* (Source Books, Gallatin, TX, 2006).

Dubro, Peggy, *Elegant Empowerment, The Evolution of Consciousness,* (Platinum Publishing, USA, 2002).

Eadie, Betty J., *Embraced by the Light,* (Bantam Books, New York, NY, 1992).

Eden, James, *Energetic Healing: The Merging of Ancient and Modern Practices,* (Plenum Press, New York, NY, 1993).

Estes, Clarissa Pinkola, Ph.D., *Women Who Run With the Wolves; Myths and Stories of the Wild Woman Archetype,* (Ballantine Books, New York, NY, 1992).

Fanning, Patrick, *Visualization for Change,* (New Harbringer Publications, Inc., 1994).

Farkas, Michael, *1-800-God-Help-Me,* (Light Technology Publishing, Sedona, AZ, 1998).

Filmore, Charles, *Jesus Christ Heals,* (Unity Classic Library, 2008).

Fiore, Edith, *The Unquiet Dead: A Psychologist Treats Spirit Possession,* (Ballantine Books, New York, NY, 1987).

Freke, Timothy & Gandy, Peter, *Jesus and the Lost Goddess,* (Three Rivers Press, New York, NY, 2001).

Gerber, Richard, *A Practical Guide to Vibrational Medicine, Energy Healing and Spiritual Transformation,* (HarperCollins Books, New York, NY, 2001).

George, Tamar, *Guardians of The Flame,* (Light Technology Publishing, Sedona, AZ, 1995).

Haffert, John, *Now The Woman Shall Conquer,* (The 101 Foundation, Inc., Asbury, NJ, 1997).

Hall, Judy, *The Art of Psychic Protection,* (Weiser Books, San Francisco, CA, 1997).

Hall, Judy, *The Crystal Bible: A Definitive Guide to Crystals,* (Walking Stick Press, Cincinnati, OH, 2004).

Hastings, Pat, *Simply a Woman of Faith: How to Live in Spiritual Power and Transform Your Life,* (Mill City Press, Minneapolis, MN, 2007).

Hathaway, William T., *Summer Snow,* (Avatar Publications, St. Albert, Alberta, CN, 2005).

Hawkins, David R., *Power vs. Force: The Hidden Determinants of Human Behavior,* (Hay House, Carlsbad, CA, 2002).

Hawkins, David R., *The Eye of the I: From Which Nothing is Hidden,* (Vertias Publishing, Sedona, AZ, 2001).

Hicks, Esther and Jerry, *Ask and It Is Given, Learning to Manifest Your Desires,* (Hay House, Inc., Carlsbad, CA, 2004).

Hicks, Esther and Jerry, *The Law of Attraction; The Basics of the Teachings of Abraham,* (Hay House, Inc., Carlsbad, CA, 2006).

Hogan, Linda, *Walk Gently Upon the Earth,* (Lulu.com, 2009).

Hollick, Malcolm, *The Science of Oneness; A Worldview for the Twenty-First Century,* (John Hunt Publishing Co., London, UK, 2006).

Holmes, Dr. Ernest, *The Science of Mind, A Philosophy, A Faith, A Way of Life,* (Penguin Putnam Inc., New York, NY, 1938).

Holmes, Dr. Ernest, *This Thing Called You,* (Penguin Putnam Inc., New York, NY, 1948).

Howell, Alice O., *The Heavens Declare: Astrological Ages and the Evolution of Consciousness,* (Quest Books, Wheaton, Il, 2006).

Hurtak, J.J., *The Book of Knowledge: The Keys of Enoch,* (The Academy For Future Sciences, Los Gatos, CA, 1977).

Jung, Carl G., *Synchronicity, An Acausal Connecting Principle,* (Bollingen Foundation, New York, NY, 1960).

Kabot-Zinn, Jon,. *Full Catastrophe Living,* (Dell Publishing, New York, NY, 1990).

King, Godfre Ray, *The I AM Discourses,* (Saint Germain Press, Mount Shasta, CA, 1940).

King, Godfre Ray, *Unveiled Mysteries,* (Saint Germain Press, Schaumburg, Il 1939).

Krieger, Dolores, *The Therapeutic Touch, How to Use Your Hands to Help or to Heal,* (Prentice Hall, Englewood Cliffs, NJ, 1979).

Kriyananda, Swami (J. Donald Walters), *The Art and Science of Raja Yoga,* (Crystal Clarity Publishers, Nevada City, CA, 2002).

Linn, Denise, *The Secret Language of Signs,* (Ballantine Books, New York, NY, 1996).

Lipton, Bruce, Ph.D., *Biology of Belief: Unleashing the Power of Consciousness, Matter, and Miracles*, (Hay House, Carlsbad, CA, 2005).

Lipton, Bruce, Ph.D., & Bhaerman, Steve B., *Spontaneous Evolution: Our Positive Future (and a Way to Get There From Here)*, (Hay House, Carlsbad, CA, 2009).

Lomonte, Cheri, *The Healing Touch of Mary,* (Divine Impressions, Austin, TX, 2005).

Long, Jeffrey, *Evidence of the Afterlife, The Science of Near-Death Experiences,* (Harper-Collins, New York, NY, 2010).

MacLaine, Shirley, *Out on a Limb*, (Bantam Books, New York, NY, 1983).

MacLaine, Shirley, *Going Within*, (Bantam Books, New York, NY, 1989).

Marciniak, Barbara, *Bringers of the Dawn: Teachings from the Pleiadians,* (Bear & Company Publishing, Rochester, VT, 1992).

Marciniak, Barbara, *Family of Light,* (Bear & Company Publishing, Rochester, VT, 1999).

Marciniak, Barbara, *Path of Empowerment, Pleiadian Wisdom for a World in Chaos,* (New World Library, Novato, CA, 2004).

Maurey, Eugene, *Exorcism: How to Clear at a Distance a Spirit Possessed Person,* (Whitford Press, West Chester, PA, 1988).

McClure, Janet, *Prelude to Ascension: Tools for Transformation,* (Light Technology Publishing, Flagstaff, AZ, 1996).

McClure, Janet, *Scopes of Dimensions: How to Experience Multi-Dimensional Reality,* (Light Technology Publishing, Sedona, AZ, 1989).

McClure, Janet, *Light Techniques That Trigger Transformation: Vywamus,* (Light Technology Publishing, Sedona, AZ, 1988).

McGowan, Kathleen, *The Expected One,* (Simon & Schuster, New York, NY, 2006).

McIntosh, John, *The Millennium Tablets,* (Light Technology Publishing, Sedona, AZ, 1996).

Megre, Vladimir, *Anastasia,* (Ringing Cedars Press, Kahului, HI, 2005).

Melchizedek, Drunvalo, *The Flower of Life,* (Red Wheel/Weiser, San Francisco, CA, 2007).

Melchizedek, Drunvalo, *Serpent of Light Beyond 2012,* (Red Wheel/Weiser, San Francisco, CA, 2007).

Myss, Caroline, *Anatomy of Spirit, The Seven Stages of Power and Healing,* (Three Rivers Press, New York, NY,1996).

Murphy, Joseph, *The Power of Your Subconscious Mind,* (Bantam Books, New York, NY, 2000).

Murphy, Joseph, *The Cosmic Energizer: Miracle Power of the Universe,* (Bantam Books, New York, NY, 1996).

Myss, Caroline, *Defy Gravity; Healing Beyond the Bounds of Reason,* (Hay House, Carlsbad, CA, 2009).

Newton, Michael, *Destiny of Souls,* (Llewellyn Publications, St. Paul, MN, 2004).

Newton, Michael, *Journey of Souls,* (Llewellyn Publications, St. Paul, MN, 2006).

Newton, Michael, *Life Between Lives,* (Llewellyn Publications, St. Paul, MN, 2006).

Orloff, Judith, *Second Sight, A Psychiatrist Clairvoyant Tells Her Extraordinary Story,* (Warner Books, Inc., New York, NY, 1996).

Oser, Andrew, *How Alternation Can Change Your Life; Finding the Rhythms of Health and Happiness,* (River Sanctuary Publishing, Felton, CA, 2010).

Page, Ken, *The Way it Works,* (Clear Light Arts, Cleveland, GA, 1997).

Pearl, Eric, *The Reconnection: Heal Others, Heal Yourself,* (Hay House Publishing, New York, NY, 2003).

Peck, M. Scott, MD, *The Road Less Traveled,* (Simon & Schuster, New York, NY, 1978).

Petrisko, Thomas W., *Call of Ages,* (Queenship Publishing Company, Santa Barbara, CA, 1995).

Petrisko, Thomas W., *The Miracle of the Illumination of All Consciences,* (St. Andrew's Productions, McKees Rock, PA, 2000).

Pinchbeck, Daniel, *2012 The Return of Quetzalcoatl,* (The Penguin Group, New York, NY, 2006).

Pursche, W.R., *Lessons to Live by : The Canine Commandments,* (Varzara House, USA, 2005).

Quan Yin, Amorah, *The Pleiadian Workbook, Awakening Your Divine KA,* (Bear & Company Publishing, Santa Fe, NM, 1996).

Quinn, Daniel, *Ishmael, An Adventure of the Mind and Spirit,* (Bantam Books, New York, NY, 1995).

Radin, Dean, Ph.D., *The Conscious Universe, The Scientific Truth of Psychic Phenomena* (HarperCollins Publishers, New York, NY, 1997).

Raphael (Ken Carey), *The Starseed Transmissions,* (Stillpoint Publishing, Walpole, NH, 1982).

Redfield, James, *The Celestine Prophecy,* (Warner Books, New York, NY, 1993).

Roeder, Dorothy, *The Next Dimension is Love: Ranoash the Ataien,* (Light Technology Publishing, Sedona, AZ, 1993).

Roeder, Dorothy, *Reach for Us: Your Cosmic Teachers and Friends,* (Light Technology Publishing, Sedona, AZ, 1995).

Ruiz, Don Miguel, *The Four Agreements,* (Amber-Allen Publishing, San Rafael, CA, 1997).

Ryden, Ruth, *The Golden Path; An Introduction to Advanced Spiritual Knowledge,* (Light Technology Publishing, Sedona, AZ, 1993).

Schuller, Robert H., *You Can Become The Person You Want To Be,* (Crystal Cathedral Ministries, Garden Grove, CA, 2007).

Scully, Nicki, *Power Animal Meditations,* (Bear & Company, Rochester, VT, 2001).

Sharp, Michael, *The Book of Life,* (Avatar Publications, St. Albert, Alberta, Canada, 2003-2006).

Sharp, Michael, *The Book of the Triumph of Spirit,* (Avatar Publications, St. Albert, Alberta, Canada, 2006).

Sharp, Michael, *The Dossier of Ascension,* (Avatar Publications, St. Albert, Alberta, Canada, 2004-2006).

www.michaelsharp.org

Shapiro, Robert, Creators & Zoosh, *Explorer Race; Creators and Friends The Mechanics of Creation,* (Light Technology Publishing, Sedona, AZ, 1997).

Shapiro, Robert, *Explorer Race; Techniques for Generating Safety,* (Light Technology Publishing, Flagstaff, AZ, 2002).

Shapiro, Robert, *The Explorer Race and Isis,* (Light Technology Publishing, Flagstaff, AZ, 2001).

Shapiro, Robert, *The Explorer Race Techniques and Jesus,* (Light Technology Publishing, Flagstaff, AZ, 2002).

Shumsky, Susan G., *Divine Revelation,* (Simon & Schuster, New York, NY, 1996).

Spalding, Baird, *Life and Teachings of the Masters of the Far East,* (DeVorss Publications, Carmarillo, CA, 1964).

St. Germain, Maureen, *Beyond The Flower of Life,* (Phoenix Rising Publishing, New York, NY, 2009).

St. Germain, Maureen, *You Are the Genie in the Bottle,* (Maureen St. Germain, 2004).

Starbird, Margaret, *The Goddess in the Gospels; Reclaiming the Sacred Feminine,* (Bear & Company, Rochester, VT, 1998).

Steiger, Brad, *Real Ghosts, Spirits, and Haunted Places,* (Visible Ink Press, Canton, MI, 2003).

Stein, Diane, *Essential Reiki, A Complete Guide to an Ancient Healing Art,* (The Crossing Press, Inc., Freedom, CA, 1996).

Stone, Joshua David, *The Complete Ascension Manual: How to Achieve Ascension In This Lifetime,* (Light Technology Publishing, Sedona, AZ, 1994).

Stone, Joshua David, *Cosmic Ascension; Your Cosmic Map Home,* (Light Technology Publishing, Sedona, AZ, 1997).

Stone, Joshua David, *Golden Keys to Ascension and Healing; Revelations of Sai Baba and the Ascended Masters,* (Light Technology Publishing, Sedona, AZ, 1998).

Szasz, T., *The Myth of Mental Illness,* (Harper and Row, New York, NY, 1974).

Tomlinson, Andy, *Healing The Eternal Soul,* (O Books, Winchester, UK, 2006).

Tolle, Eckhart, *A New Earth; Awakening to Your Life's Purpose,* (Penguin Group, New York, NY, 2005).

Virtue, Doreen, *Divine Guidance; How to Have a Dialogue with God and Your Guardian Angels,* (St. Martin's Griffin, New York, NY, 1998).

Virtue, Doreen, *Goddesses & Angels: Awakening Your Inner High-Priestess and "Source-eress,"* (Hay House, Inc. Carlsbad, CA, 2005).

Virtue, Doreen, *Healing with the Angels,* (Hay House, Inc. Carlsbad, CA, 1999).

Virtue, Doreen, *The Lightworker's Way: Awakening Your Spiritual Power to Know and Heal,* (Hay House, Inc. Carlsbad, CA, 1997).

Weil, Andrew, *Healthy Aging,* (Random House, Inc., New York, NY, 2005).

Weil, Andrew, *Spontaneous Healing,* (Ballantine Books, New York, NY, 1995).

Weil, Andrew, *The Marriage of The Sun and The Moon: A Quest for Unity in Consciousness,* (Houghton Milfflin Co., Boston, MA, 1980).

Weingard, Rev. Karen, *I Am the Party, Set for Life and Lovin' It,* (The Barclay, New York, NY, 2009).

Weiss, Brian, *Messages From The Masters,* (Warner Books, New York, NY, 2000).

Weiss, Brian, *Many Lives, Many Masters,* (Simon & Schuster, New York, NY, 1988).

Weiss, Brian, *Same Soul, Many Bodies,* (Simon & Schuster, New York, NY, 2004).

Whitfield, Barbara Harris, *Spiritual Awakenings; Insights of the Near Death Experience and Other Doorways to Our Soul,* Health Communications, Inc., Deerfield Beach, FL., 1995).

Wiseman, B., *Psychiatry The Ultimate Betrayal,* (Freedom Publishing, Los Angeles, CA, 1995).

Yogananda, Paramahansa, *Autobiography of a Yogi,* (Crystal Clarity Publishers, New York, NY, 1946).

Young, Wm. Paul, *The Shack: Where Tragedy Confronts Eternity,* (Windblown Media, Newbury Park, CA, 2007

Divine Websites

Rev. Estelle: *www. AllThingsArePossible.org*
Dr. Robert H. Schuller: *www. hourofpower.org*
Joel Osteen: *www.joelosteen.org*
Oprah Winfrey: *www.oprah.com/own*

Cindy Curran: Poet & Author, 401-615-8681, spiritualliterature@ yahoo.com

Divine DVDs

Conversations With God, Neale Donald Walsch (CWG Films, 2006).

I Am, Tom Shadyac, (Flying Eye Productions, 2011).

Michael Bernard Beckwith: Spiritual Liberation; Fulfilling Your Soul's Potential, (Beyond Words Publications, 2009).

Soul Surfer, (TriStar Pictures, 2011).

Spirit Space, A Journey into Your Consciousness, (WireWerks Films, 2008).

The Celestine Prophecy, (Sony Pictures, 2005).

The Living Matrix, New Insights into Our Bodies, Minds and Health, (LTD and Becker Massey, LLC, 2009).

The Peaceful Warrior, (Universal Studios, 2005).

The Shift, by Dr. Wayne Dyer, (Hay House, 2009).

The Shadow Effect, Debbie Ford, (Hay House, 2009).

You Can Heal Your Life, by Louise Hay, (Hay House, 2007).

What The Bleep Do We Know!?, (20th Century Fox, 2004).

Divine CDs

Karen Drucker, *All About Love,* (2004)

Karen Drucker, *Power of Women,* (2008)

Karen Drucker, *Shine,* (2007)

Pat Hastings, *Simply a Woman of Faith,* (2007)

Tom Kenyon, *White Gold Alchemy,* (2001)

Dona Oxford, *Step Up,* (2008)

David Roth, *Practice Makes Progress,* (2008).

Savannah Jack, *Savannah Jack*

Joey Stann: *Family Tree,* (2001)

Mark Stanton Welch, *Ask Your Guides,* (2000-2007)

Mark Stanton Welch, *Dance Your Spirit,* (2006)

Kristine Wilbur, *Always Here,* (2008)

Index